BEYOND GOOD AND EVIL

FRIEDRICH NIETZSCHE (1844–1900) was born in Röcken, Saxony, and educated at the universities of Bonn and Leipzig. At the age of only 24 he was appointed Professor of Classical Philology at the University of Basle, but prolonged bouts of ill health forced him to resign from his post in 1879. Over the next decade he shuttled between the Swiss Alps and the Mediterranean coast, devoting himself entirely to thinking and writing. His early books and pamphlets (*The Birth of Tragedy, Untimely Meditations*) were heavily influenced by Wagner and Schopenhauer, but from *Human, All Too Human* (1878) on, his thought began to develop more independently, and he published a series of ground-breaking philosophical works (*The Gay Science, Thus Spake Zarathustra, Beyond Good and Evil, On the Genealogy of Morals*) which culminated in a frenzy of production in the closing months of 1888. In January 1889 Nietzsche suffered a mental breakdown from which he was never to recover, and he died in Weimar eleven years later.

MARION FABER is Professor of German at Swarthmore College in Pennsylvania. Her earlier translations include Nietzsche's *Human, All Too Human* (1994) and Wolfgang Hildesheimer's *Mozart* (1983), a nominee for the American Book Award in translation.

ROBERT C. HOLUB teaches German intellectual, cultural, and literary history in the German department at the University of California, Berkeley. Among his numerous publications on these topics are *Reflections of Realism* (1991); *Jürgen Habermas: Critic in the Public Sphere* (1991); *Crossing Borders: Reception Theory, Poststructuralism, Deconstruction* (1992); and *Friedrich Nietzsche* (1995). He is the editor of *Impure Reason: Dialectic of Enlightenment in Germany* (1993), *Responsibility and Commitment* (1996), and *Heinrich Heine's Contested Identities* (1998).

OXFORD WORLD'S CLASSICS

*For over 100 years Oxford World's Classics have brought
readers closer to the world's great literature. Now with over 700
titles—from the 4,000-year-old myths of Mesopotamia to the
twentieth century's greatest novels—the series makes available
lesser-known as well as celebrated writing.*

*The pocket-sized hardbacks of the early years contained
introductions by Virginia Woolf, T. S. Eliot, Graham Greene,
and other literary figures which enriched the experience of reading.
Today the series is recognized for its fine scholarship and
reliability in texts that span world literature, drama and poetry,
religion, philosophy and politics. Each edition includes perceptive
commentary and essential background information to meet the
changing needs of readers.*

OXFORD WORLD'S CLASSICS

FRIEDRICH NIETZSCHE

Beyond Good and Evil

Prelude to a Philosophy of the Future

Translated and Edited by
MARION FABER

With an Introduction by
ROBERT C. HOLUB

OXFORD
UNIVERSITY PRESS

OXFORD

UNIVERSITY PRESS

Great Clarendon Street, Oxford OX2 6DP

Oxford University Press is a department of the University of Oxford.
It furthers the University's objective of excellence in research, scholarship,
and education by publishing worldwide in

Oxford New York

Athens Auckland Bangkok Bogotá Buenos Aires Calcutta
Cape Town Chennai Dar es Salaam Delhi Florence Hong Kong Istanbul
Karachi Kuala Lumpur Madrid Melbourne Mexico City Mumbai
Nairobi Paris São Paulo Shanghai Singapore Taipei Tokyo Toronto Warsaw

with associated companies in Berlin Ibadan

Oxford is a registered trade mark of Oxford University Press
in the UK and in certain other countries

Published in the United States
by Oxford University Press Inc., New York

Translation, Notes, Index © Marion Faber 1998
Introduction © Robert Holub 1998
Chronology © Duncan Large 1997

First published as an Oxford World's Classics paperback 1998

British Library Cataloguing in Publication Data

Data available

Library of Congress Cataloging in Publication Data

Nietzsche, Friedrich Wilhelm, 1844–1900.
[Jenseits von Gut und Böse. English]
Beyond good and evil: prelude to a philosophy of the future /
translated and edited by Marion Faber : with an introduction by
Robert C. Holub
(Oxford world's classics)
Includes bibliographical references and index.
1. Ethics. 2. Philosophy. I. Faber, Marion. II. Title.
III. Series: Oxford world's classics (Oxford University Press).
B3313.J42E5 1998 193—dc21 98–15016

ISBN 0–19–283263–8 (pbk.)

5 7 9 10 8 6

Typeset by Intype London Ltd.
Printed in Great Britain by
Clays Ltd, St Ives plc

CONTENTS

INTRODUCTION

THERE is no better introduction to the mature philosophy of Friedrich Nietzsche than *Beyond Good and Evil*. Written during the summer of 1885 and the winter of 1886, this work assumes a pivotal position in his oeuvre. It was the first published work after the monumental *Thus Spake Zarathustra*, which laid out central tenets of Nietzsche's philosophy in parabolic form. Conceived as a parody of the Bible, the four books of *Zarathustra* presented the reader with the activities and speeches of the eponymous hero, who is surely Nietzsche's spokesperson. *Beyond Good and Evil* covers some of the same ground, but in this work Nietzsche does not offer us a narrative and parables that require interpretation, but rather a series of aphorisms. Nietzsche himself was conscious of the affinities in content between *Zarathustra* and *Beyond Good and Evil*. Writing to his colleague Jacob Burckhardt, the celebrated art historian at Basle, he claimed that his new book 'says the same things as my *Zarathustra*, but differently, very differently'. But he was also aware that *Beyond Good and Evil* represents a return to earlier efforts from the 1870s and early 1880s, in which he did not communicate with his reader through a persona. In his correspondence Nietzsche called his new work a fifth *Untimely Meditation*, referring to writings of the early 1870s in which he focused on a central theme or person. And he told a prospective publisher that he was ready to publish a second volume of *Daybreak*, a collection of aphorisms that had originally appeared in 1881. Nietzsche himself thus obviously saw *Beyond Good and Evil* in a variety of contexts that related to prior endeavours, from his essayistic works written while he was still a professor of classical philology in Basle to the more monumental undertakings from his years of travel in Switzerland and Italy.

While we may agree that *Beyond Good and Evil* has affinities with several of Nietzsche's previous writings, we should be a bit wary of taking Nietzsche too literally when he makes claims about it as a continuation of earlier books. We should note, for example, that concepts central to *Zarathustra* are absent from *Beyond Good and Evil*. The 'superman' or 'overman', which was Nietzsche's catchy expression for an evolutionary overcoming of the current state of the human species, or the quasi-scientific notion of 'eternal recurrence of the same', a hypothesis that all events have already occurred and will inevitably recur again and again, are nowhere to be found in the new volume. There are ways in which Nietzsche did indeed return to criticisms of German society found in the *Untimely Meditations*, but *Beyond Good and Evil* is not as limited in scope as these earlier essays were, and certainly more philosophically mature. While Nietzsche returns to an aphoristic style, such as we find in writings from *Human, All Too Human* (1878–9) to *The Gay Science* (1882), his new work represented a major step away from his so-called positivistic phase with its reliance on a scientific model, and towards a more sceptical, more intricate, and more synthetic vision. Thus although philosophical arguments fundamental to *Zarathustra* are repeated in *Beyond Good and Evil* in a less enigmatic form, and although many of the aphorisms that find their way into the final text were sketched out in notebooks composed prior to or during the period of *Zarathustra*'s composition, *Beyond Good and Evil* represented a new and a final stage of Nietzsche's philosophy, a culmination of his thought and insight into the human condition.

Considering that *Beyond Good and Evil* is a central work by one of the most influential philosophers of the past century, it is sobering and astonishing to realize that Nietzsche had difficulty finding a publisher for it. Nietzsche's publisher for the previous decade or so had been Ernst Schmeitzner, but the two men, each for his own reasons, had become increasingly discontented with their relationship. Nietzsche was offended because Schmeitzner was devoting more of his time and energies to anti-Semitic publications and activities, and ignoring the promotion of Nietzsche's books; Nietzsche objected to the anti-Semitic movement in Germany and was particularly upset because his continued association with Schmeitzner made it seem that he harboured similar racist sympathies. Schmeitzner, for his part, was discontented with his author for the simple reason that his writings did not sell very well. He therefore tried to peddle the rights to Nietzsche's works, but no publisher was willing to meet his asking price. The tension between author and publisher reached such an impasse that Nietzsche himself published the fourth part of *Zarathustra* privately. Eventually Nietzsche initiated legal proceedings in order to acquire the rights to his work, and he pursued this goal to the end of his sane life in 1889 without success. In the spring of 1886 it was evident to Nietzsche that Schmeitzner was no longer suitable as a publisher for *Beyond Good and Evil*; but since he was unable to interest another publisher, he was forced again to pay for the printing of his book using the imprint of C. G. Naumann in Leipzig. On 21 July 1886, over two years since the public appearance of his last book, the first copies of *Beyond Good and Evil* appeared on the German book market. Nietzsche had hoped to sell 300 copies in order to cover his costs, but after a year just over 100 copies had been purchased.

One of the misconceptions surrounding *Beyond Good and Evil* from the start is that it is a book concerning mainly moral philosophy. The title leads the prospective reader to believe that Nietzsche is dealing essentially with ethical issues, but the volume that actually fits this description is *The Genealogy of Morals*, a work Nietzsche published in 1887 in order to clarify certain issues in his earlier book. The scope of *Beyond Good and Evil* is much broader, encompassing reflections on epistemology, religion, art, and current affairs. Why then did Nietzsche choose a title that suggests a more limited focus on the critique of morality? The answer is twofold. First Nietzsche believed that *Beyond Good and Evil* would be an effective title for his new work. When we examine Nietzsche's notebooks we often find him experimenting with lists of prospective books with different titles and section headers. The consummate stylist, Nietzsche was extremely conscious of selecting appropriate and striking titles for his writings. But *Beyond Good and Evil* was Nietzsche's choice for another reason. The phrase occurs first in volume one of *Human, All Too Human*, but he employs it more frequently in writings of the early and mid-1880s, especially from *Zarathustra* onwards. In these works it has a significance in moral philosophy, suggesting that we must call into question our traditional notions of good and evil as conventions rather than absolutes. But it also contains religious overtones: the German word *Jenseits* means not only 'beyond', but also refers to the afterlife. By the 1880s *Beyond Good and Evil* came to mean more than a moral imperative; it signified the place from which Zarathustra, and by extension Nietzsche himself, proclaim their philosophy. Only when we have stripped ourselves of our previous values and recognized their function in the economy of our own lives and our societies, only when we stand 'beyond good and evil', can we begin to understand the 'philosophy of the future' to which *Beyond Good and Evil* is only a prelude.

If the perspective 'beyond good and evil' is not entirely without preconceptions—and we shall see that Nietzsche harbours some of the typical prejudices of his time—then it is at least programmatically non-dogmatic, and we should not be surprised to find Nietzsche's own preface emphasizing his opposition to doctrinaire beliefs. He does this by employing an unusual metaphor. The text opens with the comparison of truth and a woman: 'Assuming that truth is a woman' (p. 3). By this time in his life Nietzsche had already acquired something of a reputation for an anti-feminist attitude, although his remarks against women's equality would become more virulent still in his final writings. Even if we excuse his most notorious misogynist remark—'You are going to women? Do not forget the whip!'—as emanating from an old woman whom Zarathustra meets and not from Zarathustra himself, Zarathustra's own comments—for example, 'Everything about woman is a riddle, and everything about woman has one solution: that is pregnancy'— are equally offensive. But at the opening of his new text Nietzsche assumes a different attitude. Here he is using the stereotypical notion of woman as an elusive being whom the philosopher must woo. Formerly, however, philosophers were rather clumsy suitors, and when they thought they had conquered truth with their dogmatic assertions, they had in reality failed. Nietzsche depicts himself on the threshold of a new era, one in which philosophers will abandon their dogmatism, rejecting accepted truths both philosophical (from Plato onward) and religious (in particular the Judaeo-Christian tradition). The preface closes by announcing the advent of new philosophers, variously called 'free spirits' and 'good Europeans', who will finally overcome the errors of their predecessors and embrace the previously enigmatic truth.

It would be a mistake to think that the 296 aphorisms that follow this preface are completely unsystematic attempts to capture this elusive truth. The aphoristic style that Nietzsche adopted for the writings of his middle period can easily produce the illusion of arbitrary ordering. *Beyond Good and Evil*, however, is one of Nietzsche's most rigorously structured works. Although each individual aphorism contains its own centre and logic, the nine sections or chapters are cohesive units that relate to an essential thematic core. Often Nietzsche will allude to themes that occurred in previous sections or anticipate future discussions, and this technique of retention and projection serves to weave together the entire text. More than his previous aphoristic writings *Beyond Good and Evil* is coherent as a totality as well as in its individual parts. Although it covers the gamut of themes that find expression in Nietzsche's mature philosophy, it is a controlled and composed text, comparable to an intricate piece of music or a finely woven tapestry. It rarely displays the frenetic, driving power of his last works, written on the brink of insanity, or the prophetic tones of *Zarathustra*, or the enthusiastic *naïveté* of his earliest writings, but perhaps for precisely these reasons, it is the most concise and compelling of Nietzsche's philosophical expositions.

Beyond Good and Evil opens with a section, 'On the Prejudices of Philosophers', in which Nietzsche undertakes a critique of the philosophical tradition in a most unusual fashion. Unlike previous philosophers, Nietzsche does not select an issue or notion and analyse it, in the process distinguishing his views from those of previous writers and erecting a body of concepts that forms a system of thought. Instead he calls into question the very basis of philosophizing. In this section the targets for his sceptical approach are philosophers themselves, their language, and the status of their writings. Philosophers, he claims, merely pose as persons seeking the truth. In actuality, the truths that they state are intimately related to their beings, indeed, to their physiological constitution. Philosophers are not objective; they are not distanced; their knowledge results from self-interest.

For they act as if they had discovered and acquired what are actually their opinions through the independent unravelling of a cold, pure, divinely unhampered dialectic . . . basically, however, they are using reasons sought after the fact to defend a pre-existing tenet, a sudden idea, a 'brainstorm', or, in most cases, a rarefied and abstract version of their heart's desire.   (p. 8; Aphorism 5)

Philosophy is therefore the epitome of a personal statement; unlike other more scientific forms of thought, it is always connected with the philosopher himself. It is 'the personal confession of its author,

a kind of unintended and unwitting memoir' (p. 8; 6). Other writers
in the nineteenth century had, of course, revealed that philosophers
or thinkers in general write from a definite perspective and defend
propositions of which they may not even be aware. Karl Marx, for
example, argued that systems of thought were ultimately ideological
reflexes that served to legitimize a dominant social order. Nietzsche
differs here from Marx, however, in that he downplays the social
situatedness of thought, but affirms even more strongly its unconscious foundation.

One of the reasons that philosophers are not conscious of the
real basis of their philosophy has to do with the subterfuge of
language. In this first book Nietzsche repeatedly notes the preva-
lence of linguistic deception. Aphorism 16 is typical in this regard.
When philosophers employ foundational notions, such as Descartes's 'I think' or Schopenhauer's 'I will', they believe they have
attained certainty or an immediate access to things as they really
are. Nietzsche, however, sees in these notions only the seduction
of words. Although we may feel that the words 'I think' are perfectly
intelligible, Nietzsche points out that they raise innumerable questions and contain several dubious presuppositions. 'If I analyse the
process expressed by the proposition "I think", I get a series of
audacious assertions that would be difficult if not impossible to
prove; for example, that *I* am the one who is thinking, that there
has to be a something doing the thinking, that thinking is an activity
and an effect on the part of a being who is thought of as a cause,
that an "I" exists, and finally, that we by now understand clearly
what is designated as thinking—that I *know* what thinking is'
(pp. 16–17; 16). Ultimately, Nietzsche suggests, our philosophical
notions are tied to a subject-centred grammar that will not allow
us to conceive of a radically different relationship to the world. For
this reason the status of philosophical statements is not one of truth
or certainty, but rather an interpretation that we impose on the
world. Concepts are not givens, but inventions; antitheses are actually falsifications, since reality consists of gradations, not
oppositions; and sensations and experiences, rather than being cap-
tured by language, are levelled and distorted by it, made common
and generalizable. Nietzsche therefore insists that we are posing
the wrong questions of philosophy. Instead of interrogating foundational concepts, we should be asking what function they play,

why they are necessary, and how they are life-preserving or life-promoting. Nietzsche's sceptical retort to the philosopher who avers the truth of the Cartesian *cogito* is simply: 'it is improbable that you are not in error, but then why must we insist on truth?' (p. 17; 16).

Nietzsche's unmasking of 'the prejudices of the philosophers' in the first section of his book is followed by a sketch of the new philosophers for whom his thought is a propaedeutic. The name he gives to this future breed of philosopher is 'free spirits', a term he had used frequently since the late 1870s. Indeed, the subtitle to *Human, All Too Human* was 'A Book for Free Spirits'. Despite his decade-long elaboration of the 'free spirit', the reader is apt to be confused about the exact nature of this term. In part Nietzsche himself accounts for this difficulty by insisting on the profundity of his thought and its inaccessibility to more mundane interpreters. He begins Aphorism 27 with the simple statement 'Making yourself understood is hard' (p. 28, 27), and proceeds to explain that his thought flows like the Ganges, while his contemporaries think like turtles or frogs. Continuing on this theme he insists in Aphorism 40 that profundity loves masks and shuns even image and parable, which would provide too direct an avenue to the profoundest things. Even when a 'secretive' man does not consciously don a mask, he will find that one has grown around him 'thanks to the constantly false, that is to say, *shallow* interpretations of his every word, his every step, every sign of life that he gives' (p. 39; 40). In these passages Nietzsche is in part venting his frustration for the poor reception and understanding of his own philosophy among contemporaries; his thought remains a philosophy of the future largely because he has found no philosophical allies in the present. And his future disciples, the coming free spirits, are vaguely defined because they have not yet taken on definite contours.

None the less the second section of *Beyond Good and Evil* allows us to detect certain characteristics that will be important for the free spirit. Above all this new philosopher will assume a place of superiority in the social and intellectual hierarchy. Nietzsche leaves no doubt that a free spirit is a superior human being '*delivered* from the crowd, the multitude, the majority, where he is allowed to forget the rule of "humanity", being the exception to it' (p. 27;

26). In several aphorisms he emphasizes a higher or loftier type of human being, one who believes and demands an 'hierarchy' (*Rangordnung*) while disdaining democracy and equal rights. For this reason Nietzsche's most extended discussion of the free spirit cautions that he not be confused with various sorts of 'freethinkers'. These 'levellers' and 'scribbling slaves of the democratic taste' (p. 40; 44) have falsely assumed the name free spirit and are the very antithesis of what Nietzsche has in mind. The Nietzschean variety will be *Versucher*, a German word that has the dual meaning of 'experimenter' and 'tempter'. They will be adherents of the 'will to power', a Nietzschean concept that explains 'all mechanical events, in so far as an energy is active in them' as well as 'our entire instinctual life' (p. 36; 36). The free spirit, like Nietzsche, will write books for the chosen few since 'books for the masses are always bad-smelling books' (p. 31; 30). Here and elsewhere in his later thought Nietzsche emphasizes an hierarchical social order based on an elusively defined notion of superiority. 'In the end', Nietzsche claims, 'things will have to be as they are and always have been: the great things are left to the great, the abysses to the profound, tenderness and thrills to the sensitive, and to sum it up in a few words, everything extraordinary to the extraordinary' (p. 40; 43). In keeping with their elevated social and intellectual status, freethinkers will also embrace a different brand of morality. In one of the most suggestive aphorisms in this section (32), Nietzsche outlines a history of moral thought. Originally actions were evaluated by their consequences in a stage Nietzsche labels 'pre-moral'. Only later was this relationship reversed: actions in the moral period, which had developed over the past ten thousand years, especially in western Europe, were regarded in terms of their origins rather than their results. Gradually the origin became identified with intentions or moral character. But the transformation of morality has not yet run its course. In the future in which free spirits will reign Nietzsche envisions a complete 'overcoming of morality'. In this 'extra-moral' stage 'an action's decisive value is demonstrated precisely by that part of it that is *not intentional*; do we not suspect that all of an action's intentionality, everything that can be seen or known about it, that can be "conscious" about it, is still part of its surface and skin—which, like all skin, reveals something, but *hides* even more?' (p. 33; 32). In this passage Nietzsche anticipates the unconscious of psychoanalysis, but he also suggests a new way to conceive of moral values, one that eradicates the notion of free will and the autonomy of the subject.

Undoubtedly the free spirits to whom Nietzsche alludes will be emancipated from traditional religion, which is the topic in the third section. Nietzsche's thoughts on religion had been developing steadily since the early 1870s. Although he was the son of a Protestant pastor, he had abandoned belief in the Christian deity rather early in life, but in the 1870s and increasingly in the 1880s he came to feel that religion in general, and especially Christianity, was responsible for the debilitating state of humanity in modern times. In *Human, All Too Human* religion was already characterized as an unnatural attempt to reinterpret our experiences. And in *The Gay Science* he had proclaimed in one of the most notorious aphorisms in his oeuvre the death of God. What Nietzsche added in the 1880s to his basic anti-religious world-view—besides a more strident rhetorical register—was an analysis of the psychology of the religious individual and an understanding of the function of religion in human society. In *Beyond Good and Evil* he maintains that original Christianity represents 'an ongoing suicide of reason' (p. 44; 46), ascribing it to an Oriental slave revolt against Roman antiquity. Like Freud after him, Nietzsche considered religion a 'neurosis' (p. 45; 47), it involves an unnatural self-denial and sacrifice. In one of his most interesting observations, Nietzsche compares the history of 'religious cruelty' to a ladder with three important rungs: the first entails the sacrifice of one's loved ones to the deity; the second demands the sacrifice of one's own instincts or inner nature; and the final rung, which we are now coming to know, involves the sacrifice of God himself for the worship of 'stone, stupidity, heaviness, fate, nothingness' (p. 50; 55). Nietzsche here suggests that our modern penchant for science or nihilism, as atheistic as it appears at first glance, is merely a replacement for religious belief.

Nietzsche is not unaware of the advantages that religion has brought to human society, even as it has debased human nature. It has helped humankind to endure an otherwise intolerable existence and has assisted us in constructing a viable social order by demanding that we love each other. But religion also has other essential socializing functions. For a particular group of people—

Nietzsche mentions the Brahmans by name—religion provides a spirituality that permits them to remove themselves from the mundane and crude world surrounding them. For those who are destined to be rulers it is one means for overcoming resistance in their subjects, since it forms a common bond with ordinary people and pacifies them into obedience. It also serves as a pedagogical and disciplinary device for the ascending classes, teaching them a certain abnegation that ennobles their spirit and allows them to rise above the common rabble. Finally, for the vast masses, religion provides a solace for their suffering and the meaninglessness of their existence, 'something that justifies their everyday lives, all the baseness, all the semi-animal poverty of their souls' (p. 55; 61). In general, however, Nietzsche's attitude towards religion is that it represents a stage of human development that must be overcome. Christianity, in particular, has led to a '*degeneration of the European race*' (p. 56; 62), and the persistence of Christian belief is a sign that the human being has not developed into a creature that is strong enough to achieve the type of self-contained nobility of spirit Nietzsche envisions.

This renewed attack on Christianity is followed by a section containing a series of 125 shorter epigrams. Each consists of a sentence or two; in contrast to the other sections, there is no extended discussion of a thought, only the core of an idea expressed in the most pithy fashion. Written in the manner of the French moralists, these maxims and reflections frequently relate to other sections in the work. For example, we find maxims about epistemology (64 or 80) and about religion (104 or 168). But we also encounter general social observations relating to women, love, happiness, and human psychology. Although this section is therefore the least interesting philosophically, it displays better than other sections Nietzsche's wit and insights into more mundane matters of the heart and the soul. This short section thus assumes the character of a true interlude, a break in the text that amuses and relaxes the reader before and after the more philosophically demanding reflections contained in the remainder of the book.

With Section V Nietzsche returns to the task of philosophy, and to his aphoristic style, focusing here on issues he had previously discussed in several writings. The first of these is the history of morality. In a sense Nietzsche, despite his extensive consideration of morality and ethics, was not a moral philosopher since he does not endeavour to write an ethical treatise or to propagate an ethical system. He resembles rather an historian or genealogist of ethics: his writings focus on the origin and function of moral value in human history. Indeed, his chief objection to previous moral philosophy is that it has sought to find a rational basis for morality in human life and has thereby avoided the fundamental problem of all morality. Nietzsche maintains that morality is neither rational nor absolute nor natural. He observes that the world has known many moral systems, each of which advances claims to universality; all moral systems are therefore particular, serving a specific purpose for their propagators or creators, and enforcing a certain regime that disciplines human beings for social life by narrowing our perspectives and limiting our horizons. Nietzsche does not simplistically assert, however, that morals deprive us of our freedom. He recognizes that there is no simple opposition between a constraining morality and a complete licence for any action. Morality, in a sense, has become 'natural' or necessary for the human being, even though it violates basic human nature or instincts. Without morality human society in general and European culture in particular would have been impossible. But we should not confuse the necessity for some kind of morality with the naturalness of any particular moral system since in their essence all moral judgements are ultimately based on capriciousness, irrationality, and the violation of natural, biological drives.

Despite Nietzsche's suggestion that there is no natural state of humankind, no pre-moral epoch in which there were no internal constraints on action, he often contrasts a quasi-mythological state of affairs, associated vaguely with pre-Socratic Greece, with the morality initiated by the Judaeo-Christian tradition. The Jews, he asserts, 'brought about that tour de force of a reversal of values' (p. 83; 195); they negated a noble order in which richness, excess, cruelty, and sensuality were validated, and substituted for it a value system in which poverty, godliness, timidity, and spirituality hold sway. This *slave revolt in morals* (p. 83; 195) disdains as evil the beast of prey and the man of prey, for Nietzsche the 'most healthy of all tropical plants and brutes' (pp. 83–4; 197), while affirming abstinence, pity, and a tolerance for suffering. The institution of the Judaeo-Christian 'herd' morality has made modern Europe possible even as it has meant an impoverishment of possibilities and human potential. Nietzsche reasons that there have always been rulers and subjects, and he recognizes that a morality preaching docile obedience is a necessity for the masses. He objects more strenuously, however, to the 'moral hypocrisy of commanders' (p. 85; 199), who portray themselves as the servants of the people, the implementers of the constitution, or the instruments of the common weal, in short, as a variation of the herd, rather than as men exercising their unbridled will to power. The ubiquity of herd morality will eventually annihilate strong and dangerous drives— Nietzsche lists 'adventurousness, recklessness, vengefulness, slyness, rapacity, lust for power' (p. 87; 201) among them; and 'everything that raises an individual above the herd and causes his neighbour to fear him' (p. 88; 201) will be condemned as evil. In Europe of the nineteenth century herd morality masquerades as the only true morality; its political components, the advocacy of democracy, equal rights, or even socialism dominate modern nations. Nietzsche's hope is that the future will bring a radical revaluation of this herd morality that will teach humans 'that their future is their *will*, that the future depends on their human will, and they will prepare the way for great risk-taking and joint experiments in discipline and breeding in order to put an end to that terrible reign of nonsense and coincidence that until now has been known as "history" ' (pp. 90–1; 203). He calls for leaders, for free spirits to liberate society from the debilitating effects of Christian-European morality.

One might suspect that these leaders will come from the educated elite, or even from the academy, but Nietzsche dispels this thought in his discussion of 'We Scholars'. This title is surely ironic; by 1886 Nietzsche no longer identified himself with academia or university affairs. Still, we should not forget that for the greater part of his adult life Nietzsche was involved in higher education as either a student or a professor. Although illness forced him to miss several semesters of teaching even when he was employed at Basle from 1869 to 1879, and compelled him to retire early thereafter, he was familiar and concerned with educational matters throughout his career. In 'We Scholars' he pursues a criticism of scholarly activity that he had inaugurated in lectures and writings from the early 1870s. Scholars must be carefully distinguished, Nietzsche asserts, from philosophers, with whom they have only a faint resemblance. The former are not noble in their heritage or thought process; a scholar is 'neither masterful nor authoritative nor even self-sufficient', but rather 'industrious, patiently joining the rank and file, conforming and moderate in his abilities and needs' (p. 96; 206). These qualities will hardly strike the reader as unequivocally desirable, and, indeed, it is Nietzsche's purpose here to present scholars as uncreative, diligent, and limited intellectual workers, who sacrifice their own subjectivity for the sake of the dubious ideal of 'objectivity' and the 'scientific method'. They are the educated counterpart to the followers of herd morality and form a contrast to the truly original, daring, and genial philosophers Nietzsche envisions as the spiritual leaders of a new epoch. These new philosophers, these men of 'tomorrow and the day after tomorrow' (p. 105; 212) distinguish themselves from both the scholarly caste and the unimaginative philosophical labourers by their relentless criticism of traditional values as well as their ability to create new values. Ultimately only a select few will qualify for the title of genuine philosopher.

What exactly will the free spirit, the new philosopher, the man of genius, or the good of tomorrow and the day after tomorrow be like? What features will he possess? How will he act differently in the world? He will certainly operate beyond good and evil, not adhering to the conventional moral codes of the Christian tradition. But can we say more about him? Nietzsche broaches this topic in his seventh section, entitled appropriately 'Our Virtues'. Like most utopian thinkers—and Nietzsche by dint of his vision of a better society in future times qualifies as a utopian thinker—to a large extent he defines the noble man of the future *ex negativo*. The free spirit of tomorrow will no longer subscribe to the truths of today; he will reject the average and the norm and validate the exception and the extraordinary. He will disabuse himself of the illusion of a disinterested and objective knowledge, understanding that knowledge is at bottom a function of the will to dominate. He will rid himself of moralities that preach equality, democracy, the general welfare, and utilitarian values, and affirm instead the natural hierarchy Nietzsche captures repeatedly in the term *Rangordnung*. He will overcome the 'historical sense', ubiquitous in nineteenth-century Europe, and appreciate in its stead 'perfection and ultimate ripeness in any culture or art, the noble element in works and people, their moment of silken seas and halcyon self-sufficiency, the golden coldness shown by every thing that has reached perfection' (p. 116; 224). More problematically Nietzsche propagates a human being that will not feel compassion with the oppressed and the unfortunate in society, and that will not seek to do away with suffering, including his own suffering. Rather, the pity this future man feels will involve the disdain for the manner in which the human race has made itself small and petty, and he will nourish suffering as the aid to 'depth, mystery, mask, spirit, cleverness, greatness' (p. 117; 225). In a controversial aphorism Nietzsche even ventures a reconsideration of cruelty as an essential part of human nature. All higher culture, all great tragedy, everything sublime, all knowledge, he contends, are ultimately based on cruelty, either towards ourselves or towards others. Above all, however, the '*very* free spirits' Nietzsche conjures up for his readers will be genuine revealers of knowledge, the knowledge that we have repressed and neglected in civilized Europe. The task Nietzsche assigns his free spirits is 'to return man to nature; to master the many conceited and gushing interpretations and secondary meanings that have heretofore been scribbled and painted over that eternal original text *homo natura*' (p. 123; 230). In terms of present values Nietzsche's free spirit will thus prove to be an 'immoralist' who affirms life and aspires to the heights of culture and creativity.

Will women also be free spirits? Nietzsche does not provide us with a definite answer, but he indicates at the end of the seventh section that women are not to be evaluated on the same basis as men. Indeed, the last eight aphorisms in this section are devoted to a virulent criticism of women's striving to attain equality and self-reliance. We have already seen that Nietzsche tended towards misogynist statements, a propensity that grew more noticeable in the 1880s, and here he is obviously reacting to the first-wave women's movement in Germany and across Europe. He is also repudiating the endeavours of women to secure admission to universities and professional careers; it was precisely during the last third of the nineteenth century that women were first able to matriculate on a regular basis at European institutions of higher education. Nietzsche considers the trend towards women's emancipation as an 'overall *uglification*' of Europe (p. 124; 232). He makes it clear that women should not seek enlightenment, that there exists an absolute and hostile antagonism between men and women, and that the advocacy of 'equal rights, equal education, equal ambitions and obligations' is 'a *typical* sign of shallowness' (p. 127; 238). Women who seek equality depart from their nature, which Nietzsche identifies with 'their genuine, predator-like, cunning suppleness, their tiger's claw beneath the glove, their naive egoism, their ineducability and inner wildness, the mystery, breadth, and range of their desires and virtues' (p. 129; 239). Nietzsche prefaces his aphorisms on women with the caveat that the truths he is going to write belong to him alone (p. 124; 231). But we should note that all his observations, whether they relate to epistemology or to current events, have the same status: they are claims he advances and wants to impress on his readers. His remarks on women are one of the more unfortunate aspects of his writings, indicating both a deep-seated prejudice that festered over time, and ultimately his inability to apply his own critical philosophical demands to the long tradition of male misogyny.

The penultimate section, entitled 'Peoples and Fatherlands', continues with themes related to current events, although it also deals briefly with ancient civilization and outstanding individuals of the nineteenth century. It opens and closes with an aphorism about Richard Wagner, the great German opera composer with whom Nietzsche was obsessed for most of his mature life, at first as a disciple, but after about 1875 increasingly as an adversary. Nietzsche's views on France and England, on which he expounds at length, are apt to strike us as somewhat quirky and slightly prejudicial: the English are not a philosophical race, Nietzsche claims, and even its most prominent intellectuals (Charles Darwin, John Stuart Mill, Herbert Spencer) are called 'respectable, but mediocre' (p. 144; 253). France, by contrast, is termed 'still, even now, the seat of the most spiritual and refined European culture and a great school of taste' (p. 145; 254); but it is difficult for Nietzsche to justify his general claims with anything but subjective impressions that often border on clichés. Ultimately Nietzsche appears to be more interested in the Germans, to whom he devotes more space, but about whom he is more derogatory. The German, he writes, is an expert on 'secret paths to chaos'; the celebrated profundity ascribed to this nation is attributed to uncertainty, shiftiness, and lack of form (pp. 134–7; 244). Nietzsche is especially critical of German anti-Semitism, with which he was personally acquainted in the person of his sister's husband, Bernhard Förster, as well as his publisher, and he inverts several of the prejudices typically levelled at the Jewish people. Nietzsche's views on Jews were complex, however, and not always flattering. While he believes that they are 'the strongest, toughest, and purest race now living in Europe' (p. 142; 251), he also makes them responsible for slave morality and its deleterious consequences. At one point he states that the Jews could gain hegemony over all of Europe if they wanted it, a statement that was as ludicrous in 1886 as it was during the Third Reich, when it was part of Nazi propaganda. But Nietzsche's vision in this section is not to validate or to deprecate any particular nation or people, but to proclaim the advent of a new united Europe. What Nietzsche envisioned is nothing like the move towards European unity we are experiencing in the late 1990s, but rather, in keeping with his elitist political and social views, entails 'the breeding of a new caste to rule over Europe' (p. 143; 251). Nietzsche's good European thus emanates from an anti-nationalist sentiment, but it does not betoken an end to hierarchical social structures.

In Nietzsche's final section he turns to a question that has been implicitly posed in earlier sections of the text: 'What is Noble?' The German term for noble is *vornehm*, a word that has the connotation of superior rank, of privilege by virtue of birth or distinction, or of some natural superiority. Nietzsche makes it obvious that genuine nobility in his sense has been damaged and made undistinguishable 'as the rule of the rabble begins, under this heavy, cloudy sky that makes everything opaque and leaden' (p. 172; 287). But he also emphasizes that the type of noble human being he envisions is desirable, indeed, that human society without noble men would be a miserable, inartistic, uncreative wasteland. His fears about the disappearance of nobility are therefore the flip side of his critique of modernity, which has led to the levelling of creativity and distinction because of the democratizing trend and the demands for equal rights. Nietzsche, continuing his anti-modernist polemic, opens this section by affirming the need for 'a great ladder of hierarchy and value differentiation between people' (p. 151; 257). Searching for a time in which nobility reigned in human affairs as well as an explanation for the demise of aristocratic regimes, he describes conflicting systems of values: one, associated with a hierarchy based on natural superiority, is the product of the nobility itself. The other, the result of the reactions of the slaves, has endeavoured to debase everything grand in the human spirit. Nietzsche's vision may have some historical foundation—although he gives few genuine historical illustrations to support his claims—but it is shocking none the less. Life itself, he asserts at one point, '*in its essence* means appropriating, injuring, overpowering those who are foreign and weaker; oppression, harshness, forcing one's own forms on others, incorporation, and at the very least, at the very mildest, exploitation' (pp. 152–3; 259). Nietzsche's argument is that these words evoke in us repulsion because of our own adherence to a morality that has degraded noble values, which he consistently regards as more natural and more life-affirming, more creative and more vital. When Nietzsche's advocacy of nobility is interpreted simply as a call for more freedom and creativity, for an end to repression and levelling of individual differences, his philosophy quite rightly meets with general approval. But the darker side of Nietzsche's views should not be ignored: at times he affirms a return to an aristocratic social order in which the happiness of the vast majority would be sacrificed for an elite caste that will produce and enjoy a European cultural renaissance.

Beyond Good and Evil is thus not an easy work to read. It is a rich and sometimes frustrating text, one that is apt to elicit from contemporary readers as many objections as affirmations. Its significance lies not only in the stylistic excellence—Nietzsche was a consummate artisan of the German language, a quality that is evident in the fine translation that follows—and in its philosophical brilliance, which is marred only occasionally by a failure to elaborate a thought or idea fully. More importantly, *Beyond Good and Evil* is a critical and reflective book, one that does not shy away from conclusions even when they are offensive, one that dares to challenge conventional truths and present utopian and perhaps dystopian visions. Behind the intricately woven themes, we sense Nietzsche grappling with the thorniest of philosophical issues, as well as with the various phenomena of modernity that appeared so suddenly and intrusively in Germany and across the continent. Nietzsche's discussions of philosophical, political, and social issues inspired several generations of thinkers to emulate, validate, and refute his contentions. No matter how we may evaluate his answers to the topics he addresses in this brilliant book, we have to admire his courage in daring to respond differently, and concede that his responses have set in motion a chain of thought that continues to occupy us today as much as it did him over a century ago. Nietzsche, disappointed with his lack of a readership during his own lifetime, commented that some people are born posthumously. The enormous influence of the philosophy articulated in *Beyond Good and Evil* offers us overwhelming evidence that Nietzsche was correct at the very least in what was almost certainly a prediction about the fate of his own writings.

TRANSLATOR'S NOTE

In undertaking this new translation of *Beyond Good and Evil* I have worked towards a semantic accuracy that is also historically appropriate. Thus I have resisted the temptation to translate with twentieth-century terms those psychoanalytic or postmodern critical concepts anticipated by Nietzsche in this 1886 text and have tried instead to use an English that is neither antiquated nor anachronistically modern. Appreciating Nietzsche's warning remark in Aphorism 28 that 'the hardest thing to translate from one language to another is the tempo of its style', I have nevertheless also tried to capture something of the tempo of Nietzsche's German in this translation. Most German philosophical writing takes the form of weighty building-blocks of variously declined nouns (unlike verb-driven English prose), and this can also be true of Nietzsche; but he usually sustains his arguments at an energetic *allegro con brio*.

Nietzsche's punctuation is somewhat idiosyncratic, and has been adapted here to retain the rhetorical thrust of his thinking without being distracting to today's reader. The most important such change has been to make distinct paragraphs of those sections set apart (and joined) by a long dash in Nietzsche's more discursive aphorisms. Recognizing that some sense of the grand wholeness of his thought may be sacrificed as a consequence (see Aphorism 247 on periodic sentences), I nevertheless considered the gains in clarity and accessibility to be more important.

While not being bound by any categorical consistency, I have usually rendered the problematic word *Geist* (which can have the sense of 'spirit', 'mind', 'wit', or 'intellect', depending on the context) as 'spirit', for in Aphorism 44 especially, Nietzsche clarifies the distinction between his own 'freier Geist' (free spirit) and other 'freethinkers'. Traditional translations of concepts that are now familiar and central to Nietzsche's thought (self-overcoming, perspective) have been retained.

The endnotes to the translation assume the reader's familiarity with prominent historical figures (Napoleon, Darwin) and Classical literary texts (*The Odyssey*), and elucidate those of Nietzsche's other allusions (Bentham, Lessing) that particularly further his arguments. The endnotes also provide translations of foreign-language phrases and explain those of Nietzsche's sometimes almost maniacal puns and plays on words that could not be reproduced in an English version.

This translation of *Beyond Good and Evil* is based on the Colli–Montinari critical edition (Berlin: Walter de Gruyter, 1968). Among previous translations of the work, those by Walter Kaufmann (1966) and R. J. Hollingdale (1973) are particularly admirable. My own translation may differ from these two in its inclination to choose Germanic rather than Latinate renderings, its non-interpretative endnotes, and its effort to capture the musical aspects of the text. My chief aim has been to provide a fluent translation for the readers of the Oxford World's Classics series.

I owe a great debt of gratitude to many people for their help with this translation: I thank Richard Eldridge, Randall Exon, Dorothea Frede, Jay Geller, Scott Gilbert, Mark Kuperberg, Amy-Jill Levine, John McNees, Rosaria Munson, Martin Ostwald, and William Turpin for their expertise. Rüdiger Bittner, especially, was a key consultant throughout the process. For advice on style, heartfelt thanks go (as usual) to Stephen Hannaford. This translation would not have been possible without the generous support of Swarthmore College. I am grateful to Judith Luna at Oxford University Press for her sustained encouragement from beginning to end. Above all, I would like to thank Joyce Crick, whose reading of the translation in its formative stages was of absolutely critical importance: she has corrected my errors, provided alternate renderings, and been in general a vigilant and astute companion in this enterprise: the quality of the translation is due in great measure to her wise judgement. Any errors or infelicities that still remain are, of course, my own.

In Aphorism 277 Nietzsche writes, 'After we have finished building our house, we notice that we have inadvertently learned something in the process, something that we absolutely *should* have known before we—began to build.' I would only add that this 'melancholy of everything *completed*' applies equally well to translations.

SELECT BIBLIOGRAPHY

Biography

Gilman, Sander L. (ed.), *Conversations with Nietzsche* (trans. David Parent, New York: Oxford University Press, 1987).

Hayman, Ronald, *Nietzsche: A Critical Life* (London: Weidenfeld and Nicolson, 1980).

Pletsch, Carl, *Young Nietzsche: Becoming a Genius* (New York: Free Press, 1991).

Anthologies

Hollingdale, R. J. (ed.), *A Nietzsche Reader* (Harmondsworth: Penguin, 1977).

Kaufmann, Walter (ed.), *Basic Writings of Nietzsche* (New York: Modern Library, 1968).

Schacht, Richard (ed.), *Nietzsche: Selections* (New York: Macmillan, 1993).

Critical Studies

Allison, David B. (ed.), *The New Nietzsche: Contemporary Styles of Interpretation* (Cambridge, Mass.: MIT Press, 1985).

Aschheim, Steven E., *The Nietzsche Legacy in Germany 1890–1990* (Berkeley and Los Angeles: University of California Press, 1992).

Behler, Ernst, *Confrontations* (trans. Steven Taubeneck, Stanford, Calif.: Stanford University Press, 1991).

Berkowitz, Peter, *Nietzsche. The Ethics of an Immoralist* (Cambridge, Mass.: Harvard University Press, 1995).

Bloom, Harold (ed.), *Friedrich Nietzsche* (New York: Chelsea House, 1987).

Danto, Arthur C., *Nietzsche as Philosopher* (New York: Columbia University Press, 1980).

Hollingdale, R. J., *Nietzsche: The Man and his Philosophy* (London: Routledge & Kegan Paul, 1965).

Holub, Robert C., *Friedrich Nietzsche* (New York: Twayne, 1995).

Irigaray, Luce, *Marine Lover of Friedrich Nietzsche* (trans. Gilliam C. Gill, New York: Columbia University Press, 1991).

Kaufmann, Walter, *Nietzsche: Philosopher, Psychologist, Antichrist* (Princeton: Princeton University Press, 1968).

Kofman, Sarah, *Nietzsche and Metaphor* (London: Athlone Press, 1993).

Magnus, Bernd, with Mileur, Jean-Pierre, and Stewart, Stanley, *Nietzsche's Case: Philosophy as/and Literature* (New York: Routledge, 1993).

Magnus, Bernd, and Higgins, Kathleen (eds.), *The Cambridge Companion to Nietzsche* (Cambridge: Cambridge University Press, 1996).

Nehamas, Alexander, *Nietzsche: Life as Literature* (Cambridge, Mass.: Harvard University Press, 1985).

Schacht, Richard, *Making Sense of Nietzsche* (Urbana: University of Illinois Press, 1994).

Sedgwick, Peter (ed.), *Nietzsche: A Critical Reader* (Oxford: Blackwell, 1995).

Solomon, Robert C. (ed.), *Nietzsche: A Collection of Critical Essays* (Notre Dame, Ind.: University of Notre Dame Press, 1980).

Stambaugh, Joan, *The Other Nietzsche* (Albany: State University of New York Press, 1993).

Strong, Tracy B., and Gillespie, Michael (eds.), *Toward New Seas: Philosophy, Aesthetics and Politics in Nietzsche* (Chicago: University of Chicago Press, 1988).

Tanner, Michael, *Nietzsche* (Oxford: Oxford University Press, 1994).

Waite, Geoff, *Nietzsche's Corps/e: Aesthetics, Politics, Prophecy, or, The Spectacular Technoculture of Everyday Life* (Durham, NC: Duke University Press, 1996).

Further Reading in Oxford World's Classics

Nietzsche, Friedrich, *On the Genealogy of Morals*, trans. and ed. Douglas Smith.

—— *Twilight of the Idols*, trans. and ed. Duncan Large.

Berkeley, George, *Principles of Human Knowledge* and *Three Dialogues*, ed. Howard Robinson.

Darwin, Charles, *The Origin of Species*, ed. Gillian Beer.

A CHRONOLOGY OF FRIEDRICH NIETZSCHE

1844   Friedrich Wilhelm Nietzsche born in Röcken (Saxony) on 15 October, son of Karl Ludwig and Franziska Nietzsche. His father and both grandfathers are Protestant clergymen.

1846   Birth of sister Elisabeth.

1849   Birth of brother Joseph; death of father.

1850   Death of brother; family moves to Naumburg.

1858–64   Attends renowned boys' boarding-school Pforta, where he excels in classics. Begins to suffer from migraine attacks which will plague him for the rest of his career.

1864   Enters Bonn University to study theology and classical philology.

1865   Follows classics professor Ritschl to Leipzig University, where he drops theology and continues with studies in classical philology. Discovers Schopenhauer's philosophy and becomes a passionate admirer.

1867   Begins publishing career with essay on Theognis; continues publishing philological articles and book reviews till 1873.

1867–8   Military service in Naumburg, until invalided out after a riding accident.

1868   Back in Leipzig, meets Richard Wagner for the first time and quickly becomes a devotee. Increasing disaffection with philology: plans to escape to Paris to study chemistry.

1869   On Ritschl's recommendation, appointed Extraordinary Professor of Classical Philology at Basle University. Awarded doctorate without examination; renounces Prussian citizenship. Begins a series of idyllic visits to the Wagners at Tribschen, on Lake Lucerne. Develops admiration for Jacob Burckhardt, his new colleague in Basle.

1870   Promoted to full professor. Participates in Franco-Prussian War as volunteer medical orderly, but contracts dysentery and diphtheria at the front within a fortnight.

1871   Granted semester's sick leave from Basle and works intensively on *The Birth of Tragedy*. Germany unified; founding of the Reich.

1872   Publishes *The Birth of Tragedy out of the Spirit of Music*, which earns him the condemnation of professional colleagues. Lectures 'On the Future of our Educational Institutions'; attends laying of foundation stone for Bayreuth Festival Theatre.

1873   Publishes first *Untimely Meditation: David Strauss the Confessor and the Writer.*

1874   Publishes second and third *Untimely Meditations: On the Use and Disadvantage of History for Life* and *Schopenhauer as Educator.* Relationship with Wagner begins to sour.

1875   Meets musician Heinrich Köselitz (Peter Gast), who idolizes him.

1876   Publishes fourth and last *Untimely Meditation: Richard Wagner in Bayreuth.* Attends first Bayreuth Festival but leaves early and subsequently breaks with Wagner. Further illness; granted full year's sick leave from the university.

1877   French translation of *Richard Wagner in Bayreuth* published, the only translation to appear during his mentally active lifetime.

1878   Publishes *Human, All Too Human: A Book for Free Spirits,* which confirms the break with Wagner.

1879   Publishes supplement to *Human, All Too Human, Assorted Opinions and Maxims.* Finally retires from teaching on a pension; first visits the Engadine, summering in St Moritz.

1880   Publishes *The Wanderer and His Shadow.* First stays in Venice and Genoa.

1881   Publishes *Daybreak: Thoughts on the Prejudices of Morality.* First stay in Sils-Maria.

1882   Publishes *The Gay Science.* Infatuation with Lou Andreas-Salomé, who spurns his marriage proposals.

1883   Publishes *Thus Spake Zarathustra: A Book for Everyone and No One,* Parts I and II (separately). Death of Wagner. Spends the summer in Sils and the winter in Nice, his pattern for the next five years. Increasingly consumed by writing.

1884   Publishes *Thus Spake Zarathustra,* Part III.

1885   *Thus Spake Zarathustra,* Part IV printed but circulated to only a handful of friends. Begins in earnest to amass notes for *The Will to Power.*

1886   Publishes *Beyond Good and Evil: Prelude to a Philosophy of the Future.* Change of publisher results in new expanded editions of *The Birth of Tragedy* and *Human, All Too Human* (now with a second volume comprising the *Assorted Opinions and Maxims* and *The Wanderer and His Shadow*).

1887   Publishes *On the Genealogy of Morals: A Polemic.* New expanded editions of *Daybreak* and *The Gay Science.*

1888   Begins to receive public recognition: Georg Brandes lectures on his work in Copenhagen. Discovers Turin, where he writes *The Wagner Case: A Musician's Problem.* Abandons *The Will to*

Power, then completes in quick succession: *Twilight of the Idols, or How to Philosophize with a Hammer* (first published 1889), *The Antichrist: Curse on Christianity* (f.p. 1895), *Ecce Homo, or How One Becomes What One Is* (f.p. 1908), *Nietzsche contra Wagner: Documents of a Psychologist* (f.p. 1895), and *Dionysus Dithyrambs* (f.p. 1892).

1889	Suffers mental breakdown in Turin (3 January) and is eventually committed to asylum in Jena. *Twilight of the Idols* published 24 January, the first of his new books to appear after his collapse.
1890	Discharged into the care of his mother in Naumburg.
1894	Elisabeth founds Nietzsche Archive in Naumburg (moving it to Weimar two years later).
1897	Mother dies; Elisabeth moves her brother to Weimar.
1900	Friedrich Nietzsche dies in Weimar on 25 August.

BEYOND GOOD AND EVIL

Prelude to
a Philosophy of the Future

PREFACE

ASSUMING that truth is a woman—what then? Is there not reason to suspect that all philosophers, in so far as they were dogmatists, have known very little about women? That if their aim was to charm a female, they have been especially inept and inapt in making advances to truth with such awful seriousness and clumsy insistence? One thing is certain: she has not let herself be charmed— and nowadays every dogmatism stands dejected and dispirited—*if* it is standing at all! For there are those who tauntingly claim that it has fallen, that all dogmatism lies defeated, even more, that it is breathing its last gasp. In all seriousness, there is good reason to hope that all philosophical dogmatizing, however solemn, conclusive, or definite its manner, may have been nothing but the infantile high-mindedness of a beginner. And we may be very near to a time when people will be constantly recognizing anew what in fact it *was* that furnished the cornerstone for those lofty, unconditional philosopher's edifices once built by the dogmatists: some folk superstition from time immemorial (such as the superstition about souls, which even today has not ceased to sow mischief as the superstition about subject and ego);* some play on words perhaps, some seductive aspect of grammar, or a daring generalization from very limited, very personal, very human, all-too-human facts. The philosophy of the dogmatists, we may hope, was only a promise reaching across millennia—as astrology used to be, in whose service more effort, money, wit, and patience were probably expended than for any real science to date: it is to astrology and its 'supernatural' pretensions in Asia and Egypt that we owe the grand style in architecture. It seems that in order to inscribe themselves into men's hearts with eternal demands, all great things must first wander the earth as monstrous and fear-inducing caricatures: dogmatic philosophy has been such a caricature, the teachings of Vedanta in Asia, for example, or Platonism in Europe. Let us not be ungrateful towards them, even though we must certainly also admit that of all errors thus far, the most grievous, protracted, and dangerous has been a dogmatist's error: Plato's invention of pure spirit and of transcendental goodness. But now that this error has been overcome, now that Europe is breathing a sigh of relief after this nightmare and in future can at least enjoy a healthier . . . sleep, we, *whose task is wakefulness itself,* have inherited all the energy that has been produced by the struggle against this error. Of course, in order to speak as he did about the spirit and the good, Plato had to set truth on its head and even deny *perspectivity,* that fundamental condition of all life; indeed, in the role of doctor, we may ask: 'What has caused such a canker on the most beautiful plant of antiquity, on Plato? Did that wicked Socrates corrupt him after all? Might Socrates really have been the corrupter of youth? And deserved his hemlock?'

But the struggle against Plato, or—to put it more clearly, for the 'common people'—the struggle against thousands of years of Christian-ecclesiastical pressure (for Christianity is Platonism for the 'common people') has created a splendid tension of the spirit in Europe such as the earth has never seen: with this kind of tension in our bow, we can now shoot at the most remote targets. To be sure, Europeans experience this tension as distress, and there have already been two elaborate attempts to loosen the bow, once by means of Jesuitism, and a second time by means of the democratic Enlightenment: with the help of freedom of the press and newspaper reading, these attempts probably did in fact make it harder for the spirit to experience itself as 'distressed'! (The Germans invented gunpowder—my respects! But they also cancelled that out by inventing the press.) But we who are not sufficiently Jesuits, nor democrats, nor even Germans, we *good Europeans* and free, *very* free spirits—we have it still, all the distress of the spirit and all the tension of its bow! And perhaps the arrow, too, the task, who knows? the *target* . . .

Sils-Maria, Upper Engadine
June 1885

SECTION ONE

ON THE PREJUDICES OF PHILOSOPHERS

I

THE will to truth, which will seduce us yet to many a risky venture, that famous truthfulness about which all philosophers to date have spoken with deference: what manner of questions has this will to truth presented for us! What strange, wicked, questionable questions! It is already a long story, and yet doesn't it seem to be just getting started? Is it any wonder that we finally grow suspicious, lose patience, turn round impatiently? That *we* learn from this Sphinx how to pose questions of our own? *Who* is actually asking us the questions here? *What* is it in us that really wants to 'get at the truth'?

It is true that we paused for a long time to question the origin of this will, until finally we came to a complete stop at an even more basic question. We asked about the *value* of this will. Given that we want truth: *why do we not prefer* untruth? And uncertainty? Even ignorance?

The problem of the value of truth appeared before us—or did we appear before it? Which of us here is Oedipus? Which the Sphinx? It is a rendezvous, so it seems, of questions and question marks.

And would you believe that in the end it seems to us as if the problem had never yet been posed, as if we were seeing it for the first time, focusing on it, *daring* it? For there is daring to it, and perhaps no daring greater.

2

'How *could* something arise from its opposite? Truth from error, for example? Or the will to truth from the will to deception? Or altruism from egoism? Or the wise man's pure, radiant contemplation from covetous desire? Such origination is impossible;

whoever dreams of it is a fool, or worse; those things of highest value must have a different origin, *their own*; they cannot be derived from this perishable, seductive, deceptive, lowly world, from this confusion of desire and delusion! Rather, their basis must lie in the womb of existence, in the imperishable, in the hidden god, in the "thing in itself"*—and nowhere else!'

Judgements of this kind constitute the typical prejudice by which we can always recognize the metaphysicians of every age; this kind of value judgement is at the back of all their logical proceedings; from out of this 'belief' of theirs, they go about seeking their 'knowledge', which they end by ceremoniously dubbing 'the truth'. The metaphysicians' fundamental belief is *the belief in the opposition of values*. It has never occurred even to the most cautious among them to raise doubts here at the threshold, where doubts would be most necessary, even though they have vowed to themselves: '*de omnibus dubitandum*'.* For may there not be doubt, first of all, whether opposites even exist and, second, whether those popular value judgements and value oppositions upon which metaphysicians have placed their seal may be no more than foreground evaluations, temporary perspectives, viewed from out of a corner perhaps, or up from underneath, a perspective from below* (to borrow an expression common to painters)? However much value we may ascribe to truth, truthfulness, or altruism, it may be that we need to attribute a higher and more fundamental value to appearance, to the will to illusion, to egoism and desire. It could even be possible that the value of those good and honoured things consists precisely in the fact that in an insidious way *they are related* to those bad, seemingly opposite things, linked, knit together, even identical perhaps. Perhaps!

But who is willing to worry about such dangerous Perhapses? We must wait for a new category of philosophers to arrive, those whose taste and inclination are the reverse of their predecessors'— they will be in every sense philosophers of the dangerous Perhaps.

And to speak in all seriousness: I see these new philosophers coming.

3

Having long kept a strict eye on the philosophers, and having looked between their lines, I say to myself: the largest part of conscious thinking has to be considered an instinctual activity, even in the case of philosophical thinking; we need a new understanding here, just as we've come to a new understanding of heredity and the 'innate'. Just as the act of birth is scarcely relevant to the entire process and progress of heredity, so 'consciousness' is scarcely *opposite* to the instincts in any decisive sense—most of a philosopher's conscious thinking is secretly guided and channelled into particular tracks by his instincts. Behind all logic, too, and its apparent tyranny of movement there are value judgements, or to speak more clearly, physiological demands for the preservation of a particular kind of life. That a certainty is worth more than an uncertainty, for example, or that appearance is worth less than 'truth': whatever their regulatory importance for *us*, such evaluations might still be nothing but foreground evaluations, a certain kind of *niaiserie*,* as is required for the preservation of beings like us. Given, that is, that man is not necessarily the 'measure of all things'* . . .

4

We do not object to a judgement just because it is false; this is probably what is strangest about our new language. The question is rather to what extent the judgement furthers life, preserves life, preserves the species, perhaps even cultivates the species; and we are in principle inclined to claim that judgements that are the most false (among which are the synthetic a priori judgements)* are the most indispensable to us, that man could not live without accepting logical fictions, without measuring reality by the purely invented world of the unconditional, self-referential, without a continual falsification of the world by means of the number—that to give up false judgements would be to give up life, to deny life. Admitting untruth as a condition of life: that means to resist familiar values in a dangerous way; and a philosophy that dares this has already placed itself beyond good and evil.

5

What provokes us to look at all philosophers with a mixture of distrust and contempt is not that we are always uncovering how guileless they are—how often and easily they lose their grasp or their way, in short how childish and childlike they are. It is rather that they are not honest enough, however loud and virtuous a racket they all make as soon as the problem of truthfulness is touched upon, even from afar. For they act as if they had discovered and acquired what are actually their opinions through the independent unravelling of a cold, pure, divinely unhampered dialectic (whereas mystics of every order, who are more honest, and more foolish, speak of 'inspiration'); basically, however, they are using reasons sought after the fact to defend a pre-existing tenet, a sudden idea, a 'brainstorm', or, in most cases, a rarefied and abstract version of their heart's desire. They are all of them advocates who refuse the name, that is in most cases wily spokesmen for their prejudices, which they dub 'truths'; and they are *very* far from having a conscience brave enough to own up to it, very far from having the good taste to announce it bravely, whether to warn a foe or a friend, or simply from high spirits and self-mockery. We have to smile at the spectacle of old Kant's hypocrisy,* as rigid as it is chaste, as he lures us onto the dialectical backroads that lead (or better, mislead) us to his 'categorical imperative',* for we are fastidious and take no small amusement in monitoring the subtle wiles of old moralists and moral preachers. Or take that hocus-pocus of mathematical form in which Spinoza armoured and disguised his philosophy ('the love of *his* wisdom'* ultimately, if we interpret the word correctly and fairly), to intimidate at the outset any brave assailant who might dare to throw a glance at this invincible virgin and Pallas Athena—how this sickly hermit's masquerade betrays his own timidity and assailability!

6

Little by little I came to understand what every great philosophy to date has been: the personal confession of its author, a kind of unintended and unwitting memoir; and similarly, that the moral (or immoral) aims in every philosophy constituted the actual seed from which the whole plant invariably grew. Whenever explaining

how a philosopher's most far-fetched metaphysical propositions
have come about, in fact, one always does well (and wisely) to ask
first: 'What morality is it (is *he*) aiming at?' Thus I do not believe
that an 'instinct for knowledge' is the father of philosophy, but
rather that here as elsewhere a different instinct has merely made
use of knowledge (and kNOwledge!)* as its tool. For anyone who
scrutinizes the basic human instincts to determine how influential
they have been as *inspiring* spirits (or demons and goblins) will find
that all the instincts have practised philosophy, and that each one
of them would like only too well to represent *itself* as the ultimate
aim of existence and as the legitimate *master* of all other instincts.
For every instinct is tyrannical; and as *such* seeks to philosophize.

Admittedly, things may be different ('better', if you like) with
scholars, the truly scientific people; they may really have something
like an instinct for knowledge, some small independent clockwork
which, when properly wound up, works away bravely *without* necessarily involving all the scholar's other instincts. That is why a
scholar's real 'interests' generally lie elsewhere entirely, in his family,
say, or in the acquisition of wealth, or in politics; indeed it is almost
a matter of indifference whether his little machine is located in this
branch of science or that, or whether the 'promising' young worker
turns out to be a good philologist or a mushroom expert or a
chemist: what he eventually becomes does not *distinguish* him.
About the philosopher, conversely, there is absolutely nothing that
is impersonal; and it is above all his morality which proves decidedly
and decisively *who he is*—that is, in what hierarchy the innermost
drives of his nature are arranged.

7

How malicious philosophers can be! I know of nothing more venomous than the joke that Epicurus* made at the expense of Plato
and the Platonists: he called them 'Dionysiokolakes'. Literally and
primarily, this means 'flatterers of Dionysus', that is, the tyrant's
appendages and toadies; but it also suggests: 'They are all *actors*,
there is nothing genuine about them' (for 'Dionysiokolax' was a
popular term for an actor). And the latter meaning contains the
real malice that Epicurus fired off at Plato: he was annoyed by
the mannered grandiosity, the theatricality that Plato and his pupils

deployed so well, and that Epicurus did not! Epicurus, the old schoolmaster of Samos, sat tucked away in his little garden in Athens and wrote three hundred books—out of fury and ambition against Plato—who knows?

It took one hundred years for Greece to realize who this garden-god Epicurus had been.

Did it realize?

8

In every philosophy there is a point when the philosopher's 'conviction' makes its entrance; or, in the language of an old mystery play:

> adventavit asinus
> pulcher et fortissimus.*

9

You want to *live* 'according to nature'? Oh you noble Stoics,* what deceit lies in these words! Imagine a creature constituted like nature, prodigal beyond measure, neutral beyond measure, with no purpose or conscience, with no compassion or fairness, fertile and desolate and uncertain all at once; imagine Indifference itself as a power: how *could* you live according to this indifference? To live—isn't that precisely the desire to be other than this nature? Doesn't life mean weighing, preferring, being unjust, having limits, wanting to be Different? And even if the real meaning of your imperative 'to live according to nature' is 'to live according to life'—how could you do *otherwise*? Why make a principle out of something that you already are and needs must be?

The truth is something else entirely: while you pretend to delight in reading the canon of your law from nature, you want the opposite, you curious play-actors and self-deceivers! In your pride you want to dictate your morality, your ideals to nature, incorporate them into nature, of all things; you demand that nature be 'according to Stoics'; you would like to make all existence exist in accordance with your own image alone—for the great and unending glorification and universalization of Stoicism! With all your love of truth, you force yourselves to stare so long, so constantly, so hypnotically at nature that you see it *falsely*, that is, stoically, and you become incapable of seeing it otherwise. And then out of some unfathomable arrogance you conceive the lunatic hope that *because* you know how to tyrannize yourself (Stoicism is self-tyranny), nature too can be tyrannized: for isn't the Stoic a *part* of nature? . . .

But this is an old, eternal story: what took place back then with the Stoics is still taking place today, whenever a philosophy begins to believe in itself. It always creates the world according to its own image, it cannot do otherwise; philosophy is this tyrannical drive itself, the most spiritual form of the will to power, to 'creation of the world', to the *causa prima*.*

10

The zeal and subtlety (I would almost like to say 'cunning') with which everyone in Europe today is raising the question 'of the real and the apparent world' give us cause for thought and for listening—and anyone who hears only a 'will to truth' in the background certainly does not have the sharpest ears. In a few rare, isolated cases a will to truth really may have played a part, an extravagant or adventurous mood, a metaphysician's craving for the lost cause, a will that ultimately prefers a handful of 'certainty' to a whole wagonload of beautiful possibilities; there may even be some puritanical fanatics of conscience* who would rather lay down their lives for a certain Nothing than for an uncertain Something. But however valiant the gestures of such virtue, this is nihilism, the sign of a despairing, mortally weary soul. With stronger, more vital thinkers, still thirsty for life, things are different: they take sides *against* appearance and are already pronouncing the word 'perspectivist' with arrogance; they take the credibility of their own body about as seriously as the credibility of the appearance that 'the earth stands still'. They seem to be ready cheerfully to let drop from their hands their surest possession (for what do we believe in more surely than our bodies?) and who knows whether at bottom they might not want to regain something that they once possessed even *more surely*, something from the old homestead of belief of earlier times, the 'immortal soul' perhaps, or 'the old god'—ideas, in short, that led to a life that was better, more robust and serene, than the one our 'modern ideas' can lead to? In this question, there is *mistrust* of modern ideas, disbelief in everything constructed yesterday and today; there may be a slight element of disgust and contempt, from those no longer able to tolerate the highly eclectic conceptual bric-a-brac that today's so-called positivism brings to the market place; those with more fastidious taste are revolted by the fairground motley and frippery of all these reality-philosophists, who have nothing new or genuine apart from their motley. We should credit the sceptical anti-realists and knowledge-microscopists of today with at least this much, I think: we have seen nothing to refute their instinct to escape from *modern* reality—their retrograde backroads are no concern of ours! What is important about them is *not* that they want to go 'back', but that they want to go—*away*! With a little *more* strength, more buoyancy, courage, artistry, they would want to go *beyond*—and not back!

11

People today are trying, it seems to me, to divert attention from Kant's real influence on German philosophy, trying especially to evade what he himself considered his great value. Kant was most proud of his table of categories; holding it in his hands he said, 'This is the most difficult thing that ever could be undertaken for the benefit of metaphysics.'

But let us understand what this 'could be' really implies! He was proud of having *discovered* in man a new faculty, the faculty to make synthetic a priori judgements. Granted that he was deceiving himself about his discovery: nevertheless, the development and rapid flowering of German philosophy stem from this pride and from the rivalry of his disciples to discover if at all possible something worthy of even more pride—and in any event 'new faculties'!

But let's think about it, it is high time. 'How are synthetic a priori judgements *possible*?' wondered Kant, and what did he answer? They are *facilitated by a faculty*:* unfortunately, however, he did not say this in four words, but so cumbersomely, so venerably, and with such an expense of German profundity and ornateness that people misheard the comical *niaiserie allemande** in such an answer. They were ecstatic about this new faculty, in fact, and the rejoicing reached its height when Kant discovered a moral faculty in man as well. (For at that time Germans were still moral, and not yet 'real-political'.*)

There followed the honeymoon of German philosophy; all the young theologians of the Tübingen Stift* headed right for the bushes—they were all looking for 'faculties'. And what all didn't they find, in that innocent, rich, still youthful era of the German spirit when the malicious elf Romanticism was still piping and singing, back when no one yet had learned to distinguish between 'finding' and 'inventing'!* They found above all a faculty for the 'extra-sensual': Schelling christened it 'intellectual intuition',* thus meeting the dearest desires of his essentially pious-desirous Germans. One can do no greater injustice to this whole arrogant, enthusiastic movement (which was youth itself, however audaciously it may have cloaked itself in grey, senile concepts) than to take it seriously and treat it with anything like moral indignation. Enough, people grew older—the dream vanished. The time came for them to rub their foreheads: they are rubbing them still today. They had been dreaming, and the first among them had been old Kant. 'Facilitated by a faculty'—that's what he had said, or at least that's what he had meant. But what kind of an answer is that? What kind of explanation? Isn't it rather simply repeating the question? How can opium make us sleep? It is 'facilitated by a faculty', the *virtus dormitiva*, answers that doctor in Molière,

> quia est in eo virtus dormitiva
> cujus est natura sensus assoupire.*

But answers like these belong in comedy, and for the Kantian question 'How are synthetic a priori judgements possible?' it is high time to substitute another question: 'Why is the belief in such judgements *necessary*?'—it is time to understand that for the purpose of preserving creatures of our kind, we must *believe* that such judgements are true; which means, of course, that they could still be *false* judgements. Or to put it more clearly, and crudely and completely: synthetic a priori judgements should not 'be possible' at all; we have no right to them, in our mouths they are only false judgements. Yet the belief in their truth happens to be necessary as one of the foreground beliefs and appearances that constitute the perspective-optics of life.

And, finally, remembering the enormous effect that 'German

philosophy' exercised throughout Europe (one understands, I hope, why it deserves quotation marks?), let no one doubt that a certain *virtus dormitiva* had a part in it: amidst the noble men of leisure, the moralists, mystics, artists, the partial Christians, and political obscurantists of every nation, people were delighted that German philosophy offered an antidote to the still overpowering sensualism pouring into this century from the previous one, in short: 'sensus assoupire' . . .

12

As regards materialistic atomism,* hardly anything has ever been so well refuted; in all Europe there is probably no scholar so unschooled as to want to credit it with serious meaning, apart from a handy everyday usefulness (that is, as a stylistic abbreviation). This we owe primarily to the Pole Boscovich,* who along with the Pole Copernicus* achieved the greatest victory yet in opposing the appearance of things. For while Copernicus convinced us to believe contrary to all our senses that the earth does *not* stand still, Boscovich taught us to renounce the last thing that 'still stood' about the earth, the belief in 'substance', in 'matter', in the bit of earth, the particle, the atom: no one on earth has ever won a greater triumph over the senses.

However, we must go even further and declare war, a merciless war unto the death against the 'atomistic need' that continues to live a dangerous afterlife in places where no one suspects it (as does the more famous 'metaphysical need').* The first step must be to kill off that other and more ominous atomism that Christianity taught best and longest: *the atomism of the soul.* If you allow me, I would use this phrase to describe the belief that holds the soul to be something ineradicable, eternal, indivisible, a monad, an atom: science must cast out *this* belief! And confidentially, we do not need to get rid of 'the soul' itself nor do without one of our oldest, most venerable hypotheses, which the bungling naturalists tend to do, losing 'the soul' as soon as they've touched on it. But the way is clear for new and refined versions of the hypothesis about the soul; in future, concepts such as the 'mortal soul' and the 'soul as the multiplicity of the subject' and the 'soul as the social construct of drives and emotions' will claim their rightful place in science. By putting an end to the superstitions that proliferated with nearly tropical abundance around the idea of the soul, the *new* psychologist has of course seemed to cast himself into a new desolation and a new distrust—it may be that the old psychologists had it easier, merrier—but he knows that he is thereby also condemned to *inventing*, and—who knows?—perhaps to *finding*.—

13

Physiologists should think twice before deciding that an organic being's primary instinct is the instinct for self-preservation. A living being wants above all else to *release* its strength; life itself is the will to power, and self-preservation is only one of its indirect and most frequent *consequences*.

Here as everywhere, in short, we must beware of *superfluous* teleological principles! And this is what the instinct for self-preservation is (which we owe to the inconsistency of Spinoza).* Such are the dictates of our method, which in essence demands that we be frugal with our principles.

14

It now may be dawning on five or six thinkers that even physics is only a way of interpreting or arranging the world (if I may say so: according to us!) and *not* a way of explaining the world. But in so far as it relies on our belief in the senses, physics is taken for more than that, and shall long continue to be taken for more, for an explanation. Our eyes and fingers speak for it, appearance and palpability speak for it: to an era with essentially plebeian tastes this is enchanting, persuasive, *convincing*, for it instinctively follows the canonized truth of ever-popular sensualism. What is clear, what 'clarifies'? First, whatever can be seen and touched—you have to take every problem at least that far. Conversely, the magic of the Platonic method consisted precisely in its *resistance to* sensuality, for this was an *aristocratic* method, practised by people who may have enjoyed senses even stronger and more clamorous than those of our contemporaries, but who sought a higher triumph by mastering them, by tossing over this colourful confusion of the senses (the rabble of the senses, as Plato called it) the pale, cold, grey nets of concepts. There was a kind of *enjoyment* in Plato's manner of overpowering and interpreting the world different from the one currently offered us by physicists, including those Darwinists and anti-teleologists among the physiological workers with their principle of the 'least possible energy'* and the greatest possible stupidity. 'Where man has nothing more to see and grasp, he has nothing more to seek'—that imperative certainly differs from Plato's, but it may be exactly right for a hardy, industrious future race of machinists and bridge-builders who have only *dirty* work to do.

15

In order to practise physiology with a good conscience, you have to believe that the sense organs are *not* phenomena in the philosophical idealist sense, for then they could not be causes! This is sensualism as a regulative hypothesis at least, if not as an heuristic principle.

What's that? And other people are actually saying that the external world is created by our sense organs? But then our body, as part of this external world, would be the creation of our sense organs! But then our very sense organs would be—the creation of our sense organs! It seems to me that this is a complete *reductio ad absurdum*:* assuming that the concept *causa sui** is something completely absurd. It follows that the outer world is *not* the creation of our sense organs—?

16

There are still some harmless self-scrutinizers who think that there are 'immediate certainties', as for example, 'I think', or, in Schopenhauer's superstition,* 'I will'—as if perception could grasp its object purely and nakedly as the 'thing in itself' without any falsification on the part of the subject or of the object. But I shall repeat a hundred times over that the 'immediate certainty', like 'absolute knowledge' and the 'thing in itself', contains a *contradictio in adjecto*:* it's time people freed themselves from the seduction of words! Let the common people think that perception means knowing-to-the-end,* the philosopher must say to himself, 'If I analyse the process expressed by the proposition "I think", I get a series of audacious assertions that would be difficult if not impossible to prove; for example, that *I* am the one who is thinking, that there has to be a something doing the thinking, that thinking is an activity and an effect on the part of a being who is thought of as a cause, that an "I" exists, and finally, that we by now understand clearly what is designated as thinking—that I *know* what thinking is. For if I had not already decided it for myself, how could I determine that what is going on is not "willing" or "feeling"? In short, saying "I think" assumes that I am *comparing* my present state with other states that I experience in myself, thereby establishing what it is: because of this reference back to another "knowledge", there is, for me at least, no immediate "certainty" here.'

Thus, instead of that 'immediate certainty' that the common people may believe in, the philosopher gets handed a series of metaphysical questions: these are actually the intellect's questions of conscience, such as, 'Where does my concept of thinking come from? Why do I believe in cause and effect? What gives me the right to talk about an "I", and beyond that an "I as cause", and beyond that yet an "I as the cause of thoughts"?' Anyone who dares to answer such metaphysical questions promptly by referring to a kind of epistemological *intuition* (like someone who says, 'I think, and know that this at least is true, real, and certain') will be met with a smile and two question marks by the philosopher of today. 'My dear sir,' the philosopher may suggest, 'it is improbable that you are not in error, but then why must we insist on truth?'

17

As regards the superstition of logicians, I never tire of underlining a quick little fact that these superstitious people are reluctant to admit: namely, that a thought comes when 'it' wants to, and not when 'I' want it to; so it is *falsifying* the facts to say that the subject 'I' is the condition of the predicate 'think'. There is thinking,* but to assert that 'there' is the same thing as that famous old 'I' is, to put it mildly, only an assumption, an hypothesis, and certainly not an 'immediate certainty'. And in the end 'there is thinking' is also going too far: even this 'there' contains an *interpretation* of the process and is not part of the process itself. People are concluding here according to grammatical habit: 'Thinking is an activity; for each activity there is someone who acts; therefore—.' Following approximately the same pattern, ancient atomism looked for that particle of matter, the atom, to complement the effective 'energy' that works from out of it; more rigorous minds finally learned to do without this 'little bit of earth' and perhaps some day logicians will even get used to doing without that little 'there' (into which the honest old 'I' has evaporated).

18

Truly, a theory is charming not least because it is refutable: that is just what attracts the better minds to it. It would seem that the theory of 'free will', which has been refuted a hundred times over, owes its endurance to this charm alone—someone is always coming along and feeling strong enough to refute it.

19

Philosophers tend to speak about the will as if everyone in the world knew all about it; Schopenhauer even suggested that the will was the only thing we actually do know, know through and through, know without additions or subtractions. But I continue to think that even in this case Schopenhauer was only doing what philosophers simply tend to do: appropriating and exaggerating a *common prejudice*. As I see it, the act of willing is above all something *complicated*, something that has unity only as a word—and this common prejudice of using only one word has overridden the philosophers' caution (which was never all that great anyway). So let us be more cautious for once, let us be 'unphilosophical'. Let us say that in every act of willing there is first of all a multiplicity of feelings, namely the feeling of the condition we are moving *away* from and the feeling of the condition we are moving *towards*; the feeling of this 'away' and this 'towards'; and then a concomitant feeling in the muscles that, without our actually moving 'arms and legs', comes into play out of a kind of habit, whenever we 'will'. Second, just as we must recognize feeling, and indeed many kinds of feeling, as an ingredient of the will, so must we likewise recognize thinking: in every act of will there is a commanding thought, and we must not deceive ourselves that this thought can be separated off from 'willing', as if we would then have any will left over! Third, the will is not merely a complex of feelings and thoughts, it is above all an *emotion*, and in fact the *emotion* of command. What is called 'freedom of the will' is essentially the emotion of superiority felt towards the one who must obey: 'I am free, "he" must obey.' This consciousness lies in every will, as does also a tense alertness, a direct gaze concentrated on one thing alone, an unconditional assessment that 'now we must have this and nothing else', an inner certainty that obedience will follow, and everything else that goes along with the condition of giving commands. A person who *wills*: this person is commanding a Something in himself that obeys, or that he thinks is obeying.

But let us now consider the strangest thing about the will, about this multifarious thing that the common people call by one word alone. In any given case, we both command *and* obey, and when we obey we know the feelings of coercion, pressure, oppression, resistance, and agitation that begin immediately after the act of will. On the other hand, we are in the habit of ignoring or over-looking this division by means of the synthetic concept 'I'. Thus, a whole series of erroneous conclusions and therefore of false assessments of the will itself has been appended to willing in such a way that the person who wills now believes with complete faith that willing *is enough* for action. Because in the vast majority of cases, willing has only occurred when there is also the *expectation* that the effect of the command—that is obedience, action—will follow, this *impression* has been translated into the feeling that there is a *necessary effect*; suffice it to say, the person willing thinks with some degree of certainty that will and action are somehow one: he attributes his success in carrying out his willing to the will itself and in this way enjoys an increase in that feeling of power that accompanies any kind of success. 'Freedom of the will'—that is the word for that complex pleasurable condition experienced by the person willing who commands and simultaneously identifies himself with the one who executes the command—as such he can share in enjoying a triumph over resistance, while secretly judging that it was actually his will that overcame that resistance. Thus the person willing adds to his pleasurable feeling as commander the pleasurable feelings of the successful executing instrument, the serviceable 'underwill' or under-soul (our body after all is nothing but a social structure of many souls). *L'effet c'est moi*:* what is occurring here occurs in every well-structured happy community where the ruling class identifies with the successes of the community as a whole. As we have said, every act of willing is simply a matter of commanding and obeying, based on a social structure of many 'souls'; for this reason a philosopher should claim the right to comprehend willing from within the sphere of ethics: ethics, that is, understood as the theory of hierarchical relationships among which the phenomenon 'life' has its origins.

20

That individual philosophical concepts are not something isolated, something unto themselves, but rather grow up in reference and relatedness to one another; that however suddenly and arbitrarily they seem to emerge in the history of thought, they are as much a part of one system as are the branches of fauna on one continent: this is revealed not least by the way the most disparate philosophers invariably fill out one particular basic schema of *possible* philosophies. Under some unseen spell they always run around the same orbit: however independent they may feel, one from the other, with their will to criticism or to system, something in them is leading them, driving them all to follow one another in a certain order—an inborn taxonomy and affinity of concepts. In truth their thinking is much less an act of discovery than an act of recognizing anew, remembering anew, a return back home to a distant, ancient universal economy of the soul from out of which those concepts initially grew: philosophizing is thus a kind of atavism of the highest order. This easily explains the strange family resemblance of all Indian, Greek, and German philosophizing. Wherever linguistic affinity, above all, is present, everything necessary for an analogous development and sequence of philosophical systems will inevitably be on hand from the beginning, thanks to the shared philosophy of grammar (I mean thanks to being unconsciously ruled and guided by similar grammatical functions), just as the way to certain other possibilities for interpreting the world will seem to be blocked. Philosophers from the Ural-Altaic linguistic zone (where the concept of the subject is least developed) will most probably look differently 'into the world' and will be found on other paths than Indo-Germans or Muslims: and in the last analysis, the spell of certain grammatical functions is the spell of *physiological* value judgements and conditions of race.

This by way of a rejection of Locke's superficiality* concerning the origin of ideas.

21

The *causa sui** is the best internal contradiction ever devised, a kind of logical freak or outrage: but because of man's excessive pride we have come to be deeply and terribly entangled with this particular nonsense. The yearning for 'freedom of the will' in the superlative metaphysical sense that unfortunately still prevails in the minds of the half-educated, the yearning to bear complete and final responsibility for one's own actions and to relieve God, the world, one's ancestors, coincidence, society from it—this is really nothing less than being that same *causa sui* and, with a daring greater than Münchhausen's,* dragging yourself by your hair out of the swamp of nothingness and into existence. Now, if someone can see through the cloddish simplicity of this famous concept 'free will' and eliminate it from his mind, I would then ask him to take his 'enlightenment' a step further and likewise eliminate from his head the opposite of the non-concept 'free will'. I mean the 'unfree will' which amounts to a misuse of cause and effect. One should not make the mistake of *concretizing* 'cause' and 'effect' as do the natural scientists (and whoever else today naturalizes in their thinking . . .), in conformity with the prevalent mechanistic foolishness that pushes and tugs at the cause until it 'has an effect'; 'cause' and 'effect' should be used only as pure *concepts*, as conventional fictions for the purpose of description or communication, and *not* for explanation. In the 'in itself' there is nothing of 'causal associations', of 'necessity', of 'psychological constraint'; the effect does *not* follow 'upon the cause', no 'law' governs it. *We* alone are the ones who have invented causes, succession, reciprocity, relativity, coercion, number, law, freedom, reason, purpose; and if we project, if we mix this world of signs into things as if it were an 'in itself', we act once more as we have always done, that is, *mythologically*. The 'unfree will' is mythology: in real life it is only a matter of *strong* and *weak* wills.

Whenever a thinker sniffs out coercion, necessity, obligation, pressure, constraint in any 'causal connection' or 'psychological necessity', it is almost always a symptom of where his own inadequacy lies: to feel this particular way is revealing—the person is revealing himself. And if I have observed correctly, the 'constraint of the will' is always conceived as a problem from two completely opposite standpoints, but always in a profoundly *personal* way: the one group will not hear of relinquishing their 'responsibility', their belief in *themselves*, their personal right to take *their* credit (the vain races are of this type); conversely, the other group wants to be responsible for nothing, guilty of nothing, and out of their inner self-contempt they yearn to *cast off* their own selves one way or another. When this latter group writes books nowadays, they tend to take up the cause of criminals; a sort of socialistic compassion is their nicest disguise. And indeed, it is surprising how much prettier the fatalism of the weak-willed can look when it presents itself as 'la religion de la souffrance humaine';* that is what *it* means by 'good taste'.

22

If you'll forgive me, an old philologist who can't give up the wickedness of pointing out examples of bad interpretative practice, the 'lawfulness of nature' that you physicists speak about so proudly, as if . . .—this only exists by grace of your interpretations, your bad 'philology'; it is not a factual matter, not a 'text', but rather no more than a naive humanitarian concoction, a contortion of meaning that allows you to succeed in accommodating the democratic instincts of the modern soul! 'Equality before the law is everywhere—nature is no different and no better than we are'— this amiable ulterior thought once again masks the plebeian's enmity towards everything privileged and autocratic, as well as a new and more subtle atheism. 'Ni dieu, ni maître'*—that's what you folks want, too. So, 'long live the law of nature!' Isn't that right? But as I say, this is interpretation, not text; and someone could come along with the opposite intention and interpretative skill who, looking at the very same nature and referring to the very same phenomena, would read out of it the ruthlessly tyrannical and unrelenting assertion of power claims. Such an interpreter would put to you the universality and unconditionality in all 'will to power' in such a way that virtually every word, even the word 'tryanny', would ultimately appear useless or at least only as a modifying, mitigating metaphor—as too human. Yet this philosopher, too, would end by making the same claims for his world as you others do for yours, namely that its course is 'necessary' and 'predictable', *not* because laws are at work in it, but rather because the laws are absolutely *lacking*, and in every moment every power draws its final consequence. And given that he too is just interpreting—and you'll be eager to raise that objection, won't you?—then, all the better.

23

Until now, all psychology has been brought to a stop by moral prejudices and fears: it has not dared to plumb these depths. If we may take previous writing as a symptom of what has also been suppressed, then no one in his thoughts has even brushed these depths as I have, as a morphology and *evolutionary theory of the will to power*. The force of moral prejudices has reached far into the most spiritual world, a world apparently cold and without premiss—and it has obviously had a harmful, inhibiting, blinding, distorting effect. A real physio-psychology must struggle with the unconscious resistances in the heart of the researcher, the 'heart' is working against it; a conscience that is still strong and hearty will be distressed and annoyed even by a theory of the reciprocal conditionality of 'good' and 'bad' instincts, which seems to be a kind of subtle immorality—and even more by a theory of the derivation of all good drives from bad ones. But granted that a person takes the emotions of hatred, envy, greed, power hunger as conditions for living, crucial and fundamental to the universal economy of life and therefore in need of intensifying if life is to be intensified, he is also a person who suffers from such an orientation in judgement as if he were seasick. And yet even this hypothesis is by no means the strangest or most painful one in this enormous, virtually new realm of dangerous insights—and in truth there are a hundred good reasons for everyone to stay away from it if he— *can*! On the other hand, once your ship has strayed onto this course: well then! All right! Grit your teeth bravely! Open your eyes! Keep your hand at the helm!—we are going to be travelling *beyond* morality, and by daring to travel there we may in the process stifle or crush whatever remnant of morality we have left—but what do *we* matter! Never yet has a *deeper* world of insight been opened to bold travellers and adventurers; and the psychologist who makes this kind of 'sacrifice' (it is *not* the *sacrifizio dell'intelletto*,* quite the contrary!) may demand at least that psychology be recognized once again as the queen of the sciences, which the other sciences exist to serve and anticipate. For psychology has once again become the way to basic issues.

SECTION TWO

THE FREE SPIRIT

24

O sancta simplicitas!* How strangely simplified and false are people's lives! Once we have focused our eyes on this wonder, there is no end to the wonderment! See how we have made everything around us bright and free and light and simple! Weren't we clever to give our senses free access to everything superficial, to give our minds a divine craving for headlong leaps and fallacies! How we have managed from the beginning to cling to our ignorance, in order to enjoy a life of almost inconceivable freedom, thoughtlessness, carelessness, heartiness, cheerfulness—to enjoy life! And only upon this foundation of ignorance, now as firm as granite, could our science be established, and our will to knowledge only upon the foundation of a much more powerful will, the will to no knowledge, to uncertainty,* to untruth—not as the opposite of the former will, but rather—as its refinement! For even if *language*, in this case as in others, cannot get past its own unwieldiness and continues to speak of oppositions where there are really only degrees and many fine differences of grade; even if we the knowing also find the words in our mouths twisted by the ingrained moral hypocrisy that is now part of our insuperable 'flesh and blood', now and then we understand what has happened, and laugh at how even the very best science would keep us trapped in this *simplified*, thoroughly artificial, neatly concocted, neatly falsified world, how the best science loves error whether it will or not, because science, being alive,—loves life!

25

After such a light-hearted introduction, it is time to attend to a serious word, one that is addressed to the most serious of people. Be on guard, all you philosophers and lovers of knowledge, and beware of turning into martyrs! Beware of suffering 'for the sake of truth'! Beware even of defending yourselves! You will ruin all the innocence and fine objectivity of your conscience; you will become obstinate in the face of objections and red rags; you will grow stupid, brutish, and bullish if in your fight against danger, defamation, accusations, expulsion, and even baser consequences of enmity you will ultimately have to play the role of defenders of truth on earth as well: as if 'truth' were such a meek and hapless woman as to need defenders! And especially such as you, gentlemen, you knights of the most sorrowful countenance,* you intellectual idlers and cobweb-spinners! In the end you know very well that it does not matter whether *you* are proved right, and likewise that no philosopher to date has been proved right, and that there is probably more value for truth in every little question mark that you place at the end of your mottoes and favourite doctrines (and occasionally after your own selves) than in all your dignified gestures and your playing the trump before plaintiffs and lawcourts! Take the side exit instead! Flee to hidden spaces! And wear your mask and your subtlety so that people will not be able to tell you apart! Or will fear you a little! And please don't forget the garden, the garden with the golden trellises! And keep people around you who are like a garden—or like music over the waters at that evening hour when day is already turning into memory: choose the *good* solitude, the free, wanton, weightless solitude that also gives you the right to remain good, in some sense at least. How venomous, how wily, how bad one becomes in every long war that cannot be waged in the open! How *personal* one becomes by holding fears for a long time, by watching long for enemies, possible enemies! Despite their most spiritual disguises and perhaps without even knowing it, these outcasts of society, these long-term fugitives, hunters' prey—and also the enforced hermits, the Spinozas or Giordano Brunos*— always end by becoming elegant avengers and poisoners (just excavate the foundation of Spinoza's ethics and theology!)—not to mention the foolish moral indignation that is the unfailing sign of a philosopher whose philosophical humour has deserted him. The philosopher's martyrdom, his 'sacrifice for truth', forces into the light whatever was lurking in him of the propagandist and the actor; and if it is true that people have regarded him with only an artistic curiosity until now, we can certainly understand why they would have the dangerous wish to see him in his degeneracy for once (degenerated to a 'martyr', to a playhouse and courthouse ranter). When we make such a wish, however, we have to be clear *what* it is that we will get to see: merely a satyr play, merely a farcical epilogue, merely the continuing proof that the actual, long tragedy *is over*—assuming that every philosophy, as it was taking shape, was one long tragedy.—

26

Every exceptional person instinctively seeks out his fortress, his secrecy, where he is *delivered* from the crowd, the multitude, the majority, where he is allowed to forget the rule of 'humanity', being the exception to it; in one case, however, an even stronger instinct pushes him, as a person of great and exceptional knowledge, towards this rule. Anyone who interacts with other people without occasionally displaying all the colours of distress (green and grey with disgust, annoyance, compassion, gloom, loneliness) is surely not a man of higher taste; but if on the other hand he declines to assume this whole dispiriting burden and keeps evading it by remaining, as described above, tucked away peaceful and proud in his fortress, then one thing is certain: he is not made for, not destined for, knowledge. For if he were, he would some day have to say to himself, 'To hell with my good taste! The rule is more interesting than the exception, more interesting than I, the exception!'—and he would go *down*, and above all, go 'into'. The study of the *average* man is a long, serious study, requiring much in the way of disguise, self-discipline, intimacy, bad company (every company is bad company except that of one's equals); it makes up a necessary part of every philosopher's biography, and it is perhaps the most unpleasant, worst-smelling part, most rife with disappointment. But if he has the good fortune that befits a fortunate child of knowledge, he will encounter others who in fact shorten and lighten his task: I mean the so-called cynics, those people who simply acknowledge what is animal-like, common, the 'rule' about themselves and yet still have enough spirituality and excitability to need to speak about themselves and their kind *in front of witnesses*—sometimes these people even wallow around in books, as in their own mire. It is only in the form of cynicism that common souls come near to being honest; and the higher man must open his ears to every kind of cynicism, whether crude or subtle, and must congratulate himself whenever he is lucky enough to hear a shameless joker or scholarly satyr raise his voice. There are even cases that mix enchantment with the disgust, when a whim of nature joins genius to such a prying goat and ape, as in the case of the Abbé Galiani,* the most profound, acute, and perhaps dirtiest man of his century—he was much more profound than Voltaire and therefore a good deal more taciturn. As I suggested, it is more common that the scholarly head is set upon an ape's body, a subtle exceptional mind above a common heart—with doctors and the physiologists of morality we find it especially often. And whenever someone speaks about human beings not bitterly, but neutrally, as if he were talking about a belly with two different needs and a head with but one; whenever someone sees, looks for, and *wants* to see only hunger, sexual desire, and vanity, as if these were the only true motives for human behaviour; whenever, in short, someone speaks 'badly' about human beings (and not even *wickedly*), then the lover of knowledge must pay close and careful attention—he must keep his ears open in general, whenever people speak without indignation. For the indignant man and whoever else uses his own teeth to mutilate and dismember himself (or God or society in place of himself) may stand higher than the laughing and self-satisfied satyr in moral terms, but in every other sense he represents the more common, more inconsequential, more uninstructive case. And only the indignant tell so many *lies*.—

27

Making yourself understood is hard—especially if you live and think *gangasrotogati*,* amidst people who all think and live differently, namely *kurmagati*, or in the best case, 'in the manner of frogs', *mandeikagati* (am I doing all I can to make myself hard to understand, too?), and we should be sincerely grateful to anyone who cares enough to achieve some subtlety as an interpreter. But as for 'good friends', who are always too comfortable and think that as friends they are entitled to be so: it is wise to start by granting them elbow room and a playground for misunderstanding—then there is still an occasion for laughing—or else just

do away with them entirely, these good friends—and laugh about
that, too!

28

The hardest thing to translate from one language to another is the
tempo of its style; this style has its basis in the character of the race,
or to speak more physiologically, in the average tempo of the race's
'metabolism'. There are some well-intended translations that are
almost counterfeits, involuntary crudifications of the original,
simply because they could not capture its bright, brave tempo, one
that leaps over, transports over all the dangers in words and things.
The German is nearly incapable of the *presto* in his language, and
we may feel free to conclude that he is therefore also incapable of
many of the most amusing and audacious nuances of free, free-
spirited thought. Just as the *buffo** and the satyr are alien to him,
body and soul, so are Aristophanes and Petronius* untranslatable
by him. The Germans have developed an excessive variety of
everything solemn, sluggish, ceremoniously clumsy, all the intermi-
nable and insufferable stylistic genres and may I be forgiven for
pointing out that even Goethe's prose, with its mixture of stiffness
and daintiness, is no exception, reflecting the 'good old days' to
which it belongs and expressing German taste in an age which there
was still such a thing as 'German taste': it was a Rococo taste, *in
moribus et artibus.** Lessing* is the exception: thanks to his actor's
nature he understood much and was skilled in much; it was not
for nothing that he translated Bayle* and liked to escape in the
company of Diderot and Voltaire and still more to the Roman
writers of comedy: even in his tempo, Lessing loved freethinking
and the escape from Germany. But how could the German language,
even in the prose of a Lessing, imitate the tempo of Machiavelli,*
who lets us breathe the fine, dry air of Florence in his *Prince* and
cannot keep from presenting the most serious business in a wild
allegrissimo, perhaps not without an artist's malicious feeling for
the contradiction he is attempting: the thoughts long, heavy, harsh,
dangerous, set to a galloping tempo of the finest, most mischievous
mood. And who could ever dare a German translation of Petronius,
whose conceits, ideas, words master the *presto* better than any
musician before him: what do all the swamps of this sick, wicked

world, or of the 'old world' matter, if you have the feet of the wind as he does, its breath and draught, the liberating mockery of a wind that makes everything healthy by making everything *run*! And as for Aristophanes, that transfiguring, complementary spirit, for whose sake one *forgives* all of ancient Greece for existing, assuming that one has grasped in all its profundity *what* it is that requires forgiving, requires transfiguring: I know of nothing that set me to musing about *Plato*'s opaqueness and sphinx-like nature as much as that fortunately preserved *petit fait*:* that under the pillow of his death bed, no 'bible', nothing Egyptian or Pythagorean or Platonic was discovered—but rather Aristophanes. How could even a Plato have endured life (a Greek life, to which he said 'no')—without an Aristophanes!

29

Only a very few people can be independent: it is a prerogative of the strong. And when independence is attempted by someone who has the right to it, but does not *need* it, we have proof that this man is probably not only strong, but bold to the point of recklessness. He ventures into a labyrinth, he multiplies life's inevitable dangers a thousandfold, and not the least among these is the absence of any person to see how and where he is going astray, becoming isolated, being rent apart piece by piece in the cave of some Minotaur of the conscience. Assuming that such a person perishes, he perishes so far away from the understanding of human beings that they do not feel it or feel for him—and he cannot go back again! Not even to the pity of humans!

30

Whenever our loftiest insights inadvertently reach the ears of people who are not constituted or destined to hear them, they must—and should!—sound foolish, or in some circumstances even criminal. Earlier philosophers (among them Indians as well as Greeks, Persians, and Muslims, people in short who believed in hierarchy and *not* in equality and equal rights) distinguished what is exoteric from what is esoteric not only by the fact that the exoteric philosopher stands on the outside, and sees, estimates, measures, and makes judgements from the outside rather than from the inside: more important is that he sees things from down below—whereas the esoteric philosopher sees things *from above*! There are heights of the soul from which vantage point even tragedy ceases to have a tragic effect; and taking all the pain of the world together, who could dare decide whether the sight of it should *necessarily* seduce and coerce us to feel pity in particular, thus redoubling the pain? . . . What serves to nourish or refresh the higher type of person must be almost poison to a very diverse and inferior type. The virtues of the ordinary man might represent vices and weaknesses in a philosopher; it could be that if a higher type of person entered a state of ruin and degeneration, he would thereby take on characteristics that would thereafter needs cause him to be revered as a saint in that lower world into which he sank. There are books that have an inverse value for body and soul depending on whether they are used by the low sort of soul, the lower life force, or the higher and more powerful; in the one case they are dangerous, erosive, disintegrative books, in the other they are calls of a herald, challenging those who are most valiant to attain *their* valour. Books for the masses are always bad-smelling books: the odour of little people clings to them. There is usually a stink wherever the common people eat and drink, and even in their places of reverence. Do not go into churches if you want to breathe *clean* air.—

31

When we are young, we revere and revile without benefit of the art of the nuance, life's greatest prize, and it is only fair that we must later repent bitterly for having pounced upon people and things with a Yes or a No. Everything is designed so that the worst of all possible tastes, our taste for the unconditional, is terribly and foolishly abused, until we learn to put some art into our feelings and even take a chance with artifice—as do the real artists of life. Young people, with their characteristic anger and awe, seem to find no peace until they have neatly falsified people and things, so that they can vent their feelings on them: youth by its very nature is something falsifying and deceptive. Later, after our young soul has been tormented by unrelieved disappointments and finally turns suspiciously back upon itself, still hot and wild even in its suspicion and pangs of conscience, then how angry we are, how impatiently we tear ourselves apart, taking vengeance for having deluded ourselves for so long, as if our delusion had been voluntary! When we make this transition, we punish ourselves by distrusting our feelings; we torture our enthusiasm with doubt, indeed we even experience our good conscience as a danger, as if it were veiling us or wearing down our finer honesty: and above all else we take sides, on principle, take sides *against* 'youth'.

A decade later, and we understand that this whole process, too, was—youth!

32

During the longest age of human history—it is called the prehistoric age—an action's value or lack of value was determined by its consequences: the action itself was taken into consideration as little as its origin. More or less as in China today, where a child's distinction or disgrace reflects back on the parent, the retroactive force of the success or failure of an action determined whether people thought well or badly of it. Let us call this period mankind's *pre-moral* period: at this time no one had heard of the imperative 'know thyself!' During the last ten thousand years, however, over large stretches of the earth, people have little by little reached the point of determining the value of an action not by its consequences but by its origins. Taken as a whole, this was a great event, a considerable refinement in perceptions and standards, with the unconscious influence of the dominance of aristocratic values and the belief in 'origins' still persisting. It was the badge of a period that we may designate in the narrower sense as the *moral* period, and it signals the first attempt at self-knowledge. Instead of consequences, origins: what a reversal of perspective! And most certainly a reversal achieved only after long struggles and hesitations! Along with it, to be sure, came an ominous new superstition, a peculiar narrowness of interpretation took hold: the origin of an action was interpreted in the most precise terms as itself originating in an *intention*; everyone was united in the belief that the value of an action lay in the value of its intention. Intention as the entire source and past history of an action: almost right up into modern times this prejudice has determined how moral judgements have been made on earth, praising, blaming, judging, philosophizing.

But now that human beings are again gaining a deeper self-awareness, shouldn't we weigh another reversal and fundamental shift in values—might we not be standing at the threshold of a period that, to put it negatively, would at first have to be described as *extra-moral*? Is not the suspicion growing, at least among us immoralists, that an action's decisive value is demonstrated precisely by that part of it that is *not intentional*; do we not suspect that all of an action's intentionality, everything that can be seen or known about it, that can be 'conscious' about it, is still part of its surface and skin—which, like all skin, reveals something, but *hides* even more? In short, we believe that the intention is but a sign or a symptom, first of all requiring interpretation, and furthermore that it is a sign with so many meanings that as a consequence it has almost none in and of itself; we believe that morality in its earlier sense, intention-morality, was a prejudice, something precipitous or perhaps preliminary, something of the order of astrology or alchemy, but in any event something that must be overcome. The overcoming of morality, or even (in a certain sense) the self-overcoming of morality: let that be the name for the long, clandestine work that was kept in reserve for the most subtle and honest (and also the most malicious) people of conscience today, living touchstones of the human heart.—

33

There's no help for it: we must haul into court and mercilessly interrogate our feelings of devotion, of sacrifice for our neighbour, the whole morality of self-renunciation, as well as the aesthetic of 'disinterested contemplation',* which the current emasculation of art is trying to use (seductively enough) to clear its conscience. 'For the sake of others', '*not* for me': these are feelings containing so much sorcery and sugar that we must be doubly distrustful of them and ask: 'Are these not perhaps—*seductions*?'

That we *like* these feelings (whether because we have them, or enjoy their fruits, or merely observe them as spectators) furnishes no argument *for* them, but rather demands that we exercise caution. So let's be cautious!

34

No matter what philosophical standpoint we may take these days, looking out from any position, the *erroneousness* of the world we think we are living in is the most certain and concrete thing our eyes can fasten on: we find a host of reasons for it, reasons that might tempt us to speculate about a deceptive principle in the 'nature of things'. But anyone who would try to claim that the falsity of the world is due to our thought process, to our 'intellect' (an honourable way out, taken by every conscious or unconscious *advocatus dei*),* anyone who takes this world with all its space, time, form, movement, to be falsely *inferred*, would at the very least have good reason to end by distrusting the thought process itself—for wouldn't this thought process have made us the victims of the greatest hoax ever? And what guarantee would we have that it wouldn't go on doing what it has always done? In all seriousness, there is something touching and awe-inspiring in the innocence of thinkers that allows them even nowadays to request *honest* answers from their consciousness: about whether it is 'substantial', for example, or why it insists on keeping the outside world at such a distance, and all sorts of other questions of that kind. The faith in 'immediate certainties' is *morally* naive, and does honour to us philosophers, but—we are not supposed to be '*only* moral' after all! In any but moral terms, our faith in immediate certainties is stupid, and does us no great honour! Maybe it is true that in bourgeois life an ever-ready distrust is taken as a sign of 'bad character' and therefore classified as imprudence: here where we are, beyond the bourgeois world and its Yes's and No's—what is there to keep us from being imprudent and saying that the philosopher has a veritable *right* to his 'bad character', as the creature who so far has always been most made a fool of on earth—these days he has a *duty* to be distrustful, to squint out as maliciously as he can from the bottom of every abyss of doubt.

Please forgive me for the joking tone of this sad caricature: for a while now, I myself have learned to think differently about deceiving and being deceived, learned to assess them differently, so I am always ready to take a few pokes at the philosophers' blind rage at being deceived. Why *not*? It is nothing but a moral prejudice to consider truth more valuable than appearance; it is, in fact, the most poorly proven assumption in the world. We should admit at least this much: there would be no life at all if not on the basis of perspectivist assessments and appearances; and if one wanted to do away with the 'apparent world' entirely, as some valiantly enthusiastic and foolish philosophers want to do, well then, assuming that people like *you* could do that—then at the very least there would be nothing left of your 'truth', either! Really, why should we be forced to assume that there is an essential difference between 'true' and 'false' in the first place? Isn't it enough to assume that there are degrees of apparency and, so to speak, lighter and darker shadows and hues of appearance—different *valeurs*,* to use the language of painters? Why should the world *that is relevant to us* not be a fiction? And if someone asks, 'But mustn't a fiction have an author?' shouldn't we answer him bluntly, '*Why?*' Mustn't this 'mustn't' be part of the fiction, too, perhaps? Aren't we allowed to be a little bit ironic, not only about predicates and objects, but also about subjects? Shouldn't the philosopher be able to rise above a faith in grammar? My respects to governesses, but isn't it about time that philosophers renounced the religion of governesses?

35

O Voltaire! O humanity! O hogwash! 'Truth' and the *search* for truth are no trivial matter; and if a person goes about searching in too human a fashion ('il ne cherche le vrai que pour faire le bien'),* I'll bet he won't find anything!

36

Assuming that nothing real is 'given' to us apart from our world of desires and passions, assuming that we cannot ascend or descend to any 'reality' other than the reality of our instincts (for thinking is merely an interrelation of these instincts, one to the other), may we not be allowed to perform an experiment and ask whether this 'given' also provides a *sufficient* explanation for the so-called mechanistic (or 'material') world? I do not mean the material world as a delusion, as 'appearance' or 'representation' (in the Berkeleian or Schopenhauerian sense), but rather as a world with the same level of reality that our emotion has—that is, as a more rudimentary form of the world of emotions, holding everything in a powerful unity, all the potential of the organic process to develop and differentiate (and spoil and weaken, too, of course), as a kind of instinctual life in which all the organic functions (self-regulation, adaptation, alimentation, elimination, metabolism) are synthetically linked to one another—as a *preliminary form* of life?

In the end, we are not only allowed to perform such an experiment, we are commanded to do so by the conscience of our *method*. We must not assume that there are several sorts of causality until we have tested the possibility that one alone will suffice, tested it to its furthest limits (to the point of nonsense, if you'll allow me to say so). We cannot evade this morality of method today: it follows 'by definition', as a mathematician would say. The question is ultimately whether we really recognize that the will can *effect* things, whether we believe in the causality of the will: if we do (and to believe in *this* is basically to believe in causality itself), we *must* experiment to test hypothetically whether the causality of the will is the only causality. A 'will' can have an effect only upon another 'will', of course, and not upon 'matter' (not upon 'nerves', for example): one must dare to hypothesize, in short, that wherever 'effects' are identified, a will is having an effect upon another will—and that all mechanical events, in so far as an energy is active in them, are really the energy of the will, the effect of the will.

Assuming, finally, that we could explain our entire instinctual life as the development and differentiation of *one* basic form of the will (namely the will to power, as *my* tenet would have it); assuming that one could derive all organic functions from this will to power and also find in it the solution to the problem of procreation and alimentation (it is all one problem), then we would have won the right to designate *all* effective energy unequivocally as: the *will to power*. The world as it is seen from the inside, the world defined and described by its 'intelligible character'*—would be simply 'will to power' and that alone.——

37

'What's that? But doesn't that mean, to speak in the vernacular, that God's been disproved, but not the devil?' On the contrary! On the contrary, my friends! And who the devil's forcing you to speak in the vernacular!——

38

Take what has happened recently, in the full light of our modern age, with the French Revolution, that gruesome and (judged from close up) superfluous farce: its noble and inspired spectators throughout Europe have been projecting their own rebellious and enthusiastic feelings onto it from afar for so long and with such passion *that the text has disappeared underneath the interpretation.* A noble posterity might one day misunderstand all of past history in a similar way, and only in so doing make the sight of it bearable.

Or rather: hasn't this already happened? Haven't we ourselves been this 'noble posterity'? And since we now recognize what we have been doing, can't we—stop it?

39

No one will very easily hold a doctrine to be true merely because it makes us happy or virtuous, with the possible exception of those dear 'idealists' who rhapsodize about goodness, truth, beauty, and let all sorts of eye-catching, obvious, and good-natured wishful thoughts swim around together in their pond. Happiness and virtue cannot be used as arguments. But we like to forget, even the thoughtful spirits among us, that whatever makes us unhappy or evil can no more be used as a counter-argument. Something might be true, even if it were also harmful and dangerous in the highest degree; indeed, it might be part of the essential nature of existence that to understand it completely would lead to our own destruction. The strength of a person's spirit would then be measured by how much 'truth' he could tolerate, or more precisely, to what extent he *needs* to have it diluted, disguised, sweetened, muted, falsified. But there can be no doubt that wicked and unhappy people are better suited to discover certain *parts* of the truth and are more likely to be successful; not to mention the wicked people who are happy—a species that the moralists have kept silent about. Perhaps harshness and cunning furnish conditions more favourable for the development of strong, independent spirits and philosophers than do that gentle, refined, accommodating good nature and skill in taking things lightly which we prize in scholars, and with good reason. Assuming, of course, that we are not restricting the concept

of 'philosopher' to the philosopher who writes books—or even sets
forth *his* philosophy in books!

We learn of one last trait in the portrait of the free-spirited
philosopher from Stendhal,* one which I must insist on underlining
for the sake of German taste, because it goes *against* German taste.
'Pour être bon philosophe,' this last great psychologist tells us, 'il
faut être sec, clair, sans illusion. Un banquier, qui a fait fortune, a
une partie du caractère requis pour faire des découvertes en philo-
sophie, c'est à dire pour voir clair dans ce qui est.'*

40

Everything deep loves a mask; the very deepest things even have a
hatred for image and parable. Wouldn't an *antithesis* be a more
fitting disguise if the shame of a god were to walk abroad? A
questionable question: it would be strange if some mystic had not
already dared to ask himself something like it. There are experiences
of such a delicate nature that it is well to conceal them by a coarse
act and make them unrecognizable; there are actions of love and
extravagant generosity after which nothing is more advisable than
to take a stick and thrash the eyewitness, thus to cloud his memory.
Some people know how to cloud and abuse their own memories,
to take revenge on this one confidant, at least: shame is inventive.
It is not the worst things that cause us the worst shame: wicked
cunning is not the only thing behind a mask—there is so much
kindness in cunning.* I could imagine that a man who had something precious and fragile to hide might roll through life as rough
and round as an old green heavily banded wine barrel: that is how
his refined shame would have it. A man whose shame is deep will
encounter even his destinies and delicate choices upon roads that
few people ever find and whose existence must be kept from his
neighbours and closest friends: his mortal danger is hidden from
their eyes, and also his regained mortal confidence. This secretive
one, whose instincts bid him speak in order to silence and be silent,
who is inexhaustible in evading communication, this person *wants*
and demands that in his stead a mask inhabit the hearts and minds
of his friends; and should it be that this is something he does not
want, then one day his eyes will be opened to the fact that a mask
of him is there nevertheless, and that that is good. Every deep

spirit needs a mask: not only that, around every deep spirit a mask is continually growing, thanks to the constantly false, that is to say, *shallow* interpretations of his every word, his every step, every sign of life that he gives.——

41

Those of us who are destined to be independent and to command must in return set ourselves our own tests—and set them at the proper time. We should not try to get out of our tests, even though they may be the most dangerous game we can play, and though they are really only tests performed for ourselves as witnesses and for no other judge. Not to be dependent on any one person, not even the most beloved—every person is a prison, and a nook. Not to be dependent on a fatherland, not even the most suffering and needy— it is certainly easier to detach your heart from a victorious fatherland. Not to be dependent on pity, not even if it were for higher men into whose extraordinary suffering and helplessness we have accidentally seen. Not to be dependent on any science, not even one that would tempt us with the most precious discoveries, seemingly reserved just for *us*. Not to be dependent even on our own detachment, on the voluptuous faraway foreignness of the bird, who constantly flies up to ever greater heights so that it can see ever more beneath it—the danger of the flier. Not to be dependent on our own virtues, nor allow our wholeness to be sacrificed to some singularity about ourselves, our 'hospitality', for example, as is the danger of dangers for ardent and generous hearts who are prodigal, almost uncaring with themselves, and practise the virtue of liberality until it is a vice. We must know how *to preserve ourselves*: the greatest test of independence.

42

A new category of philosophers is on the rise: I shall be so bold as to christen them with a name that is not without its dangers. As I divine them, as they allow themselves to be divined (for it is part of their nature to *want* to remain a riddle in some respects), these philosophers of the future might rightfully—perhaps also wrongfully—be described as *experimenters*. And this name too is ultimately only an experiment, and, if you like, a temptation.*

43

Are they new friends of 'truth', these approaching philosophers?
Probably so, for until now all philosophers have loved their truths.
But it is certain that they will not be dogmatists. It would surely
go against their pride, and also against their good taste, if their
truth had to be a truth for everyone else, too—this has been the
secret wish and ulterior thought in all earlier dogmatic endeavours.
'My judgement is *my* judgement: no one else has a right to it so
easily', as a philosopher of the future might say. We have to rid
ourselves of the bad taste of wanting to agree with many others.
'Good' is no longer good if our neighbour takes the word into his
mouth. So how could there possibly be 'common goods'! The term
contradicts itself: anything that is common never has much value.
In the end things will have to be as they are and always have been:
the great things are left to the great, the abysses to the profound,
tenderness and thrills to the sensitive, and to sum it up in a few
words, everything extraordinary to the extraordinary.

44

After all that has been said, must I still make a special point
of mentioning that they too will be free, *very* free spirits, these
philosophers of the future—just as surely as they will not be free
spirits merely, but something more, higher, greater, and fundamentally different, something that would not go unrecognized or
misidentified? But in saying this, I feel even towards them (as
towards ourselves, the free spirits who are their heralds and
forerunners!) the *obligation* to dispel for both of us a stupid old
prejudice and misunderstanding that for all too long has
enshrouded the concept 'free spirit' like a fog. In all the countries
of Europe and in America now as well, there is something that is
misusing this name: a very narrow, trapped, enchained sort of spirit
who wants more or less the opposite of what we do, by instinct
and intention—not to mention that they are bound to be the shut
windows and barred doors to those approaching *new* philosophers.
These falsely dubbed 'free spirits' belong, short and sour, to the
levellers, loquacious scribbling slaves of the democratic taste and its
'modern ideas': they are all of them people without solitude,
without their own solitude, plain well-behaved lads whose courage

and honourable propriety cannot be denied. It is just that they are unfree and laughably superficial, especially in light of their basic tendency to see, more or less, the cause of *all* human misery and failure in the structures of society up to now, thus happily managing to turn truth upside down! What they are trying with all their strength to achieve is a common green pasture of happiness for the herd, with safety, security, comfort, ease of life for everyone; their two most often recited tunes and teachings are 'Equal rights' and 'Compassion for all suffering'—and they take suffering itself as something that must be *eliminated*.

We who are the opposite, who have opened an *eye* and a conscience to the question of where and how the plant 'human being' has most vigorously grown tall, we are of the opinion that this has always happened under the opposite conditions: that the precariousness of the plant's situation had first to increase enormously; that its power of invention and disguise (its 'spirit'—) had to become subtle and daring through long periods of pressure and discipline; that its life-will had to be intensified into an unconditional power-will. We are of the opinion that harshness, violence, enslavement, danger on the street and in the heart, seclusion, stoicism, the art of the tempter and every kind of devilry, that everything evil, frightful, tyrannical, predatory, and snake-like about humans serves to heighten the species 'human being' as much as does its opposite. To say only this much, in fact, is not even saying enough, and whether we speak or are silent at this juncture, we find ourselves at the *other* end of all modern ideology and wishful thinking of the herd: as their antipodes, perhaps? Is it any surprise that we 'free spirits' are not the most communicative of spirits? That we do not wish to reveal in every case what a spirit can liberate itself *from* and what it may then perhaps be driven *to*? And as far as concerns the dangerous phrase 'beyond good and evil', it guards us at least against being misidentified: we *are* something other than 'libre-penseurs', 'liberi pensatori', 'freethinkers',* and whatever other names all these honourable advocates of 'modern ideas' might choose to call themselves by. Having been at home, or at least a guest in many countries of the spirit; having again and again escaped the pleasant, overstuffed nooks to which our special loves and hatreds, our youth, our origins, the accidents of people and books, or even the weariness of the journey have seemed to banish us; full of malice towards the temptations of dependence that lie hidden in honours or money or position or the enthusiasms of the senses; grateful in fact for distress and varying illnesses, because they have always freed us from some rule and its 'prejudice'; grateful to god, devil, sheep, and worm in us, curious to the point of vice, investigators to the point of cruelty, thoughtlessly fingering what cannot be grasped, with teeth and stomach for what is most indigestible, ready for any craft that demands sharp wits and sharp senses, ready for every venture thanks to a surplus of 'free will', with fore-souls and back-souls whose ultimate intentions no one can easily penetrate, with foregrounds and backgrounds that no foot could traverse to the end, secluded under the cloaks of light, conquerors despite our resemblance to heirs and wastrels, organizers and collectors from morn till night, misers of our wealth and of our overflowing desk-drawers, economical in learning and forgetting, inventive in schemata, sometimes proud of category tables, sometimes pedants, sometimes labouring night-owls even in bright daylight; and yes, if necessary, even scarecrows—and that is what is necessary today, in so far as we are the born, sworn jealous friends of *solitude*, our own, deepest, most midnight, midday solitude. That is the sort of human we are, we free spirits! And perhaps *you* have something of it, too, you who are approaching? You *new* philosophers?—

SECTION THREE

THE RELIGIOUS DISPOSITION

45

THE human soul and its boundaries; the dimensions that the human inner life has thus far attained, its peaks, valleys, and distances; the whole *previous* history of the soul and its as yet unexplored possibilities—for a born psychologist and lover of the 'great hunt', this is his preordained hunting ground. But how often, despairingly, must he say to himself: 'I am one man alone! Only one man alone, in this great, primeval forest!' And he wishes he had a few hundred helpers for the hunt and some well-schooled, fine-nosed blood-hounds to chase into the history of the human soul and flush out *his* game for him. In vain: again and again he discovers, bitterly and absolutely, how difficult it is to find hounds or helpers for just those things that pique his curiosity. There is no advantage to sending scholars out into new and dangerous hunting grounds, where courage, cleverness, and subtlety are required in every sense, where the '*great* hunt' (but also the great danger) begins, for scholars are no longer useful there: rather, that is just where they lose their keen eye and sensitive nose. To intuit and establish the history of the problem of *cognizance and conscience* in the soul of *homines religiosi,** for example, you might yourself have to be as deep, as wounded, as monstrous as was the intellectual conscience of Pascal.* And even then you would still have need of that vast breadth of sky above with its bright, malicious spirituality to survey this multitude of dangerous, painful experiences, order them, and force them into formulae.

But who could render me this service! And who would have time to wait for such servants to appear! Clearly, they turn up too rarely, finding them is always so improbable! In the end, if you want to know something, you must do everything *yourself*, which means that there is *much* to do!

Yet a curiosity like mine, after all, is the most pleasant of vices—

excuse me! what I meant to say is that the love of truth has its reward in heaven, and indeed even on earth.

46

The faith demanded and often achieved by early Christianity in the midst of the southern world of sceptical free spirits, where philosophical schools had not only battled for centuries but where the Roman empire had also educated men to be tolerant, is *not* the same as that naive and quarrelsome underlings' faith with which Luther, for example, or Cromwell, or any other northern barbarian of the spirit clung to their God and their Christianity. Rather, that early faith is more like Pascal's, one that has the horrible aspect of an ongoing suicide of reason—a tough, long-lived, wormlike reason that cannot be killed off all at once with one blow. From the beginning, Christian faith has meant a sacrifice: the sacrifice of freedom, pride, spiritual self-confidence; it has meant subjugation and self-derision, self-mutilation. There is cruelty and religious Phoenicianism* in this faith, which is demanded of a soft, differentiated, and often pampered conscience. This kind of faith assumes that the submission of the spirit is indescribably *painful*, that the past history and habits of this kind of spirit are resistant to the *absurdissimum*,* in which form 'faith' confronts it. Modern people, deadened to all the terms of Christian language, no longer have a feeling for the terrifying superlative, which for the ancient sensibility lay in the paradox of the formula 'God on the cross'. At no time or place has there ever been such a daring reversal, a formula so frightful, questioning, and questionable as this one: it ushered in a re-evaluation of all ancient values.

Thus did the Orient, the *profound* Orient, the Oriental slave take vengeance on Rome, with its noble and frivolous tolerance, vengeance on the Roman 'Catholicism' of faith—and it was never faith, but rather the freedom from faith, that half-stoic, smiling lack of concern for the seriousness of faith, which enraged the slaves about their masters, set them against their masters. 'Enlightenment' enrages the slave, for he wants what is unconditional; he understands only what is tyrannical, even in morality; he loves as he hates, without nuance, into the very depths, of pain, of disease— his manifold *hidden* suffering rages against that noble sensibility which seems to *deny* suffering. Indeed, scepticism about suffering, at bottom only an aristocratic moral pose, played no small role in the origins of the last great slave rebellion, which began with the French Revolution.

47

Wherever the religious neurosis has appeared on earth until now, we find it combined with three dangerous dietetic prescriptions: solitude, fasting, and sexual abstinence—though it is impossible to decide with certainty which is the cause, which the effect, and *whether* in fact there is a cause-and-effect relationship at all. This last doubt is justified if we consider that one of the most regular symptoms of religious neurosis in both savage and civilized peoples is a sudden, extravagant voluptuousness, which just as suddenly turns into spasms of penitence and a denial of the world and the will; both perhaps to be interpreted as a disguised form of epilepsy? In no area, however, should one be so ready to dismiss interpretations as here: no other archetype has given rise to such a wealth of nonsense and superstition, or held greater interest for people, even philosophers this might be the right time to cool down, to learn caution, or even better: to look away, to *go* away.

Even behind the most recent philosophy—Schopenhauer's—there still lies what is virtually the key problem, this terrifying question mark of religious crisis and religious awakening. How is the denial of the will *possible*? How is sainthood possible? That really does seem to be the question that first concerned Schopenhauer and made him into a philosopher. And so it was a genuinely Schopenhauerian consequence that his most convinced disciple (perhaps his last one, too, in Germany at least), Richard Wagner by name, should have brought his own life's work to a conclusion at just this point, introducing that terrible and eternal archetype to the stage as Kundry,* *type vécu*,* in the living flesh; at the same time psychiatrists from nearly all the countries in Europe had opportunity to study the type at close quarters, wherever the most recent epidemic of the religious neurosis—or, as I call it, the religious disposition—broke out and marched forth in the guise of the 'Salvation Army'.

If we wonder what it is that all kinds of people at all times, even philosophers, have continued to find so interesting in the whole phenomenon of the saint, the answer is surely its seeming miraculousness, the immediate *succession of opposites*, of conditions of the soul with opposite moral value: here it seemed palpable that a 'bad person' could all at once turn into a 'saint', a good person. This is where earlier psychology ran aground: was it not chiefly because it had submitted to the rule of morality, itself *believing* in moral value oppositions and seeing, reading, *interpreting* these oppositions into the text *and* facts of the case?—

What's that? A 'miracle' may be only an interpretative error? A philological failure?

48

Catholicism is much more internalized in the Latin races, it seems, than is any form of Christianity among us northerners; as a result, lack of faith means something quite different in Catholic countries as opposed to Protestant countries. In Catholic countries it means a kind of rebellion against the spirit of the race, whereas for us lack of faith seems rather to mean a return to the spirit (or lack of spirit) of our race. There can be no doubt that we northerners originate from barbarian races, even in respect to our gift for religion. We do *not* have much of a gift for it. The Celts are an exception, and for that reason provided the Christian infection with its most receptive northern soil. In France, to the extent that the pale northern sun had allowed it to bloom at all, the Christian ideal produced its last withered blossoms. As they have inherited some Celtic blood, even these last French sceptics strike us as strangely pious. For us, there is such a Catholic, un-Germanic smell to Auguste Comte's sociology,* with its Roman logic of the instincts. And such a Jesuitical smell to Saint-Beuve,* that dear and clever cicerone of Port-Royal, for all his hostility towards the Jesuits. And as for Ernest Renan:* how unintelligible to a northerner is the language of someone like Renan, in whom some ephemeral religious tension disrupts at every moment the balance of his comfortable and (in the finer sense) voluptuous soul! Just try repeating his pretty sentences—and see what a malicious and arrogant response stirs immediately in our soul, which is probably a less pretty soul, and harsher, that is, more German.

'Disons donc hardiment que la religion est un produit de l'homme normal, que l'homme est le plus dans le vrai quand il est le plus religieux et le plus assuré d'une destinée infinie ... C'est quand il est bon qu'il veut que la vertu corresponde à un ordre éternel, c'est quand il contemple les choses d'une manière désintéressée qu'il trouve la mort révoltante et absurde. Comment ne pas supposer que c'est dans ces moments-là, que l'homme voit le mieux?'* So *antipodal* to my own ears and habits are these sentences, that when I found them, my first fury had me write alongside them: 'la niaiserie religieuse par excellence!'*—until my final fury actually grew fond of them, these sentences with their upside-down truth. It is so pleasant, such a distinction, to have antipodes of one's own!

49

The astonishing thing about the ancient Greeks' religiosity is the tremendous wealth of gratitude pouring forth from it: only a very noble kind of person can face nature and life like *this*!

Afterwards, when the rabble got the upper hand in Greece, *fear* ran rampant in their religion, too; and the ground was prepared for Christianity.

50

The passion for God: there is the boorish, naive, and obtrusive kind, like Luther's (all of Protestantism lacks southern *delicatezza*).* There is an oriental deliriousness in it, like that of a slave who has undeservedly been pardoned or promoted; we find it in Augustine, for example, whose gestures and desires are offensive in their lack of any nobility. There is a feminine amorousness and desire in this passion, as it bashfully and ignorantly yearns towards a *unio mystica et physica*,* as in Madame de Guyon.* In many cases, strangely enough, it manifests itself as the disguise for the puberty of a boy or girl; and sometimes it even seems to be the hysteria of an old maid, her last ambition—in such cases, the Church has often canonized the woman.

51

Until now, the most powerful people have continued to bow down
with respect before the saint, as a riddle of self-discipline and
deliberate, ultimate renunciation: why have they bowed down?
Behind the question mark of the saint's fragile and pitiable appearance, they sensed the superior force that wished to test itself
through a discipline such as his. It was the strength of the will; in
it they recognized anew and were able to honour their own strength
and lordly pleasure: they were honouring something in themselves
when they honoured the saint. The sight of the saint also planted
a suspicion in them: 'Such a monstrous denial, so contrary to
nature, cannot have been desired for nothing,' they said to themselves and wondered. 'Maybe there is a reason for it, maybe there
is some very great danger, which the ascetic, thanks to his secret
counsellors and visitors, knows more about?' Suffice it to say, in
his presence the powerful of the world learned a new fear; they
sensed a new power, a strange enemy, still unconquered: it was the
'will to power' which brought them to a stop before the saint. They
needed to ask him—

52

The Jewish 'Old Testament', the book of divine justice, portrays
people, things, and utterances in such a grand style that nothing
in Greek or Indian writing can be compared to it. With fear and
admiration we stand in the presence of these tremendous remnants
of what man used to be, thinking sad thoughts about old Asia and
its protruding peninsula Europe—Europe which has come to
signify 'man's progress' over and against Asia. To be sure, if you
are nothing but a scrawny, tame house-pet, knowing only a house-
pet's needs (like civilized people of today, including the Christians
of 'civilized' Christianity), you will be neither amazed nor saddened
among these ruins: the taste for the Old Testament is a touchstone
for 'greatness' or 'smallness'. Perhaps you find the New Testament,
the book of mercy, more to your liking (there is much in it of the
proper, delicate, dank odour of devotees and small souls). This
New Testament, in every respect a kind of Rococo of sensibility,
has been pasted together with the Old Testament into one book,
as a 'Bible', as 'the book per se'—this is perhaps the greatest

audacity and 'sin against the spirit' that literary Europe has on its conscience.

53

What is the reason for today's atheism?

God 'the father' has been thoroughly refuted, so has 'the judge', 'the rewarder'. So has his 'free will': he does not hear—and if he did hear, he still would not be able to help. The worst part is that he seems incapable of communicating clearly: is he unintelligible?

Asking questions, listening carefully through many conversations, I have discovered that this is what has caused the demise of European theism; it seems to me that although the religious instinct is growing vigorously, it has found theism itself unsatisfying and has rejected it with profound mistrust.

54

What really is the use of all modern philosophy? Since Descartes (and more in defiance of him than because of his example) all philosophers have attempted to assassinate the old concept of the soul, under the guise of criticizing the subject-predicate concept. That is to say, they have attempted to assassinate the basic assumption of Christian doctrine. Whether overtly or covertly, modern philosophy (that is, epistemological scepticism) is *anti-Christian*, although (this is meant for finer ears) it is by no means anti-religious. In earlier times people believed in the 'soul' just as they believed in grammar and the grammatical subject. They said that 'I' is a condition, that 'think' is a predicate and thus conditioned: thinking is an activity for which a causal subject *must* be thought. And then, with admirable tenacity and cunning, people tried to see whether they might not be able to get out of this trap, whether perhaps the reverse was true: that 'think' was the condition, and 'I' the conditioned; 'I' would thus be a synthesis, which was *made* through the thinking itself. Basically, *Kant* wanted to prove that the subject could not be proved by means of the subject, nor could the object be proved either. Perhaps he was already familiar with the possibility of an *apparent existence* of the subject (that is, of the soul), this thought that was once present on earth, tremendously powerful, in the philosophy of Vedanta.

55

The great ladder of religious cruelty has many rungs, but three of them are the most important. In earlier times, people offered their god sacrifices of human beings, perhaps even those whom they loved best: to this group belong those first sacrifices of all prehistoric religions, and also the Emperor Tiberius' sacrifice in the Mithras Grotto* on the Isle of Capri, that most terrifying of all Roman anachronisms. Later, in humanity's moral epoch, people sacrificed to their God the strongest instincts that they possessed, their 'nature'; *this* is the celebratory joy that shines in the terrible glance of the ascetic, of a man living rapturously contrary to nature. Finally: what was left to sacrifice? Didn't people finally have to sacrifice everything comforting, sacred, curative, all hope, all faith in hidden harmony, in future bliss and justice? Didn't they have to sacrifice God himself, and, out of self-directed cruelty, worship stone, stupidity, heaviness, fate, nothingness? To sacrifice God for the sake of nothingness—the paradoxical mystery of this final cruelty has been reserved for the generation that is just now emerging—and all of us already know something about it.

56

Anyone who has struggled for a long time, as I have, with a mysterious desire to think down to the depths of pessimism and redeem it from the half-Christian, half-German narrowness and simplicity with which it has most recently been portrayed, namely in the form of Schopenhauerian philosophy; anyone who has truly looked with an Asiatic and super-Asiatic eye into—and underneath—the most world-denying of all possible ways of thinking (beyond good and evil and no longer helplessly deluded, like Buddha and Schopenhauer, by morality)—this person may, without really intending it, have opened his eyes to the opposite ideal: to the ideal of the most audacious, lively, and world-affirming human being, one who has learned not only to accept and bear that which has been and is, but who also wants to have it over again, *just as it was and is*, throughout all eternity, calling out insatiably *da capo*,* not only to himself, but to the whole drama, the whole spectacle, and not only to a spectacle, but ultimately to the one who has need of just this spectacle—and makes it necessary, because he continually has need of himself—and makes himself necessary—

Well? And wouldn't this then be—*circulus vitiosus deus?**

57

As his intellectual sight and insight grow stronger, the distances and, as it were, the space surrounding a man increase: his world becomes more profound; new stars, new images and riddles keep coming into view. Perhaps all the things that trained his mind's eye to see more acutely and profoundly were nothing but occasions for training, playthings for children and childish people. Perhaps the most solemn concepts, those that have triggered the greatest struggles and suffering, the concepts 'God' and 'sin', will some day seem no more important to us than the toys and pains of childhood seem to an old man—and perhaps the 'old man' will then need a different toy and a different pain—still so much a child, an eternal child!

58

Has anyone noticed the extent to which a true religious life (which includes its favourite work of microscopic self-examination, along with that state of gentle calm called 'prayer', the ongoing preparation for 'the coming of God') is dependent on external leisure or semi-leisure, by which I mean that time-honoured, guilt-free, ancestral leisure that is not entirely different from an aristocrat's feeling that work *desecrates*—that it debases soul and body? And that it is therefore the modern, noisy, time-consuming, self-congratulatory, stupidly proud work ethic more than anything else that trains and prepares us for a 'lack of faith'? Among contemporary non-religious Germans, for example, I find all kinds of 'freethinkers' with all kinds of backgrounds, but above all else a majority whose religious instincts have disintegrated over the generations because of the work ethic, so that they no longer have any idea at all of the possible use of religion, and merely take note, as it were, with a kind of dumb astonishment that religions exist in the world. These good people feel that there are enough claims on their time already, whether because of their business affairs or their recreational activities, not to mention their 'fatherland' and their newspapers and their 'family obligations': it would seem that they have no time left over for religion, especially since they never can figure out whether going to church would be classified as a new business deal or a new recreational activity—for one can't possibly go to church, they tell themselves, just to spoil one's good mood. They are not hostile to religious customs; if in certain cases someone (the state, for example) requires them to take part in such customs, they do what is required as they do other required things: with a patient, modest seriousness and without much curiosity or discomfort—they live too much outside and apart from these matters even to feel the need for their own Pro or Con. This sort of indifferent person makes up the majority of middle-class German Protestants nowadays, especially in large, hard-working centres of business and commerce, and also makes up the majority of hard-working scholars and the whole academic entourage (with the exception of the theologians, whose improbable existence gives the psychologist ever more and ever subtler riddles to unravel). Pious or even merely church-going people seldom imagine *how much* good will (wilful will, one could say) is required nowadays for a German scholar to take the problem of religion seriously; all of his craft (and, as mentioned above, the craftsmanlike work ethic to which he is bound by his modern conscience) inclines him to feel a superior, almost serene benevolence towards religion, mixed at times with a slight disdain for the 'polluted' spirit which he assumes must be at work whenever someone has joined a church. Only through the study of history (that is, *not* from personal experience) is a scholar able to treat religions with a reverent seriousness and a certain shy regard; but even if he has elevated his feeling towards them to the point of gratitude, he has in his own person still not come even one step closer to the remnants of church and piety—perhaps the reverse. He was born and raised to treat religious matters with a practical indifference that tends to be sublimated into fastidious circumspection, making him avoid contact with religious people or things; and it may be precisely because he is so deeply tolerant and humane that he tries to escape the subtle state of distress that accompanies even tolerance.

Every age has invented its own divine type of *naïveté*, which other periods may find enviable—and how much *naïveté*, how much admirable, childlike, and endlessly foolish *naïveté* lies in the scholar's faith in his own superiority, in his good conscience for being tolerant, in the simple clueless confidence with which he instinctively treats the religious person as an inferior and lower type, one that he himself has grown away from, grown beyond, grown *above*— he, the presumptuous little dwarf and vulgarian, the diligent darting headworker and handworker of 'ideas', of 'modern ideas'!

59

Whoever has looked deeply into the world will surely divine what wisdom there is in human superficiality. It is the instinct of preservation that teaches us to be fleet, light, and false. Now and then, in philosophers or artists, one finds a passionate and exaggerated worship of 'pure forms': no one should doubt that a person who so *needs* the surface must once have made an unfortunate grab *underneath* it. Perhaps these burnt children, the born artists who find their only joy in trying to *falsify* life's image (as if taking protracted revenge against it—), perhaps they may even belong to a hierarchy: we could tell the degree to which they are sick of life by how much they wish to see its image adulterated, diluted, transcendentalized, apotheosized—we could count the *homines religiosi* among the artists, as their *highest* class. For thousands of years, a deep, suspicious fear of an incurable pessimism has forced people to cling to a religious interpretation of existence: this instinctual fear senses that they might gain possession of the truth *too soon*, before they have become strong enough for it, tough enough, artist enough.

When viewed thus, piety, a 'life with God', would appear to be the most exquisite end product of the *fear* of truth; the worshipful artist's intoxication at the most persistent of all falsifications; the will to truth-reversal, to untruth at any price. Perhaps there has never yet been a more powerful device for beautifying even mankind than piety itself: it can turn humans so completely into art, surface, opalescence, kindness, that we no longer suffer when we look at them.

60

To love mankind *for the sake of God*—that has been the most noble and far-fetched feeling yet achieved by human beings. The idea that without some sanctifying ulterior motive, a love of mankind is just one *more* brutish stupidity, that the predisposition to such a love must first find its weight, its refinement, its grain of salt and pinch of ambergris in another even higher predisposition—whoever first felt and 'witnessed' this, and however much his tongue may have stuttered in attempting to express such a delicate idea: may he remain forever venerable and holy in our sight as the man who as yet has flown the highest and erred the most beautifully!

61

The philosopher as *we* understand him, we free spirits—as a person with the most wide-ranging responsibility, whose conscience encompasses mankind's overall development. this philosopher, in his efforts to improve education and breeding, will make use of religions just as he makes use of the political and economic circumstances of his time. The influence that can be exerted with the help of religion is an influence for selecting and breeding, and is always necessarily as destructive as it is creative and formative; depending on the sort of people who come under the spell and protection of religion, its influence can be manifold and diverse.

For those who are strong and independent, prepared and predestined to command, who embody the intellect and the art of a governing race, religion is one further means to overcome obstacles, to learn to rule: as a bond that ties together rulers and subjects, revealing and surrendering to the former the consciences of the latter, their hidden and innermost secret, the wish to escape the bonds of obedience. And if, because of their high spirituality, a few of these nobly-born natures are inclined to a more removed and contemplative life, reserving for themselves only the most subtle form of authority (over selected disciples or brothers of the order), they can use religion as a means to ensure their repose when confronted with the noisy exertions of the *cruder* type of authority, and their purity when confronted with the *necessary* filth of every kind of political activity. That is how the Brahmans understood it, for example: with the help of a religious organization, they gave themselves the power to appoint the kings for the common people, while they themselves remained apart and outside, feeling that their own duties were more important than those of royalty.

Meanwhile, religion also gives guidance and an opportunity to prepare for eventual authority and command to a portion of the governed, to those slowly rising classes and ranks whose successful marriage patterns have ensured that the strong desire of their will, their will to self-rule, is always growing. Religion can offer them enough incitements and temptations to go the ways of higher spirituality, to test their feelings of great self-control, silence, and solitude: asceticism and puritanism are the virtually indispensable means to educate and improve a race that wants to overcome its origin in the rabble and work itself up to eventual authority.

To the ordinary people, finally, to the vast majority who exist to serve and be generally useful and *must* exist only to that end, religion offers an inestimable contentment with their own situation and nature, an ongoing peace of heart, improved obedience, joy and sorrow shared with their own kind, and something in the way of transfiguration and beautification, something that justifies their everyday lives, all the baseness, all the semi-animal poverty of their souls. Being religious and finding a religious significance to life sheds sunshine on these constantly afflicted people, even enabling them to bear the sight of themselves; it has the same effect that Epicurean philosophy tends to have on a higher class of sufferer: refreshing, purifying, *exploiting* suffering, as it were, and ultimately even sanctifying and justifying it. There is perhaps nothing so admirable about Christianity and Buddhism as their skill in showing even the lowliest people how piety can place them within an illusory higher order of things and thus enable them to remain content with the real order, within which they certainly live a harsh (and this harshness is exactly what's needed!) life.

62

But finally, of course, to reckon up the bad side of religions like these and expose their sinister danger: there is always a dear and terrible price to pay whenever religions hold sway *not* as the philosopher's means to breed and educate, but rather on their own and *absolutely*, when they claim to be an ultimate end, rather than one means among others. Among humans as among every other species of animal, there is a surplus of deformed, sick, degenerating, frail, necessarily suffering individuals; even among humans and even considering that man is the *animal that has not yet been established*, successful cases are always the exception, the rare exception. But even worse: the higher the nature of a particular type, the greater the probability that any representative individual of that type *will not thrive*: randomness, the law of meaninglessness in the overall economy of mankind, is seen at its most terrible in its destructive effect on higher individuals, whose needs in life are subtle, manifold, and difficult to calculate.

Now how do the two above-mentioned greatest religions treat this *surplus* of failed cases? They try to preserve, try to keep alive, whatever can somehow be retained of them, indeed they take their side on principle, as religions *for the suffering*; according to these religions, all the people who suffer from life as from an illness are in the right, and they would like to ensure that any other experience of life be considered wrong and rendered impossible. However greatly one might like to value such indulgent and supportive solicitude, in that it has also included and continues to include among the suffering the highest species of humans, who until now have almost always suffered the most: nevertheless, in the last analysis, earlier religions, namely *absolute* religions are among the main reasons that the species 'human' has been stuck on a lower rung of development—they have preserved too much of what *ought to perish*. They have given us priceless gifts; and who is so richly endowed with gratitude that he would not become poor in thanking Christianity's 'spiritual people', for example, for what they have already done for Europe! And yet, after they have offered comfort to the suffering, courage to the oppressed and desperate, and been a staff and support to the dependent; after they have lured those inwardly ravaged and driven mad away from society into cloisters and spiritual prisons: what more should they have to do to work with such conviction and a good conscience for the preservation of everything sick and suffering, that is to say, to work in deed and in truth for the *degeneration of the European race*? Turn all evaluations *upside down*—*that* is what they had to do! And shatter the strong, debilitate the great hopes, question any joy in beauty, take everything autocratic, masculine, triumphant, tyrannical, all the instincts that belong to the highest and best-formed species of 'human', and twist them into doubt, pangs of conscience, self-destruction, indeed reverse all love for earthly things and for mastery of the earth into a hatred of the earth and the earthly—*that* is the task the Church set for itself and had to set for itself, until 'unworldliness', 'asceticism', and 'the higher man' fused together in its estimation into *one* feeling. Assuming that one were able to survey the strangely painful comedy of European Christianity, as coarse as it is refined, with the mocking and disinterested eye of an Epicurean god, I think there would be no end to the astonishment and laughter: doesn't it seem that for eighteen centuries one will alone has ruled over Europe, set on making man into a *sublime deformity?* But if someone with the opposite needs, no longer an Epicurean, but with some divine hammer in his hand, were to come up to this almost capriciously degenerate and stunted man that is the European Christian (Pascal, for example), would he not have to cry out in anger, in pity, in horror: 'Oh you fools, you presumptuous pitying fools, see what you have done! Was this a work for your hands! See how you have hacked up my most beautiful stone and bungled it! How could *you* presume to do such a thing!'

That is to say: Christianity has been the most disastrous form of human presumption yet. Humans who were neither high-minded nor tough enough to claim the power to work *on mankind* as its shaping artist; humans who were neither strong nor far-sighted enough to exercise a sublime self-control and *let* the foreground law of thousands of failures and defeats hold sway; humans who were not noble enough to see the unfathomably diverse hierarchy in the gulf between human and human—*these* are the people who have controlled Europe's destiny so far, with their 'equal in the eyes of God', until they have bred a diminished, almost ludicrous species, a herd animal, something good-natured, sickly, and mediocre, today's European . . .

SECTION FOUR

EPIGRAMS AND INTERLUDES

63

A TRUE teacher doesn't take anything seriously except in relation to his pupils—not even himself.

64

'Knowledge for its own sake'—that is the last snare set by morality, tangling us up in it again completely.

65

Knowledge would have only a slight allure if there weren't so much shame to overcome in achieving it.

65a

People are most dishonest in relation to their god: he *must* not sin!

66

The inclination to degrade ourselves, to allow ourselves to be robbed, lied to, and exploited, might be the shame of a god among humans.

67

The love for one individual is barbarous, for it is practised at the expense of everyone else. Even a love for God.

68

'I have done that,' says my memory. I cannot have done that—says my pride and remains unshakeable. Finally—memory yields.

69

You have been a poor observer of life if you have not also seen the hand that with kindness—kills.

70

If a person has character, he also has his typical experience that happens again and again.

71

The sage as astronomer.—As long as you still feel the stars as something 'above you', you have not yet acquired the gaze of a man of deep understanding.

72

It is not the strength of his great feelings, but rather their duration that is the mark of a great man.

73

One who reaches his ideal has by so doing gone beyond it.

73a

Some peacocks hide their peacock's tail from every eye—and call that pride.

74

A person of genius is intolerable if he does not possess at least two other things: gratitude and cleanliness.

75

The degree and nature of a person's sexuality extends into the highest pinnacle of his spirit.

76

When things are peaceful, the warlike person trips over himself.

77

We use our basic principles to tyrannize or justify or honour or scold or conceal our habits—two people with the same basic principles probably intend something basically different by them.

78

A person who despises himself still respects himself as a despiser.*

79

A heart that knows it is loved, but does not itself love, reveals its sediment—its bottom rises to the top.

80

Once a matter has been clarified it no longer concerns us.

What might that god have meant who advised: 'Know thyself!'? Might he have meant: 'Don't be concerned with yourself any more! Become objective!'?

And Socrates?

And 'the man of science'?

81

It is terrible to die of thirst on the ocean. Does your truth have to be so salty that it can no longer even—quench thirst?

82

'To pity everyone'—that would be to chastise and tyrannize *yourself*, my dear neighbour!—

83

Instinct.—When your house is on fire, you even forget to have dinner.

Yes, but you make up for it later on the ashes.

84

Women learn to hate to the same extent that they—unlearn how to beguile.

85

Men and women have the same emotions, but at a different tempo: that is why men and women never cease to misunderstand one another.

86

Behind all her personal vanity, a woman still harbours her own impersonal contempt—for 'women'.

87

Bound heart, free spirit.—If you severely bind and enchain your heart, you can give your spirit many liberties: that is what I said, once upon a time. But people don't believe me, unless they've already found it out for themselves . . .

88

We begin to distrust very clever people when they become embarrassed.

89

Dreadful experiences make us wonder whether the person who experiences them may not be something dreadful.

90

Heavy, heavy-hearted people respond to the very same thing that makes other people heavy, to love and hatred, by growing lighter and coming temporarily to their surface.

91

So cold, so icy, that you burn your fingers on him! Every hand that touches him darts back in fear!

And for that very reason, some think he is aglow.

92

Is there anyone who has not at times maintained his good reputation by sacrificing—himself?

93

In affability there is no hatred for mankind—that is why there is all too much contempt.

94

A man's maturity: having rediscovered the seriousness that he had as a child, at play.

95

Being ashamed of our immorality: that is one step on the ladder that leads to being also ashamed of our morality.

96

We should depart from life as Odysseus parted from Nausicaa—with a blessing, but not in love.

97

What's this? A great man? All I can see is the play-actor of his own ideal.

98

When we teach our conscience to do tricks, it kisses us even as it bites.*

99

The disappointed person speaks.—'I listened for an echo and all I heard was praise—'

100

Left to ourselves, we all pretend to be simpler than we are: this is how we relax from our fellow man.

101

These days a man of deep understanding could easily feel like God's incarnation as an animal.*

102

Discovering that his love is returned should actually disillusion a lover about his beloved. 'What's this? *This* person is unassuming enough to love even you? Or stupid enough? Or—or—'

103

The danger in happiness.—'Everything is turning out right for me now, from now on I'll love every turn of fate—who wants to be my fate?'

104

It is not their brotherly love, but rather the impotence of their brotherly love that keeps today's Christians from—burning us down.

105

For the free spirit, for the 'pious man of knowledge'—the *pia fraus** goes even more against the grain (of *his* 'piety') than the *impia fraus*. Hence his profound lack of understanding for the Church, proper to the type 'free spirit'—as *his* lack of freedom.

106

Through music, even our passions can enjoy themselves.

107

Once you resolve to keep your ears closed even to the best counter-argument, it shows that you have a strong character. And thus an occasional will to stupidity.

108

There is no such thing as moral phenomena, but only a moral interpretation of phenomena . . .

109

Often enough, a criminal is not up to his deed: he diminishes and debases it.

110

A criminal's lawyers are seldom contortionists enough to turn the fine horror of his deed to its perpetrator's advantage.

111

Our vanity is most resistant to wounds when our pride has just been wounded.

112

A person who feels himself predestined to observe rather than to believe finds all believers too noisy and insistent: he fends them off.

113

'You want to win him over? Then pretend to be embarrassed in his presence—'

114

The tremendous anticipation of sexual love and the shame in this anticipation spoil any sense of perspective in women from the start.

115

When neither love nor hatred plays a part, a woman's playing will be mediocre.

116

The great periods of our life occur when we gain the courage to rechristen what is bad about us as what is best.

117

The will to overcome an emotion is in the last analysis only the will of another or several other emotions.

118

There is an innocence in admiration: it occurs in one who has not yet realized that he might one day be admired.

119

An aversion to dirt can be so great that it keeps us from cleaning ourselves—from 'vindicating' ourselves.

120

Sensuality often hurries the growth of love too much, so that its roots remain weak and easy to extract.

121

It is a subtle point that God learned Greek when he decided to become a writer—and that he did not learn it better.

122

For some people, taking pleasure in praise is only a courtesy of the heart—and the exact opposite of a vanity of the mind.

123

Even cohabitation has been corrupted—by marriage.

124

A person who can exult while being burned at the stake is not triumphing over the pain but over the fact that he feels no pain where he expected to. A parable.

125

When we are forced to re-evaluate a person, we judge him harshly for the trouble he causes us in doing so.

126

A people is the detour made by nature to arrive at six or seven great men.

Yes, and then to get around them.

127

All proper women find that science is inimical to their modesty. It makes them feel as if someone wanted to take a look under their skin—or worse! under their clothes and make-up.

128

The more abstract the truth you wish to teach us, the more you must entice our senses into learning it.

129

The devil has the widest perspectives for God, and that is why he keeps so far away from him—the devil, then, as the oldest friend of knowledge.

130

A person begins to reveal what he *is* when his talent declines—when he stops demonstrating what he can *do*. Talent can also be an adornment; an adornment can also be a hiding place.

131

The sexes deceive themselves about one another: as a result, they basically honour and love only themselves (or their ideal of themselves, to express it more kindly—). Thus men want women to be peaceful—but women especially are *by their very nature* unpeaceful, like cats, however well they have learned to give the impression of peacefulness.

132

People are best punished for their virtues.

133

A person who does not know how to find the way to *his* ideal lives more frivolously and more impudently than a person with no ideal.

134

Our senses are the first origin of all credibility, all good conscience, all apparent truth.

135

Pharisaism* is not the degeneracy of a good person: rather, a good portion of it is integral to every sort of goodness.

136

One person seeks a midwife for his thoughts, another seeks to act as midwife: the origin of a good conversation.

137

In dealing with scholars and artists, we easily miscalculate in reverse: not infrequently, we find behind a remarkable scholar a mediocre person, and often, in fact, we find behind a mediocre artist—a very remarkable person.

138

What we do when dreaming, we also do when awake: we first dream up the person we are interacting with—and instantly forget that we have done so.

139

In revenge and in love, women are more barbaric than men.

140

Curious counsel.*—'To make the bond hold tight, at first give it a bite.'

141

The belly is the reason that man doesn't readily take himself for a god.

142

The most chaste saying I have heard: 'Dans le véritable amour c'est l'âme, qui enveloppe le corps.'*

143

Our vanity would like to claim that what we do best is precisely what is hardest for us to do. A note on the origin of much morality.

144

When a woman has scholarly tendencies, there is usually something wrong with her sexuality. Barrenness in and of itself predisposes to a certain masculinity of taste: for, if I may say so, the man is the 'barren animal'.

145

Comparing men and women in general, you might say that women would not have their genius for adornment if they did not have an instinct for the *supporting* role.

146

Anyone who fights with monsters should take care that he does not in the process become a monster. And if you gaze for long into an abyss, the abyss gazes back into you.

147

From old Florentine tales, and in addition—from life: *buona femmina e mala femmina vuol bastone.** Sacchetti.* Nov. 86.

148

Seducing your neighbour into a good opinion and then believing devoutly in this neighbour's opinion—in this kind of trick, who can outdo women?

149

What one age perceives as evil is usually an untimely echo of something that was once perceived as good—the atavism of an older ideal.

150

Around a hero everything becomes a tragedy, around a demigod everything becomes a satyr play; and around God everything becomes—what do you think? perhaps the 'world'?—

151

Having a talent is not enough: we also need your permission to have it—don't you think so? my good friends?

152

'Where the tree of knowledge stands, you will always find paradise'—that's what the oldest and the youngest serpents will tell you.

153

What is done out of love always takes place beyond good and evil.

154

Objections, evasions, a gay distrust, mockery—all are indications of health: everything absolute comes under pathology.

155

The feeling for the tragic decreases and increases along with sensuality.

156

Madness is rare in individuals—but in groups, political parties, nations, epochs, it is the rule.

157

The thought of suicide is a powerful solace: it helps us through many a bad night.

158

Our most powerful instinct, the tyrant in us, subjugates not only our reason, but also our conscience . . .

159

We *must* repay, both good and bad: but why especially must it be to the one who did us good or bad?

160

We no longer love our knowledge enough, once we have communicated it.

161

Poets are shameless with their experiences: they exploit them.

162

'Thy neighbour* is not your neighbour, but your neighbour's neighbour'—as every people tells itself.

163

Love exposes the great and hidden qualities in the lover—what is rare and exceptional about him: to that extent it easily conceals what is ordinary.

164

Jesus told his Jews: 'The law was meant for servants—love God as I love him, as his son! What do we sons of God care about morality!'

165

About all political parties.—A shepherd always needs to have a bell-wether, too—or else upon occasion he himself will be the sheep.*

166

It is true that we lie with our mouth; but with the grimace* we make when we do so, we still end up telling the truth.

167

In harsh people, tender feeling is a cause for shame—and something precious.

168

Christianity gave Eros poison to drink—he did not die of it, it's true, but he deteriorated, into a vice.

169

Talking a great deal about yourself can also be a means of hiding.

170

Praise is more intrusive than blame.

171

In a person of knowledge, pity has an almost comical effect, like delicate hands on a cyclops.

172

From time to time, we embrace some arbitrary person (because we cannot embrace everybody) for reasons of brotherly love: but that fact above all must be kept from the arbitrary person.

173

We do not feel hatred as long as we esteem lightly, but only when we esteem equally or highly.

174

You utilitarians, even your love for everything that is *utile** is only for the *vehicle* of your predilections—don't you really agree that the noise of its wheels is unbearable?

175

Ultimately, it is the desire, not the desired, that we love.

176

We find other people's vanity contrary to our taste only when it is contrary to our vanity.

177

In speaking about 'truthfulness', perhaps no one yet has been sufficiently truthful.

178

No one believes the foolish acts of clever men: what a loss of human rights!

179

The consequences of our actions grab us by the scruff of the neck, oblivious to the fact that we have in the meanwhile 'mended our ways'.

180

There is an innocence in lying that signals good faith in a cause.

181

It is inhuman to bless where we are being cursed.

182

The intimacy of a superior person embitters because it cannot be returned.

183

'What has shaken me is not that you lied to me, but that I no longer believe you.'—

184

There is a wantonness of goodness that strongly resembles malice.

185

'I don't like him.'
Why not?
'I am not up to him.'
Has any person ever answered thus?

TOWARDS A NATURAL HISTORY OF MORALS

186

THE moral sensibility in Europe these days is as subtle, mature, differentiated, sensitive, refined, as the relevant 'science of morality' is still young, raw, clumsy, and crude: an attractive antithesis which is sometimes revealed in the person of the moralist himself. Even the term 'science of morality', considering what it describes, is much too arrogant and offends *good* taste—which always tends to prefer more modest terms. We should sternly admit to ourselves *what* will be required in the long term, *what* the only right course is for the moment: that is, to gather the material, establish the concepts, and organize the abundance of subtle feelings and distinctions in the area of values, as they live, grow, procreate, and perish; and perhaps we should also attempt to illustrate the more frequently recurring forms of this living crystallization—in preparation for a *taxonomy* of morals. True, such modesty has not so far been the rule. The moment philosophers were concerned with morality as a science, all of them, with a ridiculous stiff solemnity, demanded of themselves something much greater, more ambitious, more solemn: they wanted to *account for* morality—and every philosopher to date has thought that he has done so; morality itself, however, was taken as a 'given'. In their clumsy pride, how remote they were from the seemingly modest task of description, forgotten in dust and decay, although even the most delicate hands and senses could hardly be delicate enough for it! Precisely because the moral philosophers knew moral *facta** only roughly, in arbitrary excerpts or random condensations, knew them as the morality of their neighbourhood, say, or of their class, their Church, the *Zeitgeist*, their climate or region; precisely because they were not well informed about peoples, epochs, past histories and were not even particularly curious about them, they never did catch sight of the real problems of morality—all of which come to light only by comparing *many* moralities. As strange as it may sound, in every previous 'science of morality' the problem of morality itself was *missing*; there was no suspicion that it might be something problematic. What the philosophers called 'accounting for morality' and expected of themselves was, viewed in the right light, only an erudite form of true *belief* in the prevailing morality, a new medium for *expressing* it, and thus itself a part of the state of affairs within a particular morality. Indeed, in the last analysis it was a way of forbidding that this morality *might be* construed as a problem—and in any event it was the opposite of a testing, analysing, doubting, dissecting of their particular belief. Just listen, for example, to the almost admirable innocence with which Schopenhauer portrays his own task, and draw your conclusions as to the scientific nature of a 'science' whose past masters still talk like children or old women: 'The principle', he writes in *The Fundamental Problems of Morality*,* 'the axiom about whose content all moralists *really* agree, *neminem laede, immo omnes, quantum potes, juva**—that is *really* the tenet that all moralists endeavour to account for—the *real* foundation of morality, which people have been seeking for thousands of years like the philosophers' stone.'

To be sure, it may be very difficult to account for the tenet he cites (everyone knows that Schopenhauer himself was not successful in doing so), and anyone who has ever thoroughly appreciated how tastelessly false and sentimental this tenet is in a world whose essence is the will to power, may want to be reminded that Schopenhauer, although he was a pessimist, *really*—played the flute. Every day, after dinner: just read what his biographer says about this. And by the way, may we not inquire whether a pessimist who denies God and the world, but *stops short* at the problem of morality, says Yes to morality, to a *laede-neminem* morality and plays the flute: well then? is this person really—a pessimist?

187

Apart from whatever value there may be in assertions such as 'a categorical imperative exists within us', we can still ask what such an assertion tells us about the person asserting it. There are moral codes that are meant to justify their author to other people; other codes are meant to soothe the author and allow him to be content with himself. Some are intended to nail him to the cross and humiliate him, others to exact vengeance for him, or hide him, or transfigure him and set him above and beyond. One moral code serves its author to forget, another to make others forget him or forget something about him. One sort of moralist would like to exercise his power and creative whims upon mankind; a different sort, and perhaps Kant himself, uses his moral code to announce: 'What is honourable about me is that I can obey—and it *should* be no different for you than for me!' In short, moral codes too are only a *sign language of emotions*.

188

Every moral code, in opposition to *laisser-aller*,* is an example of tyranny against 'nature', and against 'reason', too: but that cannot be an objection to it, or else we would have to turn around and decree on the basis of some other moral code that all kinds of tyranny and unreason were impermissible. The essential, invaluable thing about every moral code is that it is one long coercion: in order to understand Stoicism or Port-Royal* or Puritanism, just think of the coercion that every language has employed up till now in achieving its strength and freedom—the coercion of metre, the tyranny of rhyme and rhythm. How much trouble the poets and orators of every people (not to exclude certain contemporary prose writers, in whose ear an unshakeable conscience resides) have put themselves to—'for the sake of folly', as utilitarian fools say, thus fancying themselves clever; 'in subservience to tyrannical laws', as anarchists say, thus imagining themselves 'free', even freethinking. But the strange fact is that everything on earth that exists or has existed by way of freedom, subtlety, daring, dance, and perfect sureness, whether it be in ideas, or in governance, or in oratory and rhetoric, in the arts as well as in manners, has developed only by virtue of the 'tyranny of such despotic laws'; and seriously, it is very likely that *this* is what is 'nature' and 'natural'—and *not* that *laisser-aller*! Every artist knows how far from the feeling of anything-goes his 'most natural' condition is, the free ordering, arranging, deciding, shaping that occurs in his moments of 'inspiration'—and how delicately and strictly, especially at such moments, he obeys the thousandfold laws whose very exactness and rigour make mockery of all conceptual formulations (even the most solid concept, by comparison, has something muzzy, multifarious, ambiguous—). To repeat, it seems that the essential thing, both 'in heaven and on earth', is that there be a protracted period of unidirectional *obedience*: in the long run, that is how something emerged and emerges that makes life on earth worth living: virtue, for example, or art, music, dance, reason, spirituality—something transfiguring, elegant, wild, and divine. The long constraint of the spirit; the reluctant coercion in the communicability of thoughts; the thinker's self-imposed discipline to think within guidelines set up by court or Church, or according to Aristotelian assumptions; the long-standing spiritual will to interpret every event according to a Christian scheme and to rediscover and justify the Christian God in every chance incident—all this violence, arbitrariness, harshness, horror, nonsense has turned out to be the means by which the European spirit was bred to be strong, ruthlessly curious, and beautifully nimble. Admittedly, much irreplaceable energy and spirit had to be suppressed, suffocated, and spoiled in the process (for here as everywhere 'nature' reveals her true colours in all her extravagant and *indifferent* grandeur, which is infuriating but also noble). For thousands of years European thinkers thought only in order to prove something (today on the other hand we are sceptical of any thinker who 'has something to prove'). They already knew in advance what was *supposed* to emerge as a result of their most rigorous meditation, rather as once in Asian astrology, or as is still the case today in harmless Christian-ethical interpretations of immediate personal experiences 'for the glory of God' or 'for the soul's salvation'. This kind of tyranny, this despotism, this stern, grandiose stupidity *educated* the spirit: it would seem that slavery, both in the cruder and the finer sense, is also the indispensable means to discipline and cultivate* the spirit. Whichever moral code we inspect in that light, its 'nature' teaches us to hate the excessive freedom of *laisser-aller* and instils a need for limited horizons, for immediate tasks—it teaches us to *narrow our perspective*, and thus in a certain sense, to be stupid, as a precondition for life and growth. 'Thou shalt obey, obey somebody, and for a long time: *or else* you will perish and lose your last remnant of self-respect'— this seems to me to be nature's moral imperative, and to be sure it is neither 'categorical', as old Kant demanded (hence the 'or else'—), nor is it addressed to individuals (what should it care about individuals!), but rather to peoples, races, epochs, classes, and above all to the whole animal 'human', to human beings *in general*.

189

The hard-working races find it a great burden to endure leisure: it was a master stroke of the *English* instinct to keep the Sabbath so holy and humdrum that without even noticing it, the Englishman craves his weekday, his workday again. It was a sort of cleverly devised, cleverly interpolated *fasting*, the sort we so often observe in the ancient world (although with southern peoples it is not particularly in relation to work—). There have to be many different kinds of fasting; and wherever powerful instincts and habits are the rule, legislators must take care to institute intercalary days when these instincts are fettered and learn to feel hunger again. From a high enough vantage point, we can regard whole generations and epochs, the ones that appear encumbered with some moral fanaticism, as such interpolated periods of coercion and fasting, during which an instinct learns to bend down and be subjugated, but also to be *purified* and *intensified*; this kind of interpretation can apply even to certain philosophical sects (the Stoics, for example, amidst an Hellenic culture whose air had grown rank and surfeit with aphrodisiacal vapours).

And this may also serve as a hint to explain the paradox of why it was especially in Europe's most Christian period and only under the pressure of Christian value judgements that the sexual drive was sublimated into love (*amour-passion*).*

190

There is something in Plato's morality that is not really part of Plato, but is simply present in his philosophy, you might say, despite Plato: and that is Socratism, for which he was actually too noble. 'No one wants to do himself harm; therefore everything bad must occur involuntarily. For the bad man does himself harm: he would not do it if he knew that the bad was bad. In accordance, the bad man is bad only through error; if we remove his error from him, we necessarily make him—good.'*

This kind of argument reeks of the *rabble*, who focus only on the nasty consequences of a bad action and are actually judging that 'it is *stupid* to act badly' while they unhesitatingly take 'good' to be synonymous with 'useful and pleasant'. We can immediately assume that any other moral utilitarianism has a similar origin and follow our nose: we will seldom go astray.

Plato did everything he could to interpret something subtle and noble (himself, most of all) into the tenet of his teacher. He was the most audacious of interpreters, taking up the whole of Socrates as if it were nothing but a popular tune or folksong of the street, and varying it into the infinite and impossible—that is, into all of his own masks and multiplicities. To speak in jest, and with Homer to boot: what might a Platonic Socrates be, if not, Πρόσθε Πλάτων, ὄπιθεν τε Πλάτων, μέσση τε χίμαιρα.*

191

The old theological problem of 'faith' versus 'knowledge' (or, more precisely, instinct versus reason); the question of whether our value judgements give more authority to instinct than to a rationality which wishes to know that judgements and actions are made for a reason, according to a 'why', that is, according to their expedience or utility—this is the same old moral problem that first appeared in the person of Socrates and that divided opinion long before Christianity. Of course Socrates himself, his taste shaped by his talent (as a superior dialectician), at first took the side of reason; and really, what did he do throughout his life but laugh at the clumsy incompetence of his noble Athenians who like all noble men were men of instinct and never could give enough information about the reasons for their actions. In the end, however, secretly and quietly, he also laughed at himself: interrogating himself with the finest insights of his conscience, he found the same difficulty and incompetence. But why then, he argued to himself, must we free ourselves of our instincts! We have to help both them *and* reason come into their own—we have to follow our instincts, but convince our reason to lend them a helping hand with good arguments. This was the real *duplicity* of that great ironist, so full of secrets; he induced his conscience to content itself with a sort of self-deception: at bottom he had grasped the irrational aspect of moral judgements.

Plato, more innocent in such matters and lacking the plebeian's craftiness, wanted to exert all his energy (more energy than any previous philosopher had ever had!) to prove to himself that reason and instinct, left to their own devices, move towards one single goal, towards the good, towards 'God'; and ever since Plato, all theologians and philosophers have been on the same track—that is to say, up until now instinct, or as Christians say, 'faith', or as I say, 'the herd' has won the day in matters of morality. We have to make an exception of Descartes, the father of rationalism (and therefore the grandfather of the revolution), who granted authority to reason alone: but reason is only a tool, and Descartes was superficial.

192

Anyone who has studied the history of one particular science will find that its development serves as a guide to understanding the oldest and most common processes in all 'knowledge and cognition'. In both cases, the first things to develop are over-eager hypotheses, fabrications, a tried-and-true will to 'belief', a lack of scepticism or patience—only later, and never completely, do our senses learn to be fine, loyal, cautious organs of cognition. On any given occasion, our eye finds it easier to reproduce an image that it has already produced many times, rather than retain what is divergent and new about an impression: the latter requires more fortitude, more 'morality'. It is painful and difficult for the ear to hear something new; we are bad at listening to strange music. When listening to another language, we arbitrarily try to form the sounds we hear into words that sound more familiar and more like our own: that is why, for example, when Germans heard the word *arcubalista*, they fashioned it into the word 'Armbrust'.* New things also find our senses averse or hostile; and in general, with even the 'simplest' sensory processes, it is the emotions, such as fear, love, hatred, or the passive emotions associated with laziness, which *dominate*.

Just as a reader today scarcely distinguishes all the individual words (let alone syllables) on a page (of every twenty words he randomly selects five or so instead, and 'guesses' the meaning that probably corresponds to those five words), so we scarcely see a tree exactly and completely, with regard to its leaves, branches, colour, shape: it is so much easier for us to dream up something approximating a tree. Even in the middle of our strangest experiences, we still do the same thing: we fabricate the greatest portion of the experience and can barely be forced *not* to observe any one event as its 'inventor'. All of this is to say that we are from time immemorial fundamentally—*accustomed to lying*. Or, to put it more virtuously and hypocritically, more pleasantly in short: we are all artists much more than we realize.

When holding a lively conversation, I often see the face of my conversation partner in terms of the thought that he is expressing, or that I believe I have called forth in him, with a degree of clarity and precision that goes far beyond the *power* of my visual faculty—the detailed movement of muscles and expression of the eye *must* have been added by my imagination. The person was probably making a completely different face, or none at all.

193

Quidquid luce fuit, tenebris agit* but also the reverse. In the last analysis, what we experience in our dreams, assuming that we experience it often, is as much a part of the overall economy of our soul as anything that we 'really' experience. We are richer or poorer because of it, have one need the more or the less, and ultimately, in broad daylight and even in the brightest moments of our waking consciousness, we are a little like toddlers, led along by the habits of our dreams. Take a person who has often dreamt that he was flying, and finally, each time he dreams, feels that he possesses the power and skill to fly as if it were his prerogative and his own most enviable state of happiness: this person, who thinks that he is able to realize any kind of loop or angle with his slightest impulse, who has felt a certain divine light-headedness, an 'upwards' without tension or pressure, a 'downwards' without condescension or humiliation—without *gravity*!—how could a person with dream experiences and dream habits like these but find the word 'happiness' defined and coloured differently during his waking hours as well! How could he but—crave happiness *differently*? 'Soaring', as poets describe it, when held against this other 'flying', must seem to him too earthly, too muscular, too violent, indeed too 'heavy'.

194

Diversity in humans is revealed not only by the diversity of their table of goods, that is to say, that they hold varying goods to be worth striving for, and also disagree about the comparative value, the hierarchy of the goods that they appreciate in common—it is revealed even more by how they define *having* and *possessing* these goods. Regarding a woman, for example, the more modest man will consider his use of her body and his sexual pleasure as a sufficient and satisfactory sign that he has, that he possesses her; but another man, with a more suspicious and exacting thirst for possession, will see the 'question mark', will see that this kind of possession is only ostensible, and will want to conduct finer tests to learn above all whether the woman is not only giving herself to him, but is also giving up for his sake what she already has or would like to have— only *then* does he think that he 'possesses' her. Even at this point, however, a third man will still not be done with his distrust and acquisitiveness; he will wonder whether his woman, if she gives up everything for his sake, might not be doing it for some phantom of himself. He first wants her to know him thoroughly, profoundly, in order to be able to accept her love at all; he takes the risk of letting himself be solved. He feels that he possesses his beloved only when she is no longer deluded about him, when she loves him for his devilishness and secret insatiability as much as for his kindness, patience, and spirituality. One man would like to possess a people, and to this end he embraces all the higher arts of Cagliostro* and Catiline.* Another man, with a more sophisticated thirst for possession, tells himself 'one must not deceive where one would possess'—he is irritable and impatient at the idea that a mask of himself is holding sway over the hearts of his people: 'I must *allow* myself to be known, then, and meanwhile know myself.' In helpful and benevolent people one nearly always finds a clumsy cunning that first rearranges the person who is to be helped so that, for example, he 'deserves' their help, needs *their* help in particular, and will prove to be deeply grateful, dependent, subservient for all their help. With fantasies such as these they control

the needy like a piece of property, just as they are benevolent and
helpful people generally because of their desire for property. If you
cross them in the act of helping, or beat them to it, you find that
they are jealous. Parents unwittingly make their child into something that resembles them (they call it 'education'); no mother
doubts at the bottom of her heart that in her child she has given
birth to a piece of property, and no father disputes his right to be
allowed to subjugate his child to *his* concepts and judgements.
Indeed, it used to be considered proper (it was true of the old
Germans) for fathers to determine the life or death of a newborn
as they saw fit. And like fathers, so teachers, classes, priests, and
princes still see in every new person an immediate opportunity for
a new possession. Which leads us to conclude . . .

195

The Jews—a people 'born into slavery' according to Tacitus and
the entire ancient world, 'the chosen people' as they themselves
say and believe—the Jews brought about that tour de force of a
reversal of values that enabled life on earth to acquire a new and
dangerous fascination for one or two thousand years. Their pro-
phets fused 'rich', 'godless', 'evil', 'violent', 'sensuous' into one
entity, and were the first to mint the word 'world' as a curse word.
In this reversal of values (part of which is to treat the word 'poor'
as a synonym for 'saint' and 'friend') lies the significance of the
Jewish people: the *slave revolt in morals* begins with them.*

196

We can *deduce* that next to the sun there are countless numbers of
dark heavenly bodies—the ones we will never see. Confidentially,
that is a metaphor; and a moral psychologist will read the entire
celestial text only as metaphor, a sign language that is able to keep
a great deal in silence.

197

People completely misunderstand predatory animals and predatory
people (Cesare Borgia,* for example), they misunderstand 'nature'
as long as they persist in examining these most healthy of all

tropical plants and brutes (as nearly all moralists till now have done) to find their fundamental 'diseased state' or inborn 'hell'. Doesn't it seem that moralists hate the jungle and the tropics? And that the 'tropical person' must be discredited at all costs, whether as a disease or degeneration in mankind or else as his own self-punishing hell? Why should this be so? To favour the 'moderate regions'? The moderate people? The 'moral' people? The mediocre people?—

Notes for a chapter on 'morals as timidity'.

198

All those moral codes that are addressed to individuals, aimed at their so-called 'happiness'—what are they but behavioural guides in relation to the degree of *precariousness* that the individual feels about himself; recipes to counter his passions, his good and bad tendencies, if he possesses the will to power and would like to play the master; large or small titbits of shrewdness and affectation, infected with the musty smell of old home remedies and old wives' tales. And all of them in a form that is grotesque and unreasonable (because they are addressed to 'everyone', because they generalize where one ought not to generalize); all of them in unconditional language, taking themselves unconditionally; all of them seasoned not only with one grain of salt, but only becoming bearable and sometimes even tempting when they learn the trick of smelling overseasoned and dangerous, above all when they smell of 'another world'. By intellectual standards, none of this is worth very much, and it is certainly nothing like 'science', let alone 'wisdom'; rather, to say it over and over again, it is shrewdness, shrewdness, shrewdness, combined with stupidity, stupidity, stupidity. It may take the form of indifference and a marble-column-coldness against the heat of emotional folly, the remedy advised by the Stoics; or then again it may be Spinoza's laugh-no-more and weep-no-more, the destruction of the emotions by analysing and dissecting them, which he advocates with such *naïveté*; or else a toning down of the emotions to a harmless mean, where their satisfaction is permissible—moral Aristotelianism. It might even be morality as enjoyment of emotions intentionally diluted and spiritualized through the symbolism of art, as music, for example, or the love of God and of mankind for

God's sake (for in religion, the passions have their civil rights again, assuming that . . .). And finally it might even be that very welcoming, wanton devotion to the emotions as it was taught by Hafis* and Goethe, a bold dropping of the reins, the exceptional case of spiritual-carnal *licentia morum** to be found in wise old eccentrics and drunkards who 'can't do much harm any more'. Further notes for a chapter on 'morals as timidity'.

199

In every age, for as long as there have been humans, there have also been human herds (family groups, congregations, tribes, peoples, nations, churches) and always a great many followers in proportion to the small number of commanders. Considering, then, that obedi-ence has until now been bred and practised best and longest among humans, we can surely assume that everyone on average is born with a need to obey, as a kind of *formal conscience* that decrees: 'Thou shalt do certain things without question, refrain from certain things without question', in short 'thou shalt'. This need seeks to satisfy its hunger and fill its form with some content; it helps itself according to how strong, impatient, or eager it is, indiscriminately, as a gross appetite, and accepts whatever may be shouted in its ear by whichever commander (parents, teachers, laws, class prejudices, public opinions). Human development has been so strangely restricted—so laggardly, protracted, often regressing and turning round and round—because the herd instinct of obedience is inherited best, and at the cost of the skill in commanding. If we imagine this instinct taken to its ultimate excesses, we find a com-plete absence of commanders or independent people; or else they suffer inwardly from a bad conscience and feel the need to dupe themselves first in order to be able to give commands, by acting as if they too were only following orders. This really is the case in Europe today: I call it the moral hypocrisy of commanders. The only way they know to protect themselves from their own bad conscience is to behave as if they were carrying out orders from before or from above (from ancestors, the constitution, the judicial system, the laws, or even from God) or else to adopt the herd phrases that are part of the herd mentality, such as 'first servant of his people', or 'instrument for the common good'. The European herd man, on the other hand, puts on airs nowadays as if he were the only acceptable type of man, glorifying the characteristics that make him tame, docile, and useful to the herd as if they were the true human virtues: such as public spirit, benevolence, consideration, industriousness, moderation, modesty, concern, sympathy. In those cases, however, when a leader and bell-wether is thought to be indispensable, people nowadays keep trying to replace commanders with an aggregation of the cleverest herd people: this is the origin of all representative constitutions, for example. But what a blessing despite everything, what salvation from an increasingly unbearable pressure the appearance of an absolute commander is for these European herd animals—this has been demonstrated most recently by the powerful impact Napoleon had when he came on the scene. The history of Napoleon's impact is virtually the history of the higher happiness which our entire century was able to achieve in its most valuable people and moments.

200

A person who lives in an age of disintegration that mixes all the races together, will carry in his body the heritage of his multifarious origins, that is to say, contradictory and often more than merely contradictory standards and instincts that struggle with one another and seldom come to rest. Such a person, in the dimming light of a late culture, will generally be a weak person: his most heartfelt desire is that the war that he *embodies* come to an end. In agreement with a medicine and a mentality that tranquillizes (Epicureanism or Christianity, for example), he takes happiness to be essentially the happiness of rest, of tranquillity, of satiety, of ultimate oneness, to be the 'Sabbath of Sabbaths',* in the words of the sainted rhetorician Augustine, who was that kind of a man himself.

But if someone with this kind of a nature experiences the warlike oppositions within him as one stimulant and incitement to life *the more*, and if on the other hand, along with his powerful and irreconcilable instincts, he has also inherited the true, inbred expertise and cunning in waging war with himself, that is to say, self-control, self-deception: then he may develop into one of those enchantingly elusive and unfathomable men, those mysterious people who are destined for victory and for seduction, expressed most beautifully in Alcibiades* and Caesar (in whose company I would like to include the *first* European to my taste, the Hohenstaufen Frederick II),* and among artists, perhaps, Leonardo da Vinci. They appear during just those epochs when that other weak type, with its desire for rest, comes into the foreground: both types belong to one another and arise from the same causes.

201

As long as the utility that dominates moral judgements is still only the utility of the herd, as long as we confine our gaze solely to the preservation of the community, seeking out immorality exactly and exclusively in whatever seems dangerous to communal stability, there can be no 'morality of neighbourly love'. Assuming that here, too, there are already small ongoing acts of consideration, sympathy, fairness, gentleness, reciprocal help; and that at this stage of society, too, all the instincts are already at work that will later be designated by honourable names as 'virtues' and finally fit the concept 'morality'; during this period they are still in no way part of the realm of moral value judgements—they are still *extra-moral*. In the heyday of Rome for example, an act of pity was neither good nor evil, neither moral nor immoral, and even such praise as it may have received could well be accompanied by a kind of irritated disdain as soon as it was compared to an action that served to further the whole, the *res publica*.* Ultimately, 'neighbourly love' is always something secondary, in part convention and a deliberate fiction in relation to *fear of one's neighbour*. Once the social structure appears to be more or less established and secured against external dangers, it is this fear of one's neighbour that once again creates new perspectives for moral value judgements. Certain strong and dangerous instincts, such as adventurousness, recklessness, vengefulness, slyness, rapacity, lust for power, were previously not only honoured (by names other than the ones above, of course) as beneficial to the community, but they also had to be cultivated and bred, because people continually had need of them in their common danger against common enemies. But now (when there are no drainage channels for them) these same instincts are felt to be doubly dangerous and are gradually stigmatized and slandered as immoral. Now the opposite drives and tendencies gain moral respect; step by step, the herd instinct draws its consequences. The moral perspective now considers how harmful or harmless an opinion, an emotional state, a will, a talent is to the community, to equality: here again, fear is the mother of morality. When an individual's highest and strongest instincts break forth with a passion, driving him far above and beyond the average, beyond the lowlands of the herd conscience, the community's self-regard is destroyed as a result; its belief in itself, its backbone, so to speak, is shattered: and that is why people do well to stigmatize and slander just these instincts above all. Exalted, self-directed spirituality, a will to solitude, even great powers of reason are felt as a danger; everything that raises an individual above the herd and causes his neighbour to fear him is henceforth called *evil*; a proper, modest, conforming, equalizing mentality, what is *average* on the scale of desires gains a moral name and respect. Finally, when conditions are very peaceable, there is less and less opportunity or necessity for educating one's feelings to be stern and harsh; and then every kind of sternness, even in matters of justice, begins to trouble the conscience; a harsh, exalted nobility or individual responsibility is almost considered offensive and awakens distrust, whereas 'a lamb', or better yet, 'a sheep' gains in esteem. There can come a point of such sickly morbidity and pampered indulgence in the history of a society that in all due seriousness it even takes the side of the one who does it harm, the *criminal*. Punishing: society thinks there is something unfair about it—it certainly finds the idea of 'punishment' and the 'need to punish' painful and frightening. 'Isn't it enough just to render him *innocuous*? Why do we have to punish him too? Real punishment is awful!'—with this question the herd morality, the morality of timidity, draws its final conclusion. Assuming that we could entirely abolish the danger, the grounds for fear, then we would have abolished this morality as well: it would no longer be necessary, it *would deem itself* no longer necessary!

Anyone who examines the conscience of a present-day European will have to extract from his thousand moral crannies and hiding places the same imperative, the imperative of herdlike timidity: 'At some point, we want there to be *nothing more to be afraid of*!' At some point—the will and the way *to that point* is what everyone in Europe today calls 'progress'.

Let us immediately say once again what we have already said a hundred times, for nowadays ears are reluctant to hear such truths—*our* truths. We know perfectly well how offensive it sounds when someone counts man among the animals plain and simple, without metaphorical intent; but we will almost be accounted a *criminal* for always using expressions such as 'herd', 'herd instincts', and the like when speaking about people of 'modern ideas'. What's the use! We can't do otherwise, for this is just what our new insight is about. We discovered that Europe, and those countries dominated by a European influence, are now of one mind in all their key moral judgements: it is obvious that Europeans nowadays *know* that which Socrates thought he did not know, and what that famous old serpent once promised to teach—people 'know' what is good and evil. It must sound harsh and trouble the ears, then, if we insist over and over that it is the instinct of man the herd animal that thinks it knows, that glorifies itself and calls itself good whenever it allots praise or blame. This instinct has had a breakthrough, has come to predominance, has prevailed over the other instincts and continues to do so as a symptom of the increasing process of physiological approximations and resemblances. *Morality in Europe today is herd animal morality*—and thus, as we understand things, it is only one kind of human morality next to which, before which, after which many others, and especially *higher* moralities, are or should be possible. But this morality defends itself with all its strength against such 'possibilities', against such 'should be's'. Stubbornly and relentlessly it says, 'I am Morality itself, and nothing else is!' Indeed, with the help of a religion that played along with and flattered the most sublime desires of the herd animal, we have reached the point of finding an ever more visible expression of this morality even in political and social structures: the *democratic* movement is Christianity's heir. But its tempo is still far too slow and sleepy for the overeager, for patients or addicts of this above-mentioned instinct, as we can tell from the increasingly frantic howl, the ever more widely bared teeth of the anarchist dogs who now roam the alleys of European culture. They appear to be in conflict with the peaceably industrious democrats or ideologues of revolution, and even more with the foolish philosophasts and brotherhood enthusiasts who call themselves socialists and want a 'free society'; but in reality they are united with those others in their fundamental and instinctive enmity towards every form of society other than *autonomous* herds (right up to the point of even rejecting the concepts 'master' and 'servant'—*ni dieu ni maître** is a socialist motto); united in their tough resistance to every exceptional claim, every exceptional right and privilege (and thus ultimately to *all* rights, for no one needs 'rights' any longer when everyone is equal); united in their distrust of any justice that punishes (as if it were a rape of the weaker party, unjust towards the *necessary* conse- quence of all earlier society); but also just as united in their religion of pity, in their empathy, wherever there are feelings, lives, or suffering (reaching down to the animal or up to 'God'—the eccen- tric notion of 'pity for God' suits a democratic age); united one and all in their impatient cry for pity, in their mortal hatred of any suffering,* in their almost feminine incapacity to remain a spectator to it, to *allow* suffering; united in the involuntary depression and decadence which seems to hold Europe captive to a threatening new Buddhism; united in their belief in a morality of *communal* pity, as if it were Morality itself, the summit, the *conquered* summit of humankind, the only hope for the future, comfort in the present, the great redemption from all past guilt—united together in their belief in community as a *redeemer*, and thus a belief in the herd, a belief in 'themselves' . . .

203

We who hold a different belief—we who consider the democratic movement not merely a decadent form of political organization, but a decadent (that is to say, diminished) form of the human being, one that mediocritizes* him and debases his value: what can *we* set our hopes on?

On *new philosophers*, we have no other choice; on spirits that are strong and original enough to give impetus to opposing value judgements and to revalue, to reverse 'eternal values'; on forerun- ners, on men of the future, who in the present will forge the necessary link to force a thousand-year-old will onto *new* tracks. They will teach humans that their future is their *will*, that the future depends on their human will, and they will prepare the way for great risk-taking and joint experiments in discipline and breeding in order to put an end to that terrible reign of nonsense and coincidence that until now has been known as 'history' (the nonsense about the 'greatest number' is only its most recent form). To accomplish this, new kinds of philosophers and commanders will eventually be necessary, whose image will make all the secretive, frightful, benevolent spirits that have existed in the world look pale and dwarfish. The image of such leaders is what hovers before *our* eyes—may I say it aloud, you free spirits? The circumstances that would have to be in part created, in part exploited to give rise to these leaders; the probable paths and tests by which a soul would grow so great and powerful that it would feel *compelled* to accomplish these projects; a revaluation of values, under whose new hammer and pressure the conscience would be transformed into steel, the heart into bronze, so that they could bear the weight of such responsibility; the indispensability of such leaders; on the other hand, the terrible danger that they might not arrive or might go astray and degenerate—those are really the things that concern and worry *us*—do you know that, you free spirits?—those are the distant oppressive thoughts and thunderstorms that pass across the sky of *our* life. There are few pains so raw as to have once observed, understood, sympathized while an extraordinary man strayed from his path or degenerated: but a person with the rare vision to see the general danger that 'man' himself *is degenerating*, who has recognized as we have the tremendous randomness that thus far has been at play in determining the future of mankind (a play that has been guided by no one's hand, not even by 'God's finger!'), who has guessed the fate that lies hidden in all the stupid innocence and blissful confidence of 'modern ideas', and even more in the entire Christian-European morality: this person suffers from an anxiety that cannot be compared to any other. With one single glance he grasps everything that *mankind could be bred to be* if all its energies and endeavours were gathered together and heightened; with all the knowledge of his conscience, he knows how mankind's greatest possibilities have as yet been untapped, and how many mysterious decisions and new paths the human type has already encountered—he knows better yet, from his most painful memory, what kind of wretched things have usually caused the finest example of an evolving being to shatter, break apart, sink down, become wretched. The *overall degeneration of man*, right down to what socialist fools and flatheads call their 'man of the future' (their ideal!); this degeneration and diminution of man into a perfect herd animal (or, as they call it, man in a 'free society'); this bestialization of man into a dwarf animal with equal rights and claims is *possible*, no doubt about that! Anyone who has thought this possibility through to its end knows no disgust but other people—and also, perhaps, a new *project*! . . .

SECTION SIX

WE SCHOLARS

204

RUNNING the risk that moralizing, even my own, will prove to be what it always has been (an unabashed *montrer ses plaies*,* according to Balzac), I would like to try to argue against an unseemly and harmful hierarchical shift between science* and philosophy that is now threatening to develop quite unnoticed and, it seems, in good conscience. In my opinion, a person's right to speak about so elevated a question as hierarchy grows out of his *experience* (and experience, I think, always means bad experience?), so that he is not speaking about colour as the blind might do, or *against* science as women and artists might ('Oh, this nasty old science!' sighs their instinct and their shame, 'it's always *finding out* about everything!'). The scientist's Declaration of Independence, his emancipation from philosophy, is one of the more subtle influences of the democratic disposition (and indisposition): the scholar's overweening self-glorification is in full bloom everywhere these days, in its finest springtime—which is not yet to suggest that in this case self-praise smells sweet.* 'Down with all masters!'—that's what the rabble instinct is urging here too; and science, after its great success in warding off theology, whose 'handmaid' it was for too long, is now arrogantly and ignorantly intent on making laws for philosophy and taking its own turn at playing the 'master'—what am I saying? the *philosopher*. My memory (a scientific man's memory, if you permit me to say so!) is bursting with naive remarks about philosophy and philosophers that I have heard made by arrogant young natural scientists and old doctors (not to mention the most cultured and conceited* of scholars, the philologists and pedagogues, who are both by profession). Now it was an idler or specialist who instinctively resisted any kind of synthethic ability or project; now a diligent worker who had caught a whiff of *otium** and elegant voluptuousness in the philosopher's inner economy and felt compromised and diminished by it. Now it was the colour-blindness of a utilitarian who sees nothing in philosophy but a series of *refuted* systems and a wasteful display that isn't 'good for' anything. Now it was the fear of veiled mysticism and of newly defined limits to knowledge that leapt to the fore; and now a disdain for particular philosophers, unwittingly generalized into disdain for philosophy in general. But most frequently I found that underlying the young scholars' arrogant condescension towards philosophy was the bad influence of a philosopher himself, one whom they generally no longer followed, it is true, but whose spell-binding dismissive assessments of other philosophers they had not shaken off—the result then being complete annoyance with all philosophy. (It seems to me that Schopenhauer, for example, has had this kind of effect on Germany most recently—with his unintelligent wrath towards Hegel he has succeeded in wrenching a whole generation of young Germans out of their relation to German culture, a culture which, weighing everything carefully, represented a supreme divinatory refinement of the *historical sense*: but in just this area Schopenhauer himself was almost brilliantly wanting, unreceptive, un-German.) In general and on the whole, it may well have been the human, all-too-human quality of recent philosophy, its poverty in short, that has most thoroughly hampered any possible respect for philosophy and opened the gates for the rabble instinct. Let us admit to ourselves how greatly our modern world lacks the whole strain of men like Heraclitus, Plato, Empedocles, and all the other splendid, royal hermits of the spirit; and given such representatives of philosophy as the ones whom today's fashion has set at the top of the heap—and beneath respect—(like the two lions of Berlin, the anarchist Eugen Dühring* and the amalgamist Eduard von Hartmann* in Germany), how *entitled* an honest man of science is to feel that he is of a better strain and parentage. The sight of those hodgepodge philosophers who call themselves 'reality philosophers' or 'positivists' is especially capable of inspiring an ambitious young scholar's heart with dangerous distrust: at best, these people are scholars and specialists themselves, it is clear as day! Indeed, they are all of them people who have been overcome and *retrieved* by the dominion of science; at one time or another they wanted *more* of themselves, but they had no right to this 'more' and its responsibility, and now they represent in word and deed, honourably, fiercely, vengefully, a *disbelief* in the masters' task and the masterfulness of philosophy. And in the end—how could it be otherwise! Science is abloom these days, its good conscience shining from its face, while recent philosophy has gradually sunk to its dregs, awakening distrust and despondence if not scorn and pity. Philosophy reduced to a 'theory of cognition', really no more than a shy epochism and doctrine of renunciation; a philosophy that doesn't even get beyond the threshold, scrupulously *refusing* itself the right to enter: this is philosophy at its last gasp, an end, an agony, something to evoke pity. How could a philosophy like that— *be the master*!

205

The dangers for the development of a philosopher these days are truly so manifold that we may doubt whether such a fruit can ever ripen at all. The towers of knowledge have grown to enormous size, and with them the probability that a philosopher will tire even while still a learner or will come to a halt somewhere and 'specialize', so that he never arrives at his peak, that is, a grand survey, a panorama, a view *downwards*. Or he will reach the top too late, when his best period and powers are behind him; or so impaired, coarsened, and degenerated that his view, his overall value judgement no longer means very much. It is the very subtlety of his intellectual conscience that might make him linger or hesitate on his path. He fears the seduction of becoming a dilettante, a SCENTipede;* he knows only too well that a man who has lost his self-respect can no longer command, no longer *lead* in the search for knowledge, either: otherwise he would have to want to become a great actor, a philosophical Cagliostro* and pied piper of minds—in short, a seducer. This is finally a question of taste, even if it weren't a question of conscience. In addition, redoubling the philosopher's difficulty yet again, he demands of himself a judgement, a Yes or No, not about the sciences, but about life and the value of life; reluctantly, he learns to believe in his right or even duty to make such judgements, and that only on the basis of the most wide-ranging (perhaps most disruptive, destructive) experiences will he find his way—often hesitating, doubting, growing mute—to that belief and that right. For a long time now, in fact, the crowd has mistaken and misconstrued the philosopher, whether taking him to be a man of learning and ideal scholar, or God's religiously exalted, desensualized, 'desecularized' enthusiast and drunkard; and these days if we hear someone praised for living 'wisely' or 'like a philosopher', it almost always means no more than 'prudently and apart'. Wisdom: to the rabble it appears to be a form of escape, a tricky way to make a good exit from a wicked game; but the true philosopher (isn't that how *we* see it, my friends?) lives 'unphilosophically' and 'unwisely' and above all *imprudently* and feels the burdensome duty of a hundred tests and temptations in life—he is continually risking *himself*, he plays *that* wicked game . . .

206

Compared to a genius, that is to say, to a being who either *begets* or *gives birth* (both words taken in their widest sense), a scholar or average man of learning is always something of an old maid—for like her he has no familiarity with the two most highly valued functions of humankind. Indeed, as compensation we concede both of them, scholars and old maids, respectability (we make a point of respectability in such cases)—and we feel the same tinge of irritation at being obliged to concede it. Let's look at this more carefully: what is a man of learning? A common sort of man, first of all, with a common man's virtues, that is to say, neither masterful nor authoritative nor even self-sufficient. He is industrious, patiently joining the rank and file, conforming and moderate in his abilities and needs. He has an instinct for his own kind and for what his own kind requires—that little patch of independence and green meadow, for example, that enables him to work in peace; that claim to honour and appreciation (which first of all and above all assumes that he is recognized, recognizable);* that sunshine of a good name; that enduring seal upon his value and his usefulness that must continually overcome the inner *mistrustfulness* at the heart's core of all dependent people and herd animals. A scholar also has the illnesses and bad habits of the common sort, of course: he is rich in petty envy and has a lynx-eye for what is base in those other natures whose heights he is unable to reach. He is friendly, although only like someone who lets himself go, but not *stream* forth; and it is precisely when facing a man who is a broad stream that he holds himself so cold and closed—then his eye is like a glassy, impenetrable lake, no longer rippled by delight or empathy. The worst and most dangerous things that a scholar is capable of come from the instinct of his type to mediocrity, that Jesuitical mediocrity that works instinctively to destroy the extra-ordinary man and tries to break or—even better!—to loosen every tensed bow. Loosen it, that is, with deference, with a gentle hand, to be sure—in friendly sympathy *loosen* it: that is the true art of Jesuitism, which has always known how to present itself as a religion of pity.

207

However gratefully we may hail the *objective* spirit (and who has not at times been sick to death of all subjectivity with its damned ipseity!),* we must finally also learn to be cautious about our gratitude and put a stop to the exaggerated way in which intellectual selflessness and depersonalization have been praised lately as if they were an end in themselves, redeeming and transfiguring. This has tended to happen among the school of pessimists especially, who for their part do have good reasons to pay the highest honour to 'disinterested cognition'. The objective person, one who no longer curses and scolds like the pessimist, the *ideal* scholar in whom the scientific instinct blossoms fully and finally after thousands of complete or partial false starts, is certainly one of the most precious tools that exist: but he needs to be put into the hand of someone more powerful. He is only a tool; let's say that he is a *mirror*, not an 'end unto himself'. The objective man is indeed a mirror: above all, we must admit, he is accustomed to subjugating himself, with no desire other than what knowledge, what 'reflecting' can offer him. He waits until something comes along and then spreads himself out gently so that even the light footsteps of spirit-like beings gliding by will not be lost upon his surface and skin. What still adheres to him of a 'person' he considers accidental, often arbitrary, more often annoying, so completely has he come to see himself as a passageway or reflection of distant figures and events. He remembers about 'himself' with effort and often incorrectly; he easily mistakes himself for someone else; he attends poorly to his own needs, and only in this regard can he be coarse and negligent. He might suffer from bad health or from the pettiness and stuffy air of wife and friends or from a lack of comrades and company—oh, he will force himself to meditate on this suffering, but in vain! His thinking is already wandering off to the *more general* case, and by tomorrow he will know as little as he did yesterday about what might help him. He does not take himself seriously, does not take the time: he is cheerful *not* from a lack of distress, but from a lack of fingers and handles to grasp *his* distress. His typical openness towards all things and experiences, the sunny, unrestrained hospitality with which he welcomes everything that comes his way, his manner of reckless benevolence, of dangerous unconcern about Yes and No—oh, there are certainly many times when he must atone for these, his virtues! And as a human being he all too easily becomes their *caput mortuum*.* If someone expects love or hatred of him (and I mean love and hatred as God, women, and animals understand them), he will do what he can and give what he can. But no one should be surprised if this is not much, if it is just here that he turns out to be false, brittle, dubious, and rotten. His love is forced, his hatred artificial and more of a tour de force, a little show of vanity and exaggeration. For he is genuine only as long as he may be objective: only in his cheerful totalism is he still 'nature' and 'natural'. His mirroring soul, ever smoothing itself out, no longer knows how to affirm, no longer how to deny; he does not command, neither does he destroy. 'Je ne méprise presque rien',* he says with Leibniz, and we should not ignore or underestimate that 'presque'! Nor is he a model human being; he neither precedes nor follows anyone; in general he puts himself at such a distance that he has no grounds on which to take a side between good and evil. If we have for so long mistaken him for a *philosopher*, for a dictatorial breeder and tyrant of culture, we have done him far too great an honour and overlooked the most essential thing about him: he is a tool, a slave-like entity, if certainly the most sublime sort of slave, but in himself nothing—*presque rien*! The objective man is a tool, a precious, easily injured and demoralized measuring tool and artful mirror to be preserved and honoured; but he is not a goal, not a way out or up, not a complementary person in whom the *rest* of existence is justified, not a conclusion—and even less a beginning, a begetting or first cause, nothing tough, powerful, autonomous that wants to be the master:

but rather only a delicate, empty, thin, malleable vessel of forms that must first wait for some sort of content and substance in order to 'take shape' accordingly—usually a person without substance or content,* a 'selfless' person. And thus nothing for women, either, *in parenthesi*.*

208

When a philosopher today asserts that he is no sceptic (I hope this was clearly understood in the description of the objective spirit offered above?) no one is happy to hear it. People look at him rather fearfully for tell-tale signs; they would like to ask him, ask him so much . . . in fact, timid listeners (who are plentiful nowadays) conclude that he is dangerous. When he rejects scepticism, they seem to hear some far-off ominous sound, as if a new explosive were being tested somewhere, intellectual dynamite, perhaps a newly discovered Russian nihilism,* a pessimism *bonae voluntatis*￼* that does not merely say No, or will No, but—terrible thought!—*acts* No. Against that kind of 'good will' (a will to deny life truly, actively) there is admittedly no better sedative or tranquillizer today than scepticism, the dear, gentle, lulling opium of scepticism; and nowadays even Hamlet is given prescriptions by doctors of the age to ward off the 'spirit' and its underground rumbling. 'Aren't our ears filled with enough bad noises already?' asks the sceptic, as a friend of peace and almost as a kind of security police, 'this subterranean "No" is terrible! Would you please be quiet, you pessimistic moles!' The sceptic, you see, that delicate creature, is all too easily startled; his conscience has been trained to twitch and feel something like a pang at every 'No' and even at a decisive, harsh 'Yes'. Yes! and No!—that goes against his morality. Conversely, he loves to indulge his virtue with noble abstinence, as if to say with Montaigne, 'What do I know?'* Or with Socrates, 'I know that I know nothing.' Or, 'I wouldn't venture in here, no door is open to me.' Or, 'Even if the door were open, why should I go right in!' Or, 'What use are premature hypotheses? It might be in better taste to make no hypotheses at all. Must you always take something crooked and hurry to bend it straight? Always plug up every hole with some sort of wadding? Don't we have plenty of time? Doesn't time have plenty of time? Oh you daredevils, can't you just *wait*? Even uncertainty has its charms; even the Sphinx is a Circe; even Circe was a philosopher.'

That is how a sceptic comforts himself; and it is true that he has need of some comfort. For scepticism is the most spiritual expression of a certain complex physiological condition that in common parlance is called bad nerves or sickliness; it invariably presents itself whenever races or classes that have long been kept apart intermix significantly and suddenly. Because the new generation has, as it were, inherited blood in new proportions and values, everything is restless, agitated, doubtful, experimental. The best energies have an inhibiting effect; even the virtues do not allow one another to grow or prosper; body and soul lack balance, gravity, perpendicular sureness. But what is prone most of all to illness and degeneracy in these mixed breeds is the *will*: they no longer understand how to make an independent decision or to feel the brave pleasure of willing—even in their dreams they doubt the 'freedom of the will'. Our Europe of today, the scene of a ridiculously sudden experiment in the radical mixture of classes and *therefore* of races, is as a consequence thoroughly sceptical—sometimes with that agile scepticism that springs impatiently and desirously from branch to branch, sometimes sad like a rain cloud laden down with question marks: and often sick unto death of its will! Paralysis of the will: where don't you stumble across this cripple these days! And often how very dolled up! Dressed to kill! This illness comes clothed in the prettiest finery and falsehoods; and that what is displayed in shop windows these days as 'objectivity', 'scientific method', *'l'art pour l'art'*,* 'pure, will-free knowledge' is usually only decked-out scepticism and paralysis of the will—I will vouch for this diagnosis of the European disease.

The disease of the will has spread over Europe unevenly: it is most pronounced and most multifarious where culture has been domesticated longest; it disappears according to how much the 'barbarian' still (or once again) holds sway underneath the ill-fitting garments of occidental culture. In contemporary France, then, as we can so easily deduce and observe, the will is sickest of all. France has always mastered the skill of reversing even its disastrous turns of spirit into something charming and seductive, and by teaching and displaying all the glamour of scepticism it most clearly demonstrates its cultural dominance over Europe today. The strength to will, or to persist in wanting a will, is rather stronger in Germany, and in northern Germany stronger still than in central Germany; noticeably stronger in England, and in Spain and Corsica, related to phlegm in the former case, to hard heads in the latter (leaving out Italy, which is too young to know what it wants and must first prove whether it is capable of willing); but it is strongest and most astonishing in that enormous middle kingdom where Europe seems to merge with Asia again: in Russia. That is where the energy to will has long been stored up in reserve; that is where the will (whether it is a will to denial or to affirmation is unclear) waits ominously to be released, to borrow the physicists' current catch-word. Wars in India and entanglements in Asia may not be the only things necessary to relieve Europe of its greatest danger, but rather internal revolts, the empire's splintering into tiny bodies and above all the introduction of parliamentary idiocy, as well as the obligation of everyone to read the newspaper over breakfast. I say this not because I wish it: the reverse would actually be more to my liking. I am talking about an increase in the Russian threat so great that Europe would have to decide to become equally threat-ening, that is, to make use of a new ruling caste in order *to gain a will*, a terrible, long-lived will of its own that could set itself goals over millennia so that the long-drawn-out comedy of its small-state system and likewise the multiple wills of its dynasties and democracies would finally come to an end. The time for petty politics is over: even by the next century, we will be battling for mastery over the earth *forced* into politics on a grand scale.

209

To describe how far the new, warlike age upon which we Europeans are now apparently embarked may also favour the development of a different, stronger sort of scepticism, I would simply refer to a parable that friends of German history will understand. That reso-lute lover of handsome, well-built grenadiers, who as King of Prussia* fathered a military and sceptical genius (and in so doing brought into being that new type of German who has recently emerged triumphant), that dubious mad father of Frederick the Great himself had a genius's lucky grasp of one point: he knew what was lacking in Germany back then, and what deficiency was a hundred times more worrying and urgent than, say, a deficiency in education or social graces—his antipathy towards the young Frederick came from the anxiety of a deep instinct. *Men were lacking*—and to his bitterest dismay, he suspected that his own son was not enough of a man. He was wrong about that, but who in his place would not have been wrong? He watched his son succumb to atheism, *esprit*,* the epicurean light-heartedness of witty Frenchmen; he saw that great bloodsucking spider Scepticism in the background. He suspected the incurable misery of a heart that is no longer harsh enough for evil or for good, a shattered will that no longer commands, no longer *knows how to* command. But meanwhile a new, harsher, more dangerous sort of scepticism was growing in his son (who can say precisely *how greatly* it was encouraged by the father's hatred and the icy melancholy of a will grown used to solitude?), a daring, manly scepticism that is most closely related to a genius for war and conquest and that first entered Germany in the form of the great Frederick. This scepticism is disdainful and nevertheless attracts; it undermines and takes possession; it withholds belief, but does not lose itself in the process; to the spirit it gives a dangerous freedom, but the heart it keeps sternly in line. It is the *German* form of scepticism, and as an ongoing, spiritually heightened Frederickianism it has for a good while brought Europe under the dominion of the German spirit and its critical and historical mistrust. Thanks to the invincibly strong, tough, manly character of the great German philologists and critics of history (all of whom, viewed correctly, were also performers of destruction and dissolution) and despite all the Romanticism in music and philosophy, a *new* concept of the German spirit gradually established itself, showing a pronounced tendency to manly scepticism—whether as a fearless gaze, for example, or as the stern courage of a dissecting hand, or as the tenacious will to dangerous voyages of discovery, to spiritualized North Pole expeditions under desolate and dangerous skies. There is probably good reason for warm-blooded, superficial, humanly humans to cross themselves when they encounter this particular spirit: *cet esprit fataliste, ironique, méphistophélique** is what Michelet calls it, not without a shudder. But if we want to appreciate how distinctive is this fear of the 'manly' German spirit that awakened Europe from its 'dogmatic slumber',* we may remember the earlier concept that had to be overcome along with it—and how it wasn't too long ago that a mannish woman* could with unbridled arrogance dare to recommend that Europe take an interest in the Germans as gentle, good-hearted, weak-willed and poetic fools. At last we may fully understand Napoleon's astonishment upon first meeting Goethe: it reveals how the 'German spirit' had been regarded for centuries. 'Voilà un homme!'* which was to say, 'My word, this is a *man*! And I was expecting only a German!'

210

If, then, in the portrait of the philosophers of the future, some one trait makes us wonder whether they will have to be sceptics in the sense suggested above, we would still be describing only one thing about them—and *not* them themselves. They would be every bit as justified in calling themselves critics; and surely they will be men who experiment. By the name that I have dared to call them* I have already expressly underlined their acts of experimenting and their joy in experimenting: did I do this because these critics in body and soul like to make use of experiments in new, perhaps extended, perhaps more dangerous senses? Will they, in their passion for knowledge, take their daring and painful experiments farther than the soft and spoiled taste of a democratic century can sanction?

There can be no doubt that these coming men will be least able to forgo those important and not inconsiderable qualities that distinguish the critic from the sceptic; I mean the certainty of standards, the conscious use of a unified method, shrewd courage, independence, and a capacity for self-reliance. Indeed, in private they admit to a *joy* in saying No and in dissecting; they admit to a certain cruel concentration that knows how to wield the knife surely and subtly, even when the heart is bleeding. They will be *harsher* (and perhaps not always only towards themselves) than humane people may wish. They will not get involved with 'truth' just for the sake of 'liking' it or so that it can 'exalt' or 'inspire' them; rather, they will have only slight faith that it is actually *truth* that elicits these emotional pleasures. They will smile, these stern spirits, should somebody say to them, 'That thought exalts me: how can it not be true?' Or, 'That work delights me: how can it

not be beautiful?' Or, 'That artist makes me greater: how can he not
be great?' They greet all such enthusiasm, idealism, femininity,
hermaphroditism not only with a smile, but with a real disgust,
and if anyone were to follow them right into their secret heart's
chamber, he would be hard put to discover there any intention of
reconciling 'Christian sentiment' with 'ancient taste', let alone with
'modern parliamentarianism' (a reconciliation that is said to occur
even in the philosophers of our very insecure and thus very concili-
atory age). Critical discipline and such habits as lead to neatness
and rigour in matters of the spirit: these philosophers of the future
will not only demand them of themselves, but might even make a
display of them as their type of adornment—nevertheless they will
not yet want to be called critics. They deem it no little insult to
philosophy to decree, as people nowadays like to do, that 'Philosophy is criticism and critical science—and that is all it is!' Although
this evaluation of philosophy may enjoy the approval of all the
positivists in France and Germany (and it may even have flattered
the heart and taste of *Kant*: just think of the titles of his major
works), our new philosophers will say nevertheless that critics are
the tools of the philosopher, and precisely because they are tools
they are a long way from being philosophers themselves! The great
Chinaman of Königsberg,* too, was only a great critic.

211

I must insist that we finally stop mistaking philosophical workers
or learned people in general for philosophers—in this regard
especially, we should give strictly 'to each his own', and not too
much to the former or much too little to the latter. The education
of the true philosopher may require that he himself once pass
through all the stages at which his servants, the learned workers of
philosophy, remain—*must* remain. Perhaps he even needs to have
been a critic and a sceptic and a dogmatist and an historian, and
in addition a poet and collector and traveller and puzzle-solver
and moralist and seer and 'free spirit' and nearly all things, so that
he can traverse the range of human values and value-feelings and
be able to look with many kinds of eyes and consciences from the
heights into every distance, from the depths into every height, from
the corners into every wide expanse. But all these are only the

preconditions for his task: the task itself calls for something else—it calls for him to *create values*. It is the task of those philosophical workers in the noble mould of Kant and Hegel to establish and press into formulae some large body of value judgements (that is, previous value-*assumptions*, value-creations that have become dominant and are for a time called 'truths'), whether in the realm of *logic* or of *politics* (morals) or of *aesthetics*. It is incumbent upon these researchers to describe clearly, conceivably, intelligibly, manageably everything that has already taken place and been assessed, to abbreviate everything that is lengthy, even 'time' itself, and to *subdue* the entire past: a tremendous and wondrous task, the execution of which can surely satisfy any refined pride or tenacious will. *But true philosophers are commanders and lawgivers.* They say, 'This is the way it *should* be!' Only they decide about mankind's Where to? and What for? and to do so they employ the preparatory work of all philosophical workers, all subduers of the past. With creative hands they reach towards the future, and everything that is or has existed becomes their means, their tool, their hammer. Their 'knowing' is *creating*, their creating is law-giving, their will to truth is—*will to power*.

Do philosophers like these exist today? Have philosophers like these ever existed? Don't philosophers like these *have* to exist? . . .

212

More and more, I tend to think that because the philosopher is *necessarily* a man of tomorrow and the day after tomorrow, he has always been and has *had* to be in conflict with his Today: in every instance, Today's ideal was his enemy. Until now, all these extraordinary furtherers of humankind who are called philosophers (and who themselves rarely felt like lovers of wisdom, but more like disagreeable fools and dangerous question marks) have found their task, their difficult, unwanted, unrefusable task, but ultimately also the greatness of their task, in being the bad conscience of their age. By taking a vivisecting knife to the breast of the *virtues of their age*, they revealed their own secret: their knowledge of a *new* human greatness, a new, untrodden path to human aggrandizement. Time and again they uncovered how much hypocrisy, smugness, casual acquiescence,* how much falsehood was hidden under the best-honoured examples of their contemporary morality, how much virtue was *obsolete*; time and again they said, 'We must go there, out there, where all of *you* today are least at home.' Faced with a world of 'modern ideas' that would like to confine everyone to a corner and to a 'speciality', the philosopher (if philosophers could exist today) would be forced to find human greatness, the concept of 'greatness' precisely in man's breadth and variety, in his whole-ness in diversity: in fact, he would assign value and rank according to how many and how many sorts of things one person could bear, could take upon himself, by how *far* a person could extend his responsibility. These days, the spirit of the times and the virtue of the times are weakening and diluting the will; nothing is so fashion-able as weakness of will. Thus it is precisely strength of will, harshness, and a capacity for lengthy decisions that are integral to the philosopher's ideal concept of 'greatness'. This is as appropriate as was the opposite doctrine (the ideal of a stupid, renunciatory, submissive, selfless humanity) in an opposite period, one that, like the sixteenth century, suffered from the pent-up energy of the will and from the wildest floods and tidal waves of selfishness. At the time of Socrates, everyone's instinct was weary, and conservative old Athenians let themselves go ('for happiness' as they claimed, for pleasure as they behaved), still pronouncing the same splendid words that their lives had long failed to justify. At that time, *irony* may have been necessary for greatness of soul, that malicious, Socratic certainty of the old doctor and plebeian who cut mercilessly into his own flesh, as he did into the flesh and heart of the 'noble', with a gaze that said clearly enough, 'Don't dissemble in front of me! Here—we are equal!' In Europe today, by contrast, it is only the herd animal who is honoured and bestows honour; 'equal rights' can all too easily be transformed into equality of wrong (I mean, into a shared struggle against everything rare, strange, privileged, against the higher human, the higher soul, the higher duty, the higher responsibility, the creative abundance of power and elegance). And so these days, being noble, wanting to be for oneself, managing to be different, standing alone and needing to live inde-pendently are integral to the concept of 'greatness'; and the philosopher will reveal something of his own ideal when he asserts, 'The greatest person should be the one who can be most lonely, most hidden, most deviant, the man beyond good and evil, the master of his virtues, abundantly rich in will. This is what *greatness* should mean: the ability to be both multifarious and whole, both wide and full.' And to ask it once again: nowadays, is—greatness *possible*?

213

It is not easy to learn what a philosopher is, because it cannot be taught: you have to 'know' it from experience—or else you should have enough pride *not* to know it. However, the fact that everyone today speaks about things they *cannot* have experienced is most (and most unfortunately) true about the philosopher and the conditions for philosophy: only very few people are familiar with them, can be familiar with them, and all popular opinions about them are false. Thus, for example, the truly philosophical coexistence of a bold, unrestrained spirituality, running at a *presto*, and an unerring dialectical rigour and necessity is unknown to the experience of most thinkers and scholars; and so, if someone were to tell them about it, they would find it unbelievable. They imagine every necessity as distress, as a painful coercion, a having to follow; and they consider thinking itself to be something slow, hesitating, almost an affliction and often enough costing the '*sweat* of the nobility'— but on no account something light, divine, and most nearly related to dancing and high spirits! 'Thinking' and taking something 'seriously', taking it 'to heart'—they think these belong together, for that is the only way they have 'experienced' it. Perhaps artists really have a finer nose in these matters, for they know only too well that it is precisely when they no longer do anything 'arbitrarily', but rather by necessity that their feeling of freedom, subtlety, authority, of creative placing, ordering, shaping comes into its own—in short, that for them necessity and 'freedom of will' become one and the same. Ultimately, there is a hierarchy of inner states that corresponds to the hierarchy of problems; and the greatest problems mercilessly rebuff anyone who attempts to approach them without being preordained to solve them by the greatness and power of his spirituality. What good will it do if, as happens so often these days, flexible ordinary minds or inflexible, honest craftsmen and empiricists with their plebeian ambition force their way into the vicinity of these problems as into the 'holy of holies'!

But rough feet will never be permitted to tread on carpets like these; that has already been attended to in the primordial law of things; the doors stay shut to these intruders, even if they knock or pound their heads against them! We have to be born to every higher world; put more clearly, we have to be *bred* to it. We have a right to philosophy (taking the word in its finest meaning) only because of our origins—here too, ancestors, 'bloodlines' are decisive. Many generations have to have prepared the ground for the philosopher's development; each of his virtues has to have been acquired, tended, bequeathed, incorporated one by one, and not only the bold, light, delicate step and run of his thoughts, but above all his readiness for great responsibilities, the grandeur of his sovereign gaze and gaze downwards, his feeling of separation from the masses and their duties and virtues, his affable protection and defence of what is misunderstood or maligned, be it God or the devil, his enjoyment and practice of the great justice, his art of command, the expanse of his will, his lingering eye that rarely admires, rarely looks up, rarely loves . . .

SECTION SEVEN

OUR VIRTUES

214

OUR virtues?

Probably even we still have our virtues, although they will obviously not be those true-hearted, four-square virtues, the ones for which we hold our grandfathers in esteem, but also a little at a distance. We Europeans of the day after tomorrow, we the first generation of the twentieth century—with all our dangerous curiosity, our multifarious arts of disguise, our soft and, as it were, overly sweet cruelty of spirit and the senses—*if* we have virtues, they will presumably only be those that were able to coexist best with our dearest and most secret predilections, our most burning needs. Well then, let us go look for them in our labyrinths!—in the very place, admittedly, where all sorts of things can go astray, can vanish entirely. And is there anything nicer than *to look for* our own virtues? Isn't this much like saying that we *believe* in our own virtue? But this 'believing in our virtue'—isn't that essentially what used to be called a 'good conscience', that venerable, dangling conceptual pigtail" that our grandfathers attached to the back of their heads, and often enough to the back of their understanding? Thus it would seem that although we would not otherwise consider ourselves old-fashioned or venerable like our grandfathers, in one respect we are their worthy grandchildren, we last Europeans with a good conscience: we too are still wearing their pigtail.

Ah, if you only knew how soon, how very soon—things will be different! . . .

215

Just as in the starry realms it sometimes happens that two suns define the path of one single planet, or in certain cases that suns of differing colour illuminate a single planet first with red light, then with green, and then both of them at once, inundating it with colour: so we modern men, because of the complicated mechanism of our 'starry sky'—are defined by *differing* moral codes; our actions shine with differing colours in alternation, they are rarely clear— and there are a good many cases when we perform *many-coloured* actions.

216

Love your enemies? I think that lesson has been well learned: we see it demonstrated today in thousands of instances, both large and small. Indeed, we sometimes even see what is grander and more sublime: when we love, and particularly when we love most intensely, we learn how to *despise*,—but it all happens unconsciously, without commotion, without ostentation, with that modest and secretive goodness that seals the mouth against any ceremonious word or virtuous formula. Morality as an affectation—offends our taste these days. This too is a sign of progress, just as it was progress when our fathers' taste was finally offended by religion as an affectation, which includes hostility and Voltairean bitterness towards religion (and whatever else used to be part of the free-thinkers' gestural language). It is the music in our conscience, the dance in our spirit that makes all the puritanical litanies, all the philistinism and moral sermons sound so dissonant.

217

Beware of those people who place great value in being considered morally sensitive, or subtle in their moral distinctions! If ever we have observed them doing something wrong (especially *to us*), they will never forgive us for it: they will inevitably begin to slander us and tear us down out of instinct, even if they remain our 'friends'.

Blessed are the forgetful, for they shall also 'be done with' their blunders.

218

The psychologists of France (and where else can we still find psychologists these days?) are continuing to take their bitter and manifold pleasure in the *bêtise bourgeoise*,* as if ... let's just say they are revealing something by doing so. Flaubert, for example, that good citizen of Rouen, ended by being unable to see, hear, or taste anything else: it was his form of self-torture and refined cruelty. Now, for a change of pace (as things are getting boring), I would recommend something else for your delectation: that is, the unconscious cunning with which all good, fat, worthy mediocrities behave towards higher spirits and their projects, that subtle, quarrelsome, Jesuitical cunning that is a thousand times subtler than the judgement or taste of this middle class at its best—even subtler than the judgement of its victims: yet a further proof that among all the forms of intelligence that have been discovered to date, 'instinct' is the most intelligent. In short, you psychologists should study the philosophy of the 'rule' in its battle with the 'exception': there you will have a spectacle fit for the gods and for divine malice! Or to be even more contemporary: try dissecting the 'good person', the '*homo bonae voluntatis*'* . . . try dissecting *yourselves*!

219

Those who are limited in spirit prefer to take their revenge on those who are less limited by judging and condemning them morally; this also functions as a kind of indemnity for their not having been well endowed by nature, and finally a chance to acquire spirit and to *become* refined: malice spiritualizes. In the bottom of their hearts it does them good to think there is a standard that would place at their level even those who have been showered with gifts and privileges of the spirit—they fight for 'everyone's equality before God' and almost *need* to believe in God for that reason alone. Among their number are the most energetic opponents of atheism. If anyone were to tell them that 'great spirituality is far beyond comparing to any kind of goodness or respectability in a merely moral person', they would be enraged—I shall take care not to do it. I would rather flatter them with my tenet that great spirituality itself exists only as a last outgrowth of moral qualities; that it is a synthesis of all those predispositions that are ascribed to the 'merely moral' person, after having been acquired one by one, through long cultivation and practice, perhaps over whole series of generations; that great spirituality is precisely the spiritualization of justice and of a benevolent severity that knows it is charged with maintaining the *order of rank* in the world, among things themselves—and not just among people.

220

Now that it has become so common to praise 'disinterested people', we must, perhaps not without some danger, be made aware of what the common people are actually interested *in*, and what really are the things that trouble an ordinary man wholly and deeply: this includes educated people, even scholars and, if we can trust our eyes, maybe even philosophers. What we will discover is that most of what interests and attracts people of more refined and discriminating taste, anyone of a higher nature, seems completely 'uninteresting' to the average person; if he nevertheless notices that some people are devoted to such things, he calls that being 'désintéressé'* and marvels how it can be possible to act 'disinterestedly'. There have been some philosophers who (perhaps because their own experience afforded them no familiarity with a higher nature?) were even able to add a seductive and mystical aspect to this popular amazement, instead of stating the naked and downright obvious truth that a 'disinterested' action is a *very* interesting and interested action, assuming that . . . 'And what about love?'—What! Even a deed done for love is supposed to be 'unegoistical'? But you fools—! 'And praise for people who make sacrifices?'—But anyone who has truly offered a sacrifice knows that he wanted something for it and got it—perhaps something of himself in return for something of himself—that he gave up something here in order to have more there, perhaps just to be more, or at least to feel as if he were 'more'. But this is a realm of questions and answers where the more fastidious spirit does not like to dwell, for when she is asked for answers about these matters, even truth must suppress her yawns. She is a woman, after all: we should not violate her.

221

It sometimes happens, said a moralistic pedant and pettifogger, that I honour and esteem an unselfish person; I do not do so because he is unselfish, however, but rather because it seems to me that he has the right to be useful to another person at his own expense.*

Let's just say there is always the question of who *he* is, and who the *other* person is. In a person created and destined to command, for example, self-denial or humble retreat would not be a virtue, but rather the waste of a virtue: so it seems to me. Any altruistic moral code that takes itself unconditionally and addresses itself to everyone is not only sinning against taste: it is inciting to sins of omission, one *more* temptation beneath a mask of philanthropy— and particularly tempting and harmful to those who are greater, rarer, privileged. Before all else, we have to force morals to bow down before *hierarchy*, we have to make them feel guilty for their presumption—until they all finally come to a clear understanding that it is *immoral* to say, 'What's good for the goose is good for the gander.'

That's what my moralistic pedant and *bonhomme** had to say: do you think he deserved to be laughed at for thus admonishing morals to be moral? But we must not be too much in the right if we want to have the laughers on *our* side: a grain of wrong, in fact, is essential to good taste.

222

Wherever pity is being preached these days (and listening carefully, it is the only religion still being preached), the psychologist does well to keep his ears open: through all the vanity, all the noise that typifies these preachers (and all preachers), he will hear a hoarse, groaning, genuine sound of *self-contempt*. Self-contempt is a part of the gloom and ugliness that have been growing in Europe for a hundred years now (and whose first symptoms were already documented in a thoughtful letter by Galiani to Madame d'Épinay)—*and they may in fact be caused by it*! The man of 'modern ideas', that proud ape, is endlessly dissatisfied with himself, that much is sure. He suffers, and his vanity would have him feel only pity for the suffering of others.*

223

The hybrid European—a rather ugly plebeian, all in all—simply has to have a costume: he needs history as his costume storeroom. Of course, he notices that no costume quite fits him—he keeps changing and changing them. Just look at how frequently the nineteenth century has changed its preferred masquerading styles, or how it has despaired occasionally when 'nothing looks good on us'. It has not helped to present ourselves as Romantic or Classical or Christian or Florentine or Baroque or 'national', *in moribus et artibus*:* nothing 'suits'! But the 'spirit', and especially the 'historical spirit', also perceives that even such despair can be turned to its advantage: again and again a new bit of antiquity and foreignness is tried out, put on, taken off, packed up, above all *affected*. We are the first affected epoch when it comes to 'costumes', by which I mean morals, articles of belief, aesthetic tastes, and religions; we are ready as no other age has been for carnival in the grand style, for the most spiritual Shrovetide laughter and high spirits, for the transcendental height of the greatest nonsense and Aristophanic mockery of the world. Perhaps this is where we will discover the realm of our *invention*, that realm where we too can still be original, as parodists of world history, say, or as God's clowns—if nothing else about today has a future, perhaps there is still a future for our *laughter*.

<h2 style="text-align:center">224</h2>

The *historical sense* (or the ability to guess quickly the hierarchy of value judgements by which a people, a society, or an individual has lived; the 'divinatory instinct' for how these value judgements are interrelated, for how the authority of values relates to the authority of active energies): this historical sense, which we Europeans claim as if it were distinctively ours, has come to us as a result of the enchanting, mad *semi-barbarity* into which Europe has been plunged by the democratic intermingling of classes and races—only the nineteenth century knows this sense, our sixth sense. Because of such mixing, our 'modern souls' are now infused with the past history of every form and way of life, with cultures that previously existed separately close by one another or on top of one another— our instincts are now running backwards in every direction, we are ourselves a kind of chaos. And ultimately, as we mentioned, the 'spirit' perceives an advantage in all of this. Because of our semi-barbarity in body and desire, we have secret passageways to all sorts of places unknown to noble epochs, passageways above all to the labyrinth of imperfect cultures and to every kind of semi-barbarity that has ever existed on earth. And in so far as the most considerable portion of human culture to date has indeed been semi-barbarous, an 'historical sense' must almost mean a sense, an instinct for Everything, a taste and a tongue for Everything—which straightway identifies it as an *ignoble* sense. We are enjoying Homer again, for example; perhaps our happiest leap forward is that we know how to appreciate Homer, whereas people of a noble culture (seventeenth-century Frenchmen, say, like Saint-Évremond,* who reproaches him with having an *esprit vaste*,* and even Voltaire, their last echo) do not and did not know how to assimilate him so easily—and scarcely permitted themselves to enjoy him. Their palate, with its very definite Yes and No, their easily ready aversion, their hesitating reserve towards everything foreign, their fear of showing even the bad taste of lively curiosity, and in general that unwillingness of every noble and self-sufficient culture to admit to any new desire, any dissatisfaction of its own, any admiration for the foreign—all this positions them, inclines them to look unfavourably on even the best things in the world, if they are not their property or *could not* become their plunder. To such people no sense is so incomprehensible as just this historical sense with its subservient, plebeian curiosity.

It is no different with Shakespeare, that astonishing synthesis of Spanish-Moorish-Saxon taste, about whom an ancient Athenian in Aeschylus' circle would have laughed or grumbled himself to death. But it is just this wild variety, this confused mixture of the greatest delicacy, crudeness, and artificiality—that we accept with a secret familiarity and warmth; we enjoy it as a refined artistry reserved just for us and allow ourselves to be no more disturbed by the repulsive vapours and proximity of the English rabble in which Shakespearean art and taste live than if we were on the Chiaia in Naples, where we go our way enchanted and docile with our senses intact, no matter how much the sewers of the rabble's quarter are in the air.

We people with an 'historical sense', we have our virtues as such—that cannot be disputed: we are unassuming, selfless, modest, brave, full of self-control, full of devotion, very grateful, very patient, very accommodating—and with all of that we are perhaps not very 'tasteful'. Let us finally admit it to ourselves: what we people with an 'historical sense' find the hardest to grasp, to feel, to remember the taste for, remember the love for, what we approach with a fundamental bias and near-hostility, is perfection and ultimate ripeness in any culture or art, the noble element in works and people, their moment of silken seas and halcyon self-sufficiency, the golden coldness shown by every thing that has reached perfection. Perhaps our great virtue, our historical sense, necessarily stands in contrast to *good* taste, or to the very best taste at least, and we can emulate in ourselves only poorly, only hesitatingly, only with effort those brief little instances of greatest happiness and transfiguration of human life as they shine up suddenly here and there—those miracles and moments when a great energy voluntarily came to a halt before the immeasurable, the unbounded; when a fine-tuned pleasure was enjoyed to overflowing as it was suddenly restrained and frozen, stopping short and standing fast upon a ground still quivering. *Proportion* is foreign to us, let us admit it; what titillates us is precisely the titillation of the infinite, the unmeasured. Like a rider on a forward-raging steed, we drop the reins before the infinite, we modern people, we semi-barbarians—entering *our* state of bliss only when we are also most—*in danger.*

225

Whether it be hedonism, pessimism, utilitarianism, eudemonism—all of these ideas that measure the value of things according to *pleasure* or *suffering*, that is to say, according to secondary states and side-effects, are foreground ideas, and naive. Anyone conscious of having *creative* energies and an artist's conscience will look down on them not without mockery, but also not without pity. Pity for all of *you*! although it is not pity in your sense, to be sure. It is not pity for social 'misery', for 'society' and its sick and injured, for the perennially depraved and downtrodden who lie around us everywhere; even less is it pity for the grumbling, oppressed, rebellious ranks of slaves who are looking to be masters (which they call 'being free'). *Our* pity is a more elevated, more far-sighted pity—we see how *human beings* are being reduced, how all of *you* are reducing them! And there are moments when we look at *your* pity especially with an indescribable anxiety, when we defend ourselves against this pity—when we find your seriousness more dangerous than any frivolity. If possible (and no 'if possible' can be more crazy) you want *to abolish suffering*! And we?—it seems that *we* want it to be, if anything, worse and greater than before! Well-being in your sense of the word—that certainly is no goal, it seems to us to be an *end*! A condition that would immediately make people ludicrous and contemptible—make us *wish* their downfall! The discipline of suffering, *great* suffering—don't you know that this discipline *alone* has created all human greatness to date? The tension of the soul in unhappiness, which cultivates its strength; its horror at the sight of the great destruction; its inventiveness and bravery in bearing, enduring, interpreting, exploiting unhappiness, and whatever in the way of depth, mystery, mask, spirit, cleverness, greatness the heart has been granted—has it not been granted them through suffering, through the discipline of great suffering? In the human being, *creature* and *creator* are united: the human being is matter, fragment, excess, clay, filth, nonsense, chaos; but the human being is also creator, sculptor, hammer-hardness, observer-divinity, and the Seventh Day—do you understand this opposition? Do you understand that *your* pity is for the 'creature in the human being', that which must be formed, broken, forged, torn, burned, annealed, purified—that which necessarily has to *suffer* and *should* suffer? And *our* pity—do you not understand whom our *reversed* pity is intended for, when it resists your pity as the worst of all possible self-indulgences and weaknesses?

Pity *versus* pity, then!

But to repeat, there are more important problems than all those concerning pleasure and suffering and pity; and any philosophy that confines itself only to these is naive.

226

We immoralists!—This world which concerns *us*, in which *we* are called upon to fear and to love, this nearly invisible, inaudible world of subtle commanding, subtle obeying, a 'not-quite' world in every respect, prickly, insidious, jeering, tender—indeed, it is well defended against clumsy observers and familiar curiosity! We are entangled in an unyielding snare and straitjacket of duties, and *cannot* get free—in this sense we too are 'duty-bound people', even we! From time to time, it is true, we do dance in our 'chains' and in and out of our 'swords'; more often, it is no less true, we groan because of it, impatient at all the secret harshness of our fate. But whatever we may do, fools and appearances will accuse us of being 'people *without* duty'—fools and appearances will always be against us!

227

Honesty: assuming that this is our virtue, the one we cannot escape, we free spirits—well then, we shall work at it with all our malice and love, and never tire of 'perfecting' ourselves in *our* virtue, the only one remaining to us: may its brightness continue to lie over this ageing culture and its musty, murky seriousness like the gilded, azure, mocking light of evening! And if someday our honesty should nevertheless grow tired and sigh and stretch its limbs and think us too harsh and wish to have it better, easier, softer, like a pleasant vice: let us remain *harsh*, we last stoics! Let us send to its aid whatever devilry we possess: our aversion to clumsiness and sloppiness, our *nitimur in vetitum*,* our adventuring spirit, our shrewd and fastidious curiosity, our most subtle, disguised, spiritual will to power and world-overcoming that dreams and roams desirously around all the realms of the future. Let us send all our 'devils' to aid our 'god'! It is likely that people will misjudge or mistake us about this—so what! People will say, 'Their "honesty"—that is only their devilry, nothing else!'—so what! And even if they're right! Haven't all earlier gods likewise been devils rechristened into saints? And in the last analysis, what do we know about ourselves? Or what the *name* of our guiding spirit is? (We are talking about names.) Or how many spirits are lodged within us? We free spirits must take care that our honesty does not become our vanity, our ostentatious adornment, our limit, our stupidity! Every virtue has a tendency towards stupidity, every stupidity towards virtue: 'Stupid to the point of sainthood', they say in Russia,—we must ultimately take care not to become saints and bores out of honesty! Isn't life a hundred times too short to live it—in a state of boredom? You'd really have to believe in life everlasting in order to . . .

228

I hope you will forgive me for the discovery that all moral philosophy until now has been boring and belongs among the sedatives—

and that nothing in my view has compromised 'virtue' so much as the fact that its representatives are so *boring*, although I wouldn't want to deny that they can often be useful! It is very important that as few people as possible reflect on morality—and thus it is *very* important that morality should never become interesting! But not to worry! Things are the same today as they have always been: I can see no one in Europe who might entertain (or *represent*) the idea that moral reflection could be carried out in a dangerous, insidious, or seductive fashion—that it might involve one's *fate*! Just consider, for example, the inexhaustible, inevitable English utilitarians, how they amble along so awkwardly and worthily in Bentham's* footsteps (a Homeric simile says it more plainly),* just as he himself had already ambled in the worthy Helvétius's* footsteps (no, he was not a dangerous man, this Helvétius!). No new thought, no attempt to give an old thought any kind of subtle turn or wrinkle, not even a real history of earlier thoughts: an *impossible* body of literature on the whole, assuming one does not know how to pickle it with a bit of malice. For even these moralists (whom you absolutely must read with mental reservations, if you *must* read them) have been invaded by that old English vice called *cant*,* which is *moral hypocrisy*, this time hiding under the new form of scientific thinking. Nor is there a lack of secret defences against the pangs of conscience that will necessarily torment a race of former Puritans, whatever their scientific engagement with morality. (Isn't a moralist the opposite of a Puritan, in that he is a thinker who takes morality to be questionable, worthy of a question mark, in short, a problem? Mightn't moralizing—be immoral?) Ultimately all of them want to justify *English* morality, in so far as that is the best way to serve humanity or 'the common good' or 'the happiness of the greatest number'—but no! the happiness *of England*. With all their might they would like to prove to themselves that the striving for *English* happiness, which is to say for *comfort* and *fashion** (and, above all, a seat in parliament) is also the right way to virtue—indeed that whatever virtue has existed in the world has consisted in just this kind of striving. None of all these ponderous herd animals with a troubled conscience (who undertake to represent the cause of egoism as a cause of the common good) wants to understand or nose out that the 'common good' is no ideal, no goal, no concept that can somehow be grasped, but rather an

emetic—that what is right for the one may certainly *not* be right
for the other, that to demand *one* morality for all is precisely to
encroach upon the higher sort of human beings—in short, that
there is a *hierarchy* between human and human, and therefore
between morality and morality as well. They are modest and
thoroughly mediocre kinds of men, these utilitarian Englishmen,
and to repeat: in so far as they are boring, one cannot praise their
utility too highly. We should actually *encourage* them, as has been
partially attempted with the following rhyme:

> Hail, dear barrowmen, and true,
> 'The longer it takes, the better' to you,
> Ever stiffer head and knee,
> Never inspired, never the joker,
> Indestructibly mediocre,
> *Sans génie et sans esprit!**

229

In those advanced eras that are rightfully proud of their humanity,
there remains so much fear, so much *superstitious* fear of the 'wild,
savage beast' which they are so particularly proud of having tamed,
that even palpable truths remain unspoken for hundreds of years
as if by agreement because they would seem to instil new life into
that wild, finally dispatched beast. Perhaps I am risking something
by letting a truth like that escape me: let others round it up again
and give it enough to drink of the 'milk of pious thinking'* so that
it lies down again quiet and forgotten in its old corner.

People should learn to understand cruelty differently and open
their eyes; people should finally learn to be impatient, so that
presumptuous, fat errors no longer wander about, virtuous and
cheeky, like the errors concerning tragedy, for example, that have
been fattened up by old and new philosophers. Almost everything
that we call 'high culture' is based on the deepening and spiritual-
izing of *cruelty*—this is my tenet. That 'wild beast' has not been
killed off at all, it lives and thrives, it has only—made a divinity of
itself. It is cruelty that constitutes the painful voluptuousness
of tragedy; whatever pleasing effect is to be found in so-called
tragic pity or in anything sublime in fact, right up to the highest
and most delicate shivers of metaphysics, gets its sweetness solely

because it is blended with the ingredient of cruelty. What the Roman in his arena, the Christian in his raptures before the cross, the Spaniard confronting the stake or the bullfight, the Japanese of today who rushes to see tragic theatre, the working-class Parisian who is nostalgic for bloody revolutions, the female Wagnerian who lets *Tristan und Isolde* wash over her with her will exposed—what all these people are enjoying, what they aspire to drink in with mysterious ardour is the spiced brew of the great Circe 'Cruelty'. Of course, we have to get rid of that foolish psychology of earlier times that held that cruelty arises only at the sight of *another* person's suffering: there is also abundant, over-abundant pleasure in our own suffering, in making ourselves suffer. And wherever a person can be persuaded to deny himself in a *religious* sense, or to mutilate himself in the manner of Phoenicians and ascetics, or in general to become contrite, desensualized, decorporealized, to feel the puritan spasm of penitence, to dissect the conscience and make a Pascalian *sacrifizio dell'intelletto*,* he is covertly being tempted and urged forward by his cruelty, by that dangerous shiver of cruelty turned *against himself*. Finally, let us consider that even the man who seeks knowledge, by forcing his spirit to know things *contrary* to the inclination of his mind and often enough also contrary to the wishes of his heart (that is, saying No where he would like to say Yes, where he would like to love and adore) functions as an artist and transfigurer of cruelty; whenever we take on anything deeply and thoroughly, it is already a rape, a wanting to do harm to the fundamental will of the spirit, a will that is constantly drawn to appearances and surfaces—in every desire for knowledge there is already a drop of cruelty.

230

Perhaps what I have said about a 'fundamental will of the spirit' will not be immediately transparent: permit me to explain.

That imperious something that the common people call 'spirit' wants to be the master, in itself and around itself, and to feel its mastery: it has the will to go from multiplicity to simplicity, a will that binds together, subdues, a tyrannical and truly masterful will. In this regard, its needs and capacities are the same as those the physiologists claim for everything that lives, grows, and repro-

duces. The spirit's energy in appropriating what is foreign to it is
revealed by its strong tendency to make the new resemble the old,
to simplify multiplicity, to overlook or reject whatever is completely
contradictory; the spirit likewise arbitrarily underlines, emphasizes,
or distorts certain qualities and contours in everything that is
foreign to it or of the 'outer world'. Its intention in doing so is to
incorporate new 'experiences', to fit new things into old orders—
to grow, then; and more specifically, to *feel* growth, to feel an
increase in strength. This same will is served by an apparently
opposite instinct of the spirit: a sudden decision for ignorance, for
arbitrary conclusions, a closing of the shutters, inwardly saying No
to this thing or that, a refusal to let things draw near, a kind of
defensive posture against much potential knowledge, being content
with darkness, with a limited horizon, saying Yes to ignorance and
affirming it; all this activity is necessary according to the degree of
the spirit's appropriating energy, its digestive energy, to keep to the
same metaphor—and indeed the 'spirit' really resembles nothing
so much as a stomach.

Likewise relevant here is the spirit's occasional will to allow itself
to be deceived, accompanied perhaps by the mischievous intuition
that things are *not* this way or that, that we are just allowing
them to be taken this way or that; a joy in every uncertainty and
ambivalence; an exulting self-satisfaction in the arbitrary confine-
ment and privacy of a nook, in things that are all too close, in
foreground things, in what has been enlarged, reduced, slanted,
prettified; a self-satisfaction in the arbitrariness of all these
expressions of power. Also relevant here, finally, is the spirit's not
inconsiderable readiness to deceive other spirits and go among them
in disguises, that constant pressure and stress of a creating, shaping,
transforming energy; it enables the spirit to enjoy its multiple masks
and slynesses, and also its feeling of security—its Protean arts are
just what defend and hide it best!

This will to appearance, to simplification, to masks, to cloaks, in
short, to the surface (for every surface is a cloak) is *countered* by
the sublime tendency of the man in search of knowledge to take
and to *want* to take things deeply, multifariously, profoundly, as a
kind of cruelty of intellectual conscience and aesthetic taste that
every courageous thinker will recognize in himself, if he has spent
an appropriate amount of time in tempering and sharpening his

self-critical eye and if he is accustomed both to severe discipline and to severe words. He will say, 'There is something cruel in the propensity of my spirit'—let virtuous and amiable people try to talk him out of it! In truth, it would sound nicer if people could talk about us, whisper about us, praise us (the free, *very* free spirits) for 'excessive honesty', say, instead of for cruelty. And might *that* really be what they will praise us for—when we are dead? Meanwhile (for there is still time until then) there is probably no one as disinclined as we to deck ourselves out in such spangled, sparkly moral language: all our previous work has soured us to the cheerful pomposity of just this kind of taste. They are beautiful, glittering, jingling, festive words: honesty, love of truth, love of wisdom, sacrifice for knowledge, the heroism of truthfulness—there is something about them that makes one swell with pride. But we hermits and marmots, we have long ago convinced ourselves in all the privacy of our hermit's conscience, that even this worthy linguistic ostentation belongs with the old adornments, the mendacious trash and gold dust of unconscious human vanity, and that even under this kind of flattering paint and concealing gilt the horrible original text *homo natura** must still be glimpsed. For to return man to nature; to master the many conceited and gushing interpretations and secondary meanings that have heretofore been scribbled and painted over that eternal original text *homo natura*; to ensure that henceforth man faces man in the same way that currently, grown tough within the discipline of science, he faces the *other* nature, with unfrightened Oedipus-eyes and plugged Odysseus-ears, deaf to the seductive melodies of the old metaphysical birdcatchers who have too long been piping at him, 'You are more! You are greater! You are of a different origin!'—that may be a strange and crazy project, but it is a *project*—who could deny that! Why have we chosen it, this crazy project? Or to ask it another way, 'Why bother with knowledge?'

Everyone will ask us about it. And we, pressed in this way, we who have asked ourselves just the same thing a hundred times over, we have found and do find no better answer . . .

231

Learning transforms us: it acts as all nourishment does, doing more than just 'keeping us going'—as physiologists know. But at the bottom of everyone, of course, way 'down there', there is something obstinately unteachable, a granite-like spiritual *Fatum*,* predetermined decisions and answers to selected, predetermined questions. In addressing any significant problem an unchangeable 'That-is-I' has its say; for example, a thinker cannot learn to change his ideas about man and woman, but can only learn his way through to the end, only discover to the limit what is firmly 'established' in his mind about them. Very soon we solve certain problems with solutions that inspire strong belief distinctively in *us*; perhaps we will go on to call them our 'convictions'. Later—we see in them only footprints on the way to self-knowledge, signposts to the problem that we *are*—more correctly, to the great stupidity that we are, to our spiritual *Fatum*, to our *unteachable* essence, way 'down there'.

After paying myself such a generous compliment, perhaps I may be allowed to enunciate some truths about 'women', assuming that henceforth people will know from the start how much these are simply—*my* truths.

232

Women want to be autonomous: and to that end they have begun to enlighten men about 'women per se'—*that* is one of the worst signs of progress in Europe's overall *uglification*. For look at all the things brought to light by these clumsy experiments in female scientific thinking and self-revelation! Women have so much reason for shame; there is so much hidden in women that is pedantic, superficial, carping, pettily presumptuous, pettily unbridled and immodest (just notice their interactions with children!), so much that has heretofore been most effectively repressed and subdued by their ultimate fear of males. God forbid that the 'Eternal-Boring'* in women (they are rich in it!) ever dares to come out, or that they begin completely and by conviction to forget their cleverness and their arts, those of grace, playfulness, bidding care begone, easing our burdens and taking the world lightly, their subtle readiness for pleasant desires! Already we hear female voices that frighten us, by holy Aristophanes! with medically precise threats about all the things that women *want* from men. Doesn't it show the very worst taste when women set about being scientific in this way? Until now, thank goodness, enlightenment was a man's business, a man's gift—and so men remained 'among themselves'. And ultimately, when-ever we read something a woman has written on 'women', we can reserve our mistrust about whether women actually *want* to be enlightened about themselves—whether they *can* want it . . . Now, if women are not doing it to get themselves some new *adornment* (self-adornment is part of the Eternal-Feminine, isn't it?), then they wish to instil fear: perhaps they want to dominate. But they do not *want* truth—what do women care about truth! From the beginning, nothing has been more alien to women, more repellent, more inimical than truth—their great art is the lie, their highest concern appearance and beauty. Let us admit it, we men: it is precisely *this* art and *this* instinct that we honour and love about women: we who have it difficult in life and are glad to relax in the company of creatures with hands, glances, and tender follies to make our seriousness, our difficulty and depth seem almost like folly. Finally, I would ask whether any woman herself has ever conceded that a woman's brain can be deep, a woman's heart just? And isn't it true on the whole that until now 'women' have been disdained most of all by women—and certainly not by us men?

We men now wish that women would stop compromising them-selves by their enlightenment, just as men once showed their concern and protection for women when the Church decreed: *mulier taceat in ecclesia!** It happened for the good of women when Napoleon gave the all-too-eloquent Madame de Staël* to under-stand: *mulier taceat in politicis!*—and I think it will be a real friend of women who calls out to them today: *mulier taceat de muliere!*

233

It is a sign of corrupt instincts (not to mention bad taste) when a woman points to Madame Roland,* say, or Madame de Staël or Monsieur George Sand,* as if they could prove something *on behalf* of 'women per se'. Men consider the above-named women the three *comical* females per se (nothing more!), actually the best unwitting *counter-arguments* to emancipation and female tyranny.

234

Stupidity in the kitchen; women as cooks; the frightful thoughtlessness that goes into providing nourishment for families and heads of households! Women don't understand what food *means*—and yet they want to be cooks! If women were sentient beings they would in their thousands of years of cooking experience have discovered the most important physiological facts and taken over the healing art! Because of bad cooks—because of the utter lack of rationality in the kitchen, human development has been longest delayed, worst compromised: things are not much better even today. A lecture for young ladies.

235

There are phrases and fillips of the spirit, there are adages, a little handful of words that can suddenly crystallize a whole culture, a whole society. Among them is that casual remark of Madame de Lambert to her son: 'Mon ami, ne vous permettez jamais que de folies, qui vous feront grand plaisir'*—incidentally the cleverest and most maternal remark ever made to a son.

236

What Dante and Goethe believed about women (the former when he sang, '*ella guardava suso, ed io in lei*',* the latter when he translated it as 'The Eternal-Feminine draws us *on high*'): I would expect that every finer woman will resist this belief, for *this* is precisely what she believes about the Eternal-Masculine . . .

237

Seven Women's Proverbs

How the dullest times will flee us, when a man creeps by to see us.

*

Age, oh dear! and books are sure to strengthen even the weakest virtue.

*

Black garments and a silent tongue suit every woman old and young.

*

Who has my greatest thanks and true? God!—and then my seam-
stress, too.

*

Young: a cave bedecked with flowers. Old: the dragon's out and
glowers.

*

Noble pedigree, handsome brow, and a man to boot, I'll take *him*
now!

*

The speech is short, the meaning long*—Mistress Ass will get it
wrong!

237

Until now men have treated women like birds that have strayed
down to them from some height: as something more fine, delicate,
wild, strange, sweet, soulful but as something that must be locked
up so that it does not fly off.

238

To address the fundamental problem of 'man and woman' in the
wrong way, either by denying a most profound antagonism and
the need for an eternal-hostile alertness, or by dreaming perhaps
of equal rights, equal education, equal ambitions and obligations:
that is a *typical* sign of shallowness, and any thinker who has
demonstrated that he is shallow (shallow in his instinct!) in this
dangerous area may generally be considered not only suspicious,
but also revealed, exposed: he will probably be too 'short' for all
the fundamental questions of life or of the life to come and be
unable to reach down to *any* depth. A deep man, on the other
hand, deep both in spirit and in desire, deep in a benevolence that
is capable of rigour and harshness and easily mistaken for them,
can think about women only like an *Oriental*: he has to conceive
of woman as a possession, as securable property, as something
predetermined for service and completed in it. He has to rely on
the tremendous reason of Asia, on Asia's superior instincts, as the
Greeks once did, Asia's best students and heirs who, as we know,
with the *growth* of their culture and the expansion of their strength
from Homer up to the time of Pericles became progressively *more*

severe towards women, in short, more Oriental. How necessary, how logical, how even humanly desirable this was: let us meditate on this in private!

239

In no other age have men ever treated the weaker sex with such respect as in our own—it is part of our democratic inclinations and basic taste, as is our irreverence for old age. Is it any wonder that this respect is already being abused? They want more; they are learning to make demands; they end by considering that modicum of respect almost irritating, preferring to compete, or even to battle for their rights: let's just say women are becoming shameless. And let us add at once that they are also becoming tasteless. They are forgetting how to *fear* men—but a woman who 'forgets how to fear' is abandoning her most womanly instincts. It is fair enough, even understandable enough if women dare to assert themselves when the fear-inducing element in men (let's put it more definitively: when the *man* in men) is no longer desired or cultivated; what is harder to understand is that this is enough to result in—the degeneration of women. This is happening today; let's make no mistake about it! Wherever the industrial spirit has triumphed over the military or aristocratic spirit, women are striving for the economic and legal independence of office clerks: 'Women as clerks' is written over the entrance-way to our developing modern society. While they are gaining these new rights, aiming to become 'master', and writing about women's 'progress' on their flags and banners, it is terribly clear that the opposite is happening: *women are regressing*. Ever since the French Revolution, women's influence in Europe has *decreased* to the same extent that their rights and ambitions have increased; and thus the 'emancipation of women', in so far as women themselves (and not only shallow males) are demanding and encouraging it, turns out to be a curious symptom of increasing weakness and dullness in the most womanly instincts. There is *stupidity* in this movement, an almost masculine stupidity, which a truly womanly woman (who is always a clever woman) would have to be utterly ashamed of. To lose the scent for which battleground best leads to victory; to neglect the practice of her true defensive arts; to let herself go ahead of a man, perhaps even 'up to a book', where she had earlier been well behaved and subtly, cleverly humble; to work with virtuous audacity against man's belief in a fundamentally alien ideal, *cloaked* in the shape of woman, in some Eternal- and Necessary-Feminine; to disabuse men volubly and emphatically of the notion that women should be kept, provided for, protected, indulged like delicate, strangely wild, and often pleasant domestic animals; to gather indignantly painstaking evidence of everything about the position of women in our own and earlier social orders that suggested the slave or bondman (as if slavery were a counter-argument and not rather a condition for every higher culture, every heightening of culture)—what does all this mean, if not a disintegration of womanly instincts, a defeminization? To be sure, there are enough idiotic women-lovers and female-corrupters among scholarly asses of the male gender who are advising women to defemininize themselves in this way and to imitate all the stupidities that are infecting 'men' in Europe, European 'masculinity'—those who would like to bring woman down to the level of 'general education', or even to reading the newspaper and politicking. Some of them would even like to make women into freethinkers and literati, as if a woman without piety were not something wholly repellent or ludicrous for a deep and godless man. Women's nerves are being destroyed almost everywhere by the most pathological and dangerous kinds of music (our modern German music), making women every day more hysterical and less competent for their first and last profession, the bearing of healthy children. In general, these men want to 'cultivate' women still more and, as they say, make the 'weaker sex' *strong* through culture, as if history did not teach as forcefully as could be that the 'cultivation' of a person was always accompanied by a weakening, that is to say, the weakening, splintering, debilitating of his *strength of will*; and that the most powerful and influential women in the world (not least Napoleon's mother) owed their power and superiority over men to their strength of will—and not to the schoolmasters! What makes us respect and often enough fear women is their *nature*, which is 'more natural' than man's, their genuine, predator-like, cunning suppleness, their tiger's claw beneath the glove, their naive egoism, their ineducability and inner wildness, the mystery, breadth, and range of their desires and virtues . . . What makes us feel pity for this dangerous and beautiful cat 'woman' despite all

our fear is that she seems to be more suffering, vulnerable, needy
of love, and condemned to disappointment than any other animal.
Fear and pity: man has always stood before woman with feelings
like these, with one foot deep in the tragedy that tears him apart
as it delights him—. Well then? And this is now to draw to an
end? And women are to *lose* their magic spell? Women are gradually
to be turned into bores? Oh, Europe! Europe! We know the horned
animal* that you have always found most attractive, that is always
threatening you! Your old tale could become 'history' once again—
a tremendous stupidity could gain mastery of you once again and
carry you off! And no God would be hidden underneath it, no!
Just an 'idea', a 'modern idea'! . . .

SECTION EIGHT

PEOPLES AND FATHERLANDS

240

ONCE again for the first time I have heard—Richard Wagner's *Meistersinger* Overture: it is a gorgeous, florid, weighty, and autumnal work of art, one proud enough to assume that to understand it, the music of two centuries is still alive to its listeners. It does honour to us Germans that such pride is not misplaced! What flowing energies, what seasons and climates are intermingled here! Now it strikes us as archaic, now foreign, tart, and overly green; it is both arbitrary and stiffly traditional; often mischievous, more often blunt and crude it has courage and fire and at the same time the slack, faded skin of fruits that ripen too late. It streams forth wide and full: and then suddenly there is a moment of inexplicable hesitation, a kind of gap that springs up between cause and effect, a pressure that makes us dream, almost a nightmare*— but then the old stream rolls on expansively again, exuding contentment, the most various contentment, past and present happiness, *very much* including the artist's happiness with himself, which he has no interest in concealing, his astonished, happily shared knowledge that he is master of the techniques he is employing, his new, new-won, untried artistic techniques as they seem to be revealed to us. Nothing beautiful, on balance, nothing of the South, nothing of the fine, bright, southern sky, nothing of gracefulness, no dancing, scarcely a will to logic; a certain clumsiness, in fact, which the artist even stresses as if he wanted to tell us, 'This is intentional'; a ponderous draping, something arbitrarily barbaric, ceremonious, a glittering of venerable and erudite jewels and laces; something German in the best and worst senses of the word, something multifarious, unformed, and inexhaustible in the German way; a certain German massiveness and abundance of soul that is not afraid to be hidden by the artful trappings of decadence—that may in fact need them in order to feel truly at ease; an honest-to-goodness symbol of the German soul, young and at the same time out of date, overly rotten and yet overly rich with the future. This kind of music best expresses my view of the Germans: they are of the day before yesterday and the day after tomorrow—*they have yet to find their Today.*

241

We 'good Europeans'—we too have our hours of indulging in a hearty fatherland-ism, falling back with a thump into old loves and impasses (I've just given an example of it), hours flooded through with feelings for the nation, patriotic anguish, and all sorts of other archaic emotional convulsions. Spirits more lumbering than our own may take longer periods of time to complete what we limit to hours, what we exhaust within hours, some of them requiring six months, others half a lifetime, according to the speed and strength of their digestion and their 'metabolism'.* Indeed, I could imagine that even within our quick-moving Europe, some dull, sluggish races might need half-centuries to overcome these atavistic attacks of fatherland-ism and attachment to the soil, and return to reason, that is to say, to being 'good Europeans'. And as I digress about this possibility, I chance to overhear the conversation of two old 'patriots' (both of them were apparently hard of hearing and therefore spoke all the louder).

'*That fellow** has about as much understanding and appreciation of philosophy as a peasant or a fraternity student,' said one of them, 'he is still innocent. But what good does that do nowadays? This is the age of the masses: they're all grovelling before anything that smacks of the masses. That's how it is in politics, too. They think that any politician who erects some new Tower of Babel for them, some monstrosity of power and empire, is "great". What use is it that those of us who are more cautious and reserved are not yet ready to abandon our old belief that only a great thought can endow a deed or cause with greatness. Assuming that a politician were to place his people in the situation of having to embark on "large-scale politics", which they were by nature poorly inclined or prepared to do, requiring them to sacrifice their old and certain virtues for the sake of a new, dubious mediocrity—assuming a politician were to sentence his people to "politicking" in general,

although they used to have better things to do and think about and
could not at the bottom of their hearts rid themselves of a cautious
disdain for the restlessness, vacuousness, and noisy wrangling of
truly political peoples: assuming that such a politician would rouse
the sleeping passions and desires of his people, turn their previous
shyness and pleasure as bystanders into a defect, their foreignness
and secret infinitude into a sin, devalue in their eyes their dearest
inclinations, reverse their conscience, make their spirit narrow, their
taste "national"—well then! Such a politician, one who would do all
this, whose people would have to atone for him forever afterwards, if
they had an afterwards, such a politician would be *great*?'

'Certainly!' the other old patriot answered him vehemently,
'otherwise he wouldn't have *been able* to do it! Do you think it was
mad to want that kind of thing? But maybe all greatness was mere
madness at first!'

'A misuse of language!' objected his partner loudly. 'Strength!
Strength! Strength and madness! *Not* greatness!'

The two old men had obviously become heated by yelling their
'truths' at one another in this fashion. But I, happy to be above
and beyond them, reflected on how quickly a strong man will find
a stronger master, and also that spiritual shallowness in one people
is balanced out by greater depth in another.

242

Whether we seek the distinctiveness of today's Europeans in what
we call 'civilization' or 'humanization' or 'progress', or whether we
withhold our praise or blame and simply use the political term:
Europe's *democratic* movement—behind all the moral and political
foregrounds that such terms describe, a tremendous *physiological*
process is occurring and continually gaining momentum. Europeans
are coming to resemble one another more and more, and are more
and more free of the conditions that would give rise to races
connected by climate and class. They are increasingly independent
of any *particular* environment that might inscribe its identical
demands into their bodies and souls over the course of centuries—
that is to say, an essentially supernational and nomadic type of
man is slowly emerging, one that is distinguished, physiologically
speaking, by having a maximum of adaptive skills and powers. This

process of the *evolving European*, which can be delayed by great relapses in tempo but may as a result very well grow with new force and depth (like the Storm and Stress of 'national feeling' still raging even now, for example, or the recent emergence of Anarchism): this process probably ends with results that were least anticipated by its naive sponsors and apologists, the apostles of 'modern ideas'. The same new conditions that typically give rise to ordinary and mediocre men (serviceable, industrious, diversely useful and handy herd-animal men) are also those most suited to producing exceptional men of the most dangerous and attractive qualities. For while it is quite impossible for this adaptability (which tries out ever-changing conditions and starts a new project in every generation, almost in every decade) to promote the *powerfulness* of the type; and while such future Europeans will probably give the overall impression of being diverse, loquacious, weak-willed, and extremely handy workers who *need* a master, a commander, like their daily bread; and while, finally, the democratization of Europe will end by procreating a type that has been developed in the subtlest sense to be *slaves*—the *strong* man, in the individual and exceptional case, will have to turn out even stronger and richer than he ever would have done before, owing to the impartiality of his training, owing to the tremendous diversity of his activities, arts, and masks. That is to say, the democratization of Europe is at the same time an involuntary contrivance for the breeding of *tyrants*—understanding the word in every sense, even the most spiritual.

243

I am glad to hear that our sun is moving rapidly on a course towards the constellation *Hercules*: and I hope that people on this planet will imitate the sun in this respect. And we ahead of all the rest, we good Europeans!

244

There was a time when people were in the habit of distinguishing the Germans as 'deep'. Now, when the most successful example of the new Germanness craves honours of quite a different sort and may wish that deep things were more 'dashing', it may be almost timely and patriotic to wonder whether we were deluding ourselves about our earlier reputation; to wonder, in short, whether German depth may not be something fundamentally different and worse—and something, thank God, that we are about to succeed in eliminating. So let's try to change our thinking about German depth: all it requires is a little vivisection of the German soul.

The German soul is above all multifarious, having diverse sources, being more layered and pieced together than truly constructed—this is because of its origins. Any German bold enough to claim that 'two souls reside, alas, within my breast'* would be grossly abusing the truth or more correctly falling short of the truth by many souls. As a people in whom there is a most tremendous mixture and mingling of the races, with a possible preponderance of the pre-Aryan element, as a 'people of the middle' in every sense, the Germans are more incomprehensible, vast, contradictory, alien, incalculable, surprising, even frightening than are other peoples to themselves—they escape *definition* and for that reason alone are the despair of the French. It is characteristic of the Germans that they can never exhaust the question 'What is German?' Kotzebue* surely knew his Germans well enough: 'We have been recognized', they called out to him joyfully—yet *Sand* also thought he knew them. Jean Paul* knew what he was doing when he furiously declared his opposition to Fichte's mendacious, but patriotic flatteries and exaggerations—yet it is probable that Goethe did not agree with Jean Paul about the Germans, even if he thought he was right about Fichte. I wonder what Goethe really thought about the Germans?

But Goethe never commented clearly on so much that surrounded him, and throughout his life managed to keep a refined silence: he probably had his good reasons. What is certain is that it was neither the 'Wars of Liberation' nor the French Revolution that caused him to brighten up a bit: the event that made him rethink his *Faust*, indeed the whole 'human' problem, was the appearance of Napoleon. We have observations of Goethe's, made as if he were speaking from a foreign country, which condemn with impatient harshness those things that Germans count as a source of pride: at one point he defines the famous German *Gemüt** as 'indulging one's own and other people's weaknesses'. Is he wrong about that? It is characteristic of the Germans that people are rarely

completely wrong about them. The German soul contains within
it a maze of passageways; there are caverns in it, hiding places,
castle keeps; its disorder has much of the charm of the mysterious;
a German knows about the secret paths to chaos. And just as each
thing loves its own image, so the German loves clouds and everything that is unclear, evolving, dusky, damp and ominous: whatever
is uncertain, unformed, shifting, growing he feels as 'deep'. The
German himself *is* not, he *is becoming*, he 'is developing'. Thus
'development' is the brilliant, truly German discovery in the great
realm of philosophical formulae: a governing concept that, along
with German beer and German music, is working at Germanizing
all of Europe. Foreigners remain attracted and transfixed at the
riddles posed by the essential contradictions at the bottom of
the German soul (which Hegel put into a system and Richard
Wagner more recently put to music). 'Good-natured and malicious':
that kind of juxtaposition, nonsensical in relation to any other
people, is unfortunately all too often justified in Germany: just go
to live for a while among the Swabians! The ungainliness and social
tastelessness of the German scholar are frighteningly compatible
with the airy boldness of his inner tightrope dance, which all the
gods have already learned to fear. If you want to see the 'German
soul' demonstrated *ad oculos*,* just take a look at German taste,
German arts and customs: what a boorish indifference to 'taste'! See
how the noblest and the commonest things are juxtaposed! How
messy and rich this whole inner economy is! The German is
weighed down by his soul; he is weighed down by everything that
he experiences. He has trouble digesting his events, he never has
'done' with them; German depth is often merely a heavy, sluggish
'digestion'. And just as all chronic patients, all dyspeptics prefer
to be comfortable, so the German loves to be 'open' and 'upright':
how *comfortable* it is to be open and upright!

Today, this friendly, receptive, cards-on-the-table aspect of
German *honesty* may be the most dangerous and most successful
disguise that the German has mastered: it is his true Mephisto-
phelian art; it will 'take him far'! The German lets himself go,
looks on with faithful, empty, blue German eyes—and presto!
foreigners confuse him with his dressing gown!—That is to say,
whatever 'German depth' may be (might we even consent to laugh
at it, just between ourselves?), we will do well to continue to honour

its image and good name and not sell our old reputation as a deep people too cheaply in exchange for Prussian 'dash' and Berlin wit and sand.* It is prudent for a people to be taken for, to *allow* itself to be taken for deep, for awkward, for good-natured, for honest, for imprudent: it might even—be deep! And finally, we should do honour to our name—it's not for nothing that we are called the 'Teuton' people, the 'two-timing' people.*

245

The 'good old' days are over, they sang their last in Mozart: how fortunate are *we* that his Rococo still speaks to us, that his 'good company', his fond raptures, his childlike pleasure in embellishments and chinoiserie, his courtesy of the heart, his need for daintiness, infatuation, springing dances, teary-eyed bliss, his belief in the South may still appeal to some *remnant* in us! Alas, this too will pass, one day. But who can doubt that the understanding and savouring of Beethoven will pass far sooner! For he was only the last note in a transition or break in styles, and *not*, like Mozart, the last note of a great, centuries-long European taste. Beethoven is the transitional product of an old, crumbling soul that is constantly breaking apart and an overly young future soul that is constantly *approaching*; his music glows in that twilight of everlasting loss and everlasting, excessive hope—the same light that bathed Europe when it dreamed along with Rousseau, when it danced around the Revolution's tree of liberty and finally almost made an Idol of Napoleon. But now, how quickly *this* particular feeling is fading, how difficult it is today even to *know* about this feeling—how alien to our ear is the language of Rousseau, Schiller, Shelley, Byron, in all of whom *together* the same European destiny found its way to the Word that sang in Beethoven!

The German music that followed belongs to Romanticism, that is, to an historically speaking even shorter, more fleeting, more superficial movement than was that other great interlude, Europe's transition from Rousseau to Napoleon and to the emergence of democracy. Weber: but what do *we* care about *Oberon* or the *Freischütz* today! Or Marschner's *Hans Heiling* and *Vampyr*! Or even Wagner's *Tannhäuser*! This music has died away, even if it hasn't yet been forgotten. Furthermore, all this Romantic music was not noble enough, not music enough to maintain its legitimacy any-where but in the theatre and before the crowd; it was second-class music from the start and rarely came to the attention of real musicians. Things were different with Felix Mendelssohn, that halcyon master whose lighter, purer, more cheerful soul made him quickly celebrated and just as quickly forgotten—as a beautiful *episode* in German music. But as for Robert Schumann, who took everything seriously and was also taken seriously from the start (he is the last composer to have founded a school): don't we privately consider it a stroke of luck, a relief, a liberation that this particular Schumannesque Romanticism has been overcome? Schumann, seeking refuge in the 'Saxon Switzerland'* of his soul, half of him like Werther,* half like Jean Paul, certainly not like Beethoven! Certainly not like Byron. (His *Manfred* music is a mistaken misun-derstanding to the point of injustice.) Schumann: with his essentially *small* taste (a dangerous tendency, that is,—among Germans doubly dangerous—to quiet lyricism and intoxication of the emotions), always walking apart, withdrawing and retreating shyly, a noble reed of a boy who revelled utterly in anonymous happiness and sorrow, from the start a sort of a girl and *noli me tangere*:* this Schumann was already only a *German* musical phenomenon, not a European one as Beethoven was, as Mozart has been to an even greater extent—in him German music was threatened by its greatest danger: to cease being *the voice of Europe's soul* and to deteriorate into mere fatherland-ism.

246

What a torture are books written in German for anyone with a *third* ear! How resentfully we face the slowly circling swamp of sounds without resonance, of rhythms without dance that Germans call a 'book'. And what about the German who *reads* books! How lazily, reluctantly, badly he reads! How many Germans have the knowledge—and expect it of themselves—that there is *art* in every good sentence—art that must be perceived if the sentence is to be understood! Misunderstand its tempo, for example, and the sen-tence itself is misunderstood! Let no one doubt how crucial its syllables are to its rhythm; let us feel the intention and the delight in interrupting an all-too-rigorous symmetry; let us open up our keen, patient ears to every *staccato*, every *rubato*; let us guess the sense behind a sequence of vowels and diphthongs, and how delicately and richly they can acquire and change colour by their juxtaposition: who among book-reading Germans is sufficiently willing to acknowledge such duties and demands and listen carefully to all this linguistic art and intention? In the end, people don't 'have an ear for it': and thus the strongest stylistic contrasts are not heard, and the finest artistry is *wasted* as upon the deaf.

These were my thoughts as I noticed how two prose masters were grossly and ignorantly mistaken for one another: one who lets his words drop down sluggish and cold as from the ceiling of a damp cave (he is counting on their muted sounds and resonances) and another who handles his language like a pliant sword and from his shoulders down to his toes feels the dangerous happiness in a trembling, razor-sharp blade that wants to bite, cut, zing.

247

How little German style has to do with sound or with hearing is demonstrated by the fact that even our good musicians write badly. A German does not read aloud, so as to be heard, but merely with his eyes: he puts his ears into his desk-drawer beforehand. When the ancients read something (it did not happen too often), they would read it aloud, in a loud voice, in fact; if a person read quietly to himself, people were surprised and wondered privately about his reasons. In a loud voice: that means with all the swelling, modulating, shifting of tone and all the tempo changes that the ancient *public* world enjoyed. At that time the laws of literary style were the same as those of oratory; and these laws depended in part on the astonishing training and subtle needs of ear and larynx, and in part on the strength, endurance, and power of ancient lungs. A periodic sentence in the ancient sense is above all a physiological whole, in so far as it is encompassed by one sole breath. A period in the manner of Demosthenes or Cicero, swelling twice and sinking twice and all in the span of one breath: this is a pleasure for the *ancients*, who had learned from their own training to appreciate the virtue of such a sentence, how rare and difficult it is to enunciate it. *We* really have no right to the *grand* period, we moderns, in every sense the short-winded! These ancients were themselves all oratorical dilettantes, after all, and thus connoisseurs, and thus critics—that is how they pushed their orators to the extremes. Similarly, every Italian in the last century, male and female, knew how to sing, and as a consequence vocal virtuosity (and thus also the art of melody) reached a high point. In Germany, however (up until the most recent times, when a kind of grandstand eloquence has been shyly and clumsily testing its wings), there was actually only one form of public and *more-or-less* artistic oratory—and that is what was delivered down from the pulpit. Only the preachers in Germany knew what a syllable, what a word is worth, to what degree a sentence can resound, leap, plunge, run along, run down; only they had a conscience in their ears, and often enough a bad conscience: for there are plenty of reasons why Germans in particular achieve excellence in oratory only rarely and almost always too late. That is why the masterpiece of German prose is, appropriately, the masterpiece of its greatest preacher: the *Bible* has been the best German book so far. Compared to Luther's Bible, practically everything else is only 'belles lettres'—a thing that was not grown in Germany and therefore did not and will not grow its way into German hearts, as the Bible has done.

248

There are two kinds of genius—one that primarily begets and wants to beget, and another that likes to be fructified and give birth. And among peoples of genius there are likewise those upon whom the womanly problem of pregnancy and the secret task of shaping, ripening, perfecting have devolved (the Greeks, for example, were a people of this kind, as were the French); and others who must fructify and become the cause of new orders of life (like the Jews, the Romans, and, may we modestly inquire, the Germans?). These peoples are tormented and thrilled by unknown fevers and irresistibly urged out of themselves, infatuated and lusting after foreign races (the ones that 'can be fructified') and at the same time power-hungry like everything that knows itself to be full of procreative powers and thus 'full of God's grace'. These two kinds of genius seek one another out like man and woman; but they also misunderstand one another—like man and woman.

249

Each people has its own hypocrisy, which it calls its virtues.

We do not know what is best about ourselves—we cannot know it.

250

What does Europe owe to the Jews?

Many things, both good and bad, and one thing above all, at once the best and the worst: the grand moral style, the horror and majesty of everlasting demands, everlasting meanings, the whole sublime romanticism of moral questions—and thus the most attractive, insidious, and choice part of those kaleidoscopic shifts and seductions to life in whose afterglow the sky of our European culture, its evening sky is now flickering—perhaps flickering out. For this, we artists among the spectators and philosophers look to the Jews with—gratitude.

251

If a people suffers, *wants* to suffer from national nervous fever and political ambition, it must be expected that various clouds and disturbances will pass across its spirit, little attacks of acquired stupidity, in short. With today's Germans, for example, it is now the anti-French stupidity, now the anti-Jewish, now the anti-Polish, now the Christian-Romantic, now the Wagnerian, now the Teutonic, now the Prussian (just think of those pitiful historians, those Sybels and Treitzschkes with their heavily bandaged heads), and whatever else they are called, these little becloudings of the German spirit and conscience. May I be forgiven that I too, during a short, hazardous stay in a very infected area, did not remain entirely spared by the disease and, like everyone, began to think about things that were none of my business: the first sign of political infection. About the Jews, for example: just listen.

I have never yet met a German who might have been well disposed to Jews; and however unconditionally all careful and political people may reject real anti-Semitism, even their care and politics are not really directed at the type of feeling per se, but rather at its dangerous extremes, especially if these extreme feelings are expressed reprehensibly or tastelessly—we must not deceive

ourselves about that. That Germany has *more than enough* Jews,
that German stomachs, German blood have found it difficult (and
will continue to find it difficult) to deal with even this amount of
'Jew' (which the Italian, the Frenchman, the Englishman have dealt
with, thanks to their stronger digestions): a general instinct states
this in clear language, and we must listen to that instinct and act
accordingly. 'Do not allow any new Jews to enter! And bar especially
those doors that face East (and also towards Austria)!' Thus decrees
the instinct of a people whose kind is still weak and inchoate,
making it easily vulnerable to obliteration or elimination by a
stronger race. But the Jews are without doubt the strongest,
toughest, and purest race now living in Europe; they know how to
succeed under even the worst conditions (better in fact than under
favourable ones) by means of certain virtues that we today would
like to label vices—they owe it above all to their resolute faith that
has no need to feel ashamed at 'modern ideas'. They change, *if*
they change, only in the way the Russian Empire makes its con-
quests: like an empire that takes its time and did not just develop
overnight—that is to say, according to the principle 'As slowly as
possible!' Any thinker who has Europe's future on his conscience
must in any proposal he makes about that future take the Jews into
account like the Russians, as they are obviously the surest and most
likely elements in the great game and struggle of forces. What we
in Europe today call a 'nation' and what is actually more of a *res
facta* than *nata* (sometimes even easily confounded with a *res ficta
et picta*)* is certainly something evolving, young, easily displaced,
not yet a race, let alone the sort of *aere perennius** that is the Jewish
kind: these 'nations' should refrain from becoming the Jews' hot-
headed enemies or competitors! If they wanted to (or if they were
forced to it, as the anti-Semites seem to want them to be), the Jews
could gain the upper hand, could in fact quite literally rule over
Europe, that much is clear—just as clear as the fact that they are
not planning or working towards that end. For the time being, what
they want and wish for, even with a certain urgency, is rather to
be wholly absorbed by Europe, into Europe; they yearn to be
established, legitimate, respected somewhere at last, and to set an
end to their nomadic life as 'wandering Jews'. And we should heed
and welcome this strong desire (that in itself may already express
a softening of Jewish instincts)—in that spirit it might be proper

and useful to reprimand all the anti-Semitic loudmouths in the land. We should welcome them with great caution, with selectivity, more or less as the English nobility does. It is obvious that the stronger and better-established types of the new German (an aristocratic officer from the March of Brandenburg, for example) could have to do with them most freely. It might be of diverse interest to see whether his inherited skill in commanding and obeying (the aforementioned province is the classic case for both at the moment) could be added to, bred together with their genius for money and patience (and especially some of their spirit and spirituality, both of which are sadly wanting in the aforementioned place). But this is where I should interrupt the cheerful Germanizing of my oration, for I am already touching on my *serious* concern, the 'European problem' as I understand it, the breeding of a new caste to rule over Europe.

252

They are not a philosophical race, these Englishmen: Bacon represents an *attack* on the philosophical spirit in general; Hobbes, Hume, and Locke a century-long degradation and devaluation of the concept 'philosopher'. Kant rose and raised himself up to rebel *against* Hume; Schelling had the *right* to say of Locke: 'je méprise Locke'.* In their struggle against the doltish mechanistic English ideas about the world, Hegel and Schopenhauer (along with Goethe) were in agreement, those two inimical brother geniuses of philosophy who strove towards opposite poles of the German spirit and thereby did wrong by each other as only brothers can.

Carlyle,* that rhetorician and quasi-actor, that tasteless, addle-pated Carlyle knew well enough what England lacks and has always lacked; behind passionate masks he tried to hide what he knew about himself, which was what Carlyle *lacked*: real spiritual *power*, spiritual vision of real *depth*—in short, philosophy.

Typically, this kind of unphilosophical race adheres strictly to Christianity: it *needs* to be disciplined by Christian 'moralizing' and humanization. Because Englishmen are gloomier, more sensual, wilful, and brutal than Germans, the coarser of the two, they are also more pious: they are simply more *in need* of Christianity. In this English Christianity, finer noses will even sense a genuine

English after-smell of spleen and alcoholic excess, to cure which they have good reason to use Christianity—a subtler poison, that is, to counteract a cruder; and in clumsy peoples a subtler form of poison is progress indeed, a step on the way to spiritualization. English clumsiness and boorish solemnity are most successfully disguised or (more accurately) explained and reinterpreted by Christian gesture and prayer and the singing of psalms; and truly, in a drunken and profligate beast who has been taught to make moral grunts, once by the power of Methodism and again more recently by the 'Salvation Army', a penitent's spasm really may be the relatively highest 'human' achievement that it can aspire to: this much we can easily admit. But what also offends us about the most human Englishman is his lack of music, to speak metaphorically (and non-metaphorically): in the movements of his body and soul he has no tempo, no dance, not even a desire for tempo and dance, for 'music'. Just listen to him speak; just look at how the most beautiful Englishwomen *walk*—there are no more beautiful doves or swans in any land on earth, but when all is said and done: just listen to them sing! But I am demanding too much . . .

253

There are truths best perceived by mediocre minds, because they are most suited to them; there are truths that have charms and seductive powers only for mediocre spirits: we are being forced just now to embrace this perhaps unpleasant tenet, ever since the spirit of respectable, but mediocre Englishmen (I am thinking of Darwin, John Stuart Mill, and Herbert Spencer) has begun to gain the upper hand in the middle region of European taste. Indeed, who would question that it is occasionally useful for *these* kinds of spirits to be dominant? It would be a mistake to expect lofty-natured, daring spirits to be especially adept at ascertaining lots of common little facts and forcing them into conclusions: rather, as they are exceptions themselves, they do not even start out in any propitious relationship to 'rules'. In the end they have more to do than merely to perceive, and that is to *be* something new, to *signify* something new, and to *represent* new values! The chasm between knowledge and ability is perhaps greater and also more sinister than we think:

a person of ability in the grand style, a creative person may have to be a person lacking in knowledge—while making scientific discoveries in the manner of Darwin, on the other hand, might require a certain narrowness, dryness, and diligent meticulousness, in short, something English.

Finally, let us not forget that there has already been a time when the English, a profoundly average people, caused the European spirit to sink into an overall depression: what we call 'modern ideas' or 'eighteenth-century ideas' or 'French ideas' (that is, what the *German* spirit opposed with deep revulsion) had an English origin, there can be no doubt about that. The French were just the apes and actors of these ideas, also their best soldiers, as well as their first and most complete, unfortunate *victims*: the damnable Anglomania of 'modern ideas' has made the *âme française** so thin and haggard that we can scarcely credit our memory of its sixteenth and seventeenth centuries, with their deep, passionate strength, their inventive elegance. But we must cling fiercely to this tenet of historical fairness and defend it against the moment and appearances: European *noblesse** (in feeling, taste, custom—in short, in every great sense of the word) is *France's* invention and accomplishment, while European commonness, the plebeianism of modern ideas is—*England's*.

254

France is still, even now, the seat of the most spiritual and refined European culture and a great school of taste. but you have to know how to find this 'France of good taste'. Its members keep themselves well hidden—there may be only a small number of people in whom it is alive and well, nor are they necessarily the steadiest on their feet, some of them fatalists, melancholics, invalids, some of them spoiled or affected, people whose *ambition* it is to remain hidden. All of them have one thing in common: they keep their ears closed to the raving stupidity and noisy chatter of the democratic bourgeoisie. To be sure, a France that is increasingly stupid and coarse is thrashing around in the foreground—at Victor Hugo's funeral it recently held a veritable orgy of bad taste and simultaneous self-admiration. And there is something else they share: a great will to defend themselves against spiritual Germanization—

and an even greater inability to do so! Schopenhauer may already have become more at home, more indigenous in this spiritual France (which is also a pessimistic France) than he ever was in Germany. Not to mention Heinrich Heine, who long ago entered the flesh and blood of Paris's finer and more ambitious poets; or Hegel, who today exercises an almost tyrannical influence in the figure of Taine* (the *first* living historian). But as far as Richard Wagner goes, we can predict that the more French musicians learn to shape themselves according to the true needs of the *âme moderne*,* the more they will 'Wagnerize'—they're already doing enough of it!

Nevertheless, there are still three things that the French can point to with pride as their particular heritage and an abiding sign of their old cultural superiority over Europe, however much their aesthetic taste has been voluntarily or involuntarily Germanized or vulgarized: first, the capacity for artistic passions, devotion to 'form', for which the phrase *l'art pour l'art*,* along with a thousand others, was invented; for three hundred years France has never lacked these qualities; its respect for the 'small number' repeatedly gave rise to a kind of literary chamber music that is hard to find in the rest of Europe.

The second thing on which the French can base their superiority over Europe is their old, heterogeneous, *moralistic* culture, which enables one to find even in lightweight newspaper novelists or chance *boulevardiers de Paris** a psychological sensitivity and curiosity which Germans, for example, have not the slightest idea of (let alone the thing itself!). To achieve it, the Germans would need a few moralistic centuries such as the French, as mentioned, did not spare themselves; to call the Germans 'naive' as a consequence is fashioning praise out of a shortcoming. (As a contrast to the Germans' inexperience and innocence in *voluptate psychologica*,* which is not totally unrelated to the tedium of their social intercourse, and as a most successful expression of a genuinely French curiosity and inventive talent in this realm of tender shivers, let us take Henri Beyle,* that remarkable, anticipatory and pioneering man who ran at a Napoleonic tempo through *his* Europe, through several centuries of the European soul, an explorer on the scent of this soul. It took two generations even to *catch up* with him somehow, to have a second guess at some of the riddles that tormented and delighted him, this strange Epicurean and question mark of a man who was France's last great psychologist.)

There is yet a third claim to superiority: the nature of the French people offers a tolerably successful synthesis of North and South, enabling them to comprehend much and to do much else that an Englishman will never comprehend. Their temperament, periodically inclining towards and away from the South, occasionally bubbling over with Provençal and Ligurian blood, protects them from the horrible northern grey-on-grey, the sunless world of spectral concepts and anaemia: our *German* aesthetic disease, against whose excesses people today are unequivocal in prescribing blood and iron,* that is to say, 'politics on a grand scale' (submitting to a dangerous cure that has taught me to wait and wait, but not as yet to hope). Even now in France there is still a predisposition to understand and accommodate those rarer and rarely satisfied people who are too expansive to find their satisfaction in any kind of fatherland-ism and know how to love what is southern about the North and what is northern about the South those born Mediterraneans,* the 'good Europeans'.

Their music has been composed by *Bizet*, this last genius, who envisioned a new seductive beauty and discovered a bit of *the South in music*.

255

With respect to German music, I feel that some caution is in order. Assuming that a person loves the South as I do, as a great school of convalescence for our most spiritual and most sensual selves, as a vast abundance of sun and sunny transfigurations cast over a tyrannical, self-worshipping existence: now, this kind of a person will learn to be somewhat cautious about German music, because while it is undermining his aesthetic taste, it is also undermining his health. Whenever such a person, a southerner not by heritage but by *faith*, dreams about the future of music,* he must also dream about redeeming northern music and must have in his ears the prelude to a deeper, more powerful, perhaps more evil and mysterious music, a supra-German music that does not pale, wither, die away as does all German music at the sight of a voluptuous blue sea and heavenly Mediterranean light, a supra-European music that holds its own even at brown desert sunsets, whose soul is kindred to the palm tree and is at ease roaming among great, beautiful, solitary beasts of prey . . . I could imagine a music whose rarest enchantment would be that it no longer knows anything of good and evil, though it might be touched here and there by a sailor's longing for home, by a few golden shadows and tender weaknesses: an art that would see from afar the colours of a declining, now almost unintelligible *moral* world seeking refuge in it, an art that would be hospitable and deep enough to receive these late-coming refugees.

<h2 style="text-align:center">256</h2>

Owing to the unhealthy alienation that national madness has planted and continues to plant between the peoples of Europe, and owing also to short-sighted and quick-handed politicians whom this madness has helped to place on top of the heap and who have no idea how far the divisive politics they pursue can of necessity only be an interim politics—owing to all that and to other unutterable things, people nowadays are overlooking or arbitrarily and mendaciously reinterpreting the most unambiguous signs that suggest that *Europe wants to be one*. All of this century's deeper and more generous individuals have actually directed the mysterious labour of their souls towards preparing a path to a new *synthesis* and experimentally anticipating the European of the future. Only in their foreground or their weaker hours, as in their old age, did they join the 'fatherlanders'—they were merely taking a rest from themselves when they became 'patriots'. I am thinking of people like Napoleon, Goethe, Beethoven, Stendhal, Heinrich Heine, Schopenhauer: do not hold it against me if I also count Richard Wagner among them: his own misunderstandings should not mislead us— geniuses of his sort are seldom privileged to understand themselves. Nor should we be misled by the rude noises that the French are now making in cutting themselves off from Richard Wagner in self-defence: it is nevertheless a fact that Richard Wagner and *late French Romanticism* of the 1840s are most closely and intimately bound together. They are akin, fundamentally akin in all the heights and depths of their desires: it is Europe, one single Europe whose soul is longing, urging itself outwards, upwards by means of this abundant, impetuous art—to what destination? Into some new light? Towards some new sun? But who would try to articulate exactly what all these masters of new linguistic forms themselves could not clearly articulate? What is certain is that they were all tormented by the same Storm and Stress, that they all went about *seeking* in the same way, these last, great seekers! All of them with eyes and ears ruled by literature (the first artists educated in world literature);* usually writers themselves, in fact, poets, intermediaries and interminglers of the arts and the senses (as a musician, Wagner should be classified among the painters, as a poet among the musicians, as an overall artist among the actors); all of them fanatics of *expression* 'at all costs' (I single out Delacroix, Wagner's closest relative); all of them great explorers in the realm of the sublime, also of the hideous and horrible, and even greater explorers of effect, of presentation, of the art of the shop window; all of them talents far beyond their own genius—virtuosi through and through, with uncanny access to everything that seduces, tempts, forces, overturns; born enemies of logic and straight lines, desirous of the foreign, the exotic, the monstrous, the crooked, the self-contradictory; as people, Tantaluses of the will, arriviste plebeians who knew they were incapable of an aristocratic tempo, a *lento*, whether in living or creating (just think of Balzac, for example); unflagging workers, nearly destroying themselves by their work; moral antinomians and rebels, ambitious and insatiable without equilibrium or pleasure; all of them ultimately shattered and brought low by the Christian cross (and that is as it should be, for which of them would have been deep and original enough for a philosophy of the *Antichrist*?); on the whole an audaciously daring, splendidly powerful, high-flying and upward-wrenching sort of higher men who first had to teach their century (and it is a century of the *crowd*!) the concept of the 'higher man' . . .

Let Richard Wagner's German friends deliberate about whether there is something particularly German in Wagnerian art, or whether it is not its very distinction that it derives from *supra-German* sources and impulses: for in these reflections let us not underestimate just how essential a role in the cultivation of his type was played by Paris, a city he longed for out of a deep instinct in his most crucial period, and how the whole manner of his appearance, his self-apostleship could be perfected only by having encountered the model of the French socialists.* When we compare more subtly, we may credit it to Richard Wagner's German nature that he carried everything out more forcefully, boldly, harshly, ambitiously than a Frenchman of the nineteenth century could do (for we Germans are still closer to barbarism than the French are). Indeed, for the entire, so aged Latin race, the oddest thing that Richard Wagner ever created may be forever and not just for today inaccessible, unintuitable, inimitable: the figure of Siegfried, that *very free* man, who may indeed be far too free, too harsh, too cheerful, too healthy, too *anti-Catholic* for the taste of old and crumbling civilized peoples. In fact, he may even have been a sin against Romanticism, this anti-Romantic Siegfried: ah well, in his dreary old age Wagner richly made up for this sin when (anticipating an aesthetic taste that has meanwhile turned into politics) he began, with his characteristic religious vehemence, to preach, if not to walk, *the road to Rome*.

So that no one will misunderstand these last words of mine, I will also make use of some vigorous rhymes to reveal my intent to less finely tuned ears—what I would say *against* 'late Wagner' and his *Parsifal* music.

> —Can this be German?—
> This fevered shrieking from a German heart?
> A German body rends itself apart?
> German the priest's hands' invocation,
> Sweet-incensed senses-titillation?
> And German this halting, dashing, reeling,
> This incoherent ding-dong pealing?
> This nuns' eye-rolling, Ave-churchbell chiming,
> The fake-ecstatic, pious rhyming?
> —Can *this* be German?—
> You stand now at the threshold: so take heed!
> For what you hear is *Rome—Rome's Wordless Creed!**

SECTION NINE

WHAT IS NOBLE?

Distance from the herd!

257

IN the past, every elevation of the type 'human being' was achieved by an aristocratic society—and this will always be the case: by a society that believes in a great ladder of hierarchy and value differentiation between people and that requires slavery in one sense or another. Without the *grand feeling of distance* that grows from inveterate class differences, from the ruling caste's constant view downwards onto its underlings and tools, and from its equally constant practice in obeying and commanding, in holding down and holding at arm's length—without this grand attitude, that other, more mysterious attitude could never exist, that longing for ever greater distances within the soul itself, the development of ever higher, rarer, more far-flung, extensive, spacious inner states, in short, the elevation of the type 'human being', the continual 'self-overcoming of the human', to use a moral formula in a supra-moral sense. To be sure, we must not give in to any humanitarian delusions about these aristocratic societies' historical origins (that is, about the preconditions for that elevation of the type 'human'): the truth is harsh. Let us not mince words in describing to ourselves the *beginnings* of every previous higher culture on earth! People who still had a nature that was natural, barbarians in every terrible sense of the word, predatory humans, whose strength of will and desire for power were still unbroken, threw themselves upon the weaker, more well-behaved, peaceable, perhaps trading or stockbreeding races, or upon old, crumbling cultures whose remaining life-force was flickering out in a brilliant fireworks display of wit and depravity. At the beginning, the noble caste was always the barbarian caste: its dominance was not due to its physical strength primarily, but rather to its spiritual—these were the *more complete* human beings (which at every level also means the 'more complete beasts').

258

Corruption, as the expression of impending anarchy among the instincts and of the collapse of the emotional foundations called 'life': this corruption will vary fundamentally according to the form of life in which it manifests itself. When for example an aristocracy like pre-Revolutionary France tosses away its privileges with sublime revulsion and sacrifices itself to its excess of moral feeling, this is corruption: it was really only the final act of that centuries-long corruption that caused the aristocracy to abandon its tyrannical authority bit by bit and reduce itself to a *function* of the monarchy (and ultimately in fact to its ornament and showpiece). The crucial thing about a good and healthy aristocracy, however, is that it does *not* feel that it is a function (whether of monarchy or community) but rather its *essence* and highest justification—and that therefore it has no misgivings in condoning the sacrifice of a vast number of people who must *for its sake* be oppressed and diminished into incomplete people, slaves, tools. Its fundamental belief must simply be that society can *not* exist for its own sake, but rather only as a foundation and scaffolding to enable a select kind of creature to ascend to its higher task and in general to its higher *existence*— much like those sun-loving climbing plants on Java (called *sipo matador*) whose tendrils encircle an oak tree so long and so repeatedly that finally, high above it but still supported by it, they are able to unfold their coronas in the free air and make a show of their happiness.—

259

To refrain from injuring, abusing, or exploiting one another; to equate another person's will with our own: in a certain crude sense this can develop into good manners between individuals, if the preconditions are in place (that is, if the individuals have truly similar strength and standards and if they are united within one single social body). But if we were to try to take this principle further and possibly even make it the *basic principle of society*, it would immediately be revealed for what it is: a will to *deny* life, a principle for dissolution and decline. We must think through the reasons for this and resist all sentimental frailty: life itself *in its essence* means appropriating, injuring, overpowering those who are foreign and weaker; oppression, harshness, forcing one's own forms on others, incorporation, and at the very least, at the very mildest, exploitation—but why should we keep using this kind of language, that has from time immemorial been infused with a slanderous intent? Even that social body whose individuals, as we have just assumed above, treat one another as equals (this happens in every healthy aristocracy) must itself, if the body is vital and not moribund, do to other bodies everything that the individuals within it refrain from doing to one another: it will have to be the will to power incarnate, it will want to grow, to reach out around itself, pull towards itself, gain the upper hand—not out of some morality or immorality, but because it is *alive*, and because life simply *is* the will to power. This, however, more than anything else, is what the common European consciousness resists learning; people everywhere are rhapsodizing, even under the guise of science, about future social conditions that will have lost their 'exploitative character'—to my ear that sounds as if they were promising to invent a life form that would refrain from all organic functions. 'Exploitation' is not part of a decadent or imperfect, primitive society: it is part of the *fundamental nature* of living things, as its fundamental organic function; it is a consequence of the true will to power, which is simply the will to life.

Assuming that this is innovative as theory—as reality it is the *original fact* of all history: let us at least be this honest with ourselves!

260

While perusing the many subtler and cruder moral codes that have prevailed or still prevail on earth thus far, I found that certain traits regularly recurred in combination, linked to one another—until finally two basic types were revealed and a fundamental difference leapt out at me. There are *master moralities* and *slave moralities*.* I would add at once that in all higher and more complex cultures, there are also apparent attempts to mediate between the two moralities, and even more often a confusion of the two and a mutual misunderstanding, indeed sometimes even their violent juxtaposition—even in the same person, within one single breast. Moral value distinctions have emerged either from among a masterful kind, pleasantly aware of how it differed from those whom it mastered, or else from among the mastered, those who were to varying degrees slaves or dependants. In the first case, when it is the masters who define the concept 'good', it is the proud, exalted states of soul that are thought to distinguish and define the hierarchy. The noble person keeps away from those beings who express the opposite of these elevated, proud inner states: he despises them. Let us note immediately that in this first kind of morality the opposition 'good' and 'bad' means about the same thing as 'noble' and 'despicable'—the opposition 'good' and *'evil'* has a different origin. The person who is cowardly or anxious or petty or concerned with narrow utility is despised; likewise the distrustful person with his constrained gaze, the self-disparager, the craven kind of person who endures maltreatment, the importunate flatterer, and above all the liar: all aristocrats hold the fundamental conviction that the common people are liars. 'We truthful ones'—that is what the ancient Greek nobility called themselves. It is obvious that moral value distinctions everywhere are first attributed to *people* and only later and in a derivative fashion applied to *actions*: for that reason moral historians commit a crass error by starting with questions such as: 'Why do we praise an empathetic action?' The noble type of person feels *himself* as determining value—he does not need approval, he judges that 'what is harmful to me is harmful per se', he knows that he is the one who causes things to be revered in the first place, he *creates values*. Everything that he knows of himself he reveres: this kind of moral code is self-glorifying. In the foreground is a feeling of fullness, of overflowing power, of happiness in great tension, an awareness of a wealth that would like to bestow and share—the noble person will also help the unfortunate, but not, or not entirely, out of pity, but rather from the urgency created by an excess of power. The noble person reveres the power in himself, and also his power over himself, his ability to speak and to be silent, to enjoy the practice of severity and harshness towards himself and to respect everything that is severe and harsh. 'Wotan placed a harsh heart within my breast,' goes a line in an old Scandinavian saga: that is how it is written from the heart of a proud Viking—and rightly so. For this kind of a person is proud *not* to be made for pity; and so the hero of the saga adds a warning: 'If your heart is not harsh when you are young, it will never become harsh.' The noble and brave people who think like this are the most removed from that other moral code which sees the sign of morality in pity or altruistic behaviour or *désintéressement*;* belief in ourselves, pride in ourselves, a fundamental hostility and irony towards 'selflessness'—these are as surely a part of a noble morality as caution and a slight disdain towards empathetic feelings and 'warm hearts'.

It is the powerful who *understand* how to revere, it is their art form, their realm of invention. Great reverence for old age and for origins (all law is based upon this twofold reverence), belief in ancestors and prejudice in their favour and to the disadvantage of the next generation—these are typical in the morality of the powerful; and if, conversely, people of 'modern ideas' believe in progress and 'the future' almost by instinct and show an increasing lack of respect for old age, that alone suffices to reveal the ignoble origin of these 'ideas'. Most of all, however, the master morality is foreign and embarrassing to current taste because of the severity of its fundamental principle: that we have duties only towards our peers, and that we may treat those of lower rank, anything foreign, as we think best or 'as our heart dictates' or in any event 'beyond good and evil'—pity and the like should be thought of in this context. The ability and duty to feel enduring gratitude or vengefulness (both only within a circle of equals), subtlety in the forms of retribution, a refined concept of friendship, a certain need for enemies (as drainage channels for the emotions of envy, combativeness, arrogance—in essence, in order to be a good *friend*): these are the typical signs of a noble morality, which, as we have suggested, is not the morality of 'modern ideas' and is therefore difficult to sympathize with these days, also difficult to dig out and uncover.

It is different with the second type of morality, *slave morality*. Assuming that the raped, the oppressed, the suffering, the shackled, the weary, the insecure engage in moralizing, what will their moral value judgements have in common? They will probably express a pessimistic suspicion about the whole human condition, and they might condemn the human being along with his condition. The slave's eye does not readily apprehend the virtues of the powerful: he is sceptical and distrustful, he is *keenly* distrustful of everything that the powerful revere as 'good'—he would like to convince himself that even their happiness is not genuine. Conversely, those qualities that serve to relieve the sufferers' existence are brought into relief and bathed in light: this is where pity, a kind, helpful hand, a warm heart, patience, diligence, humility, friendliness are revered—for in this context, these qualities are most useful and practically the only means of enduring an oppressive existence. Slave morality is essentially a morality of utility. It is upon this hearth that the famous opposition 'good' and '*evil*' originates— power and dangerousness, a certain fear-inducing, subtle strength that keeps contempt from surfacing, are translated by experience into evil. According to slave morality, then, the 'evil' person evokes fear; according to master morality, it is exactly the 'good' person who evokes fear and wants to evoke it, while the 'bad' person is felt to be despicable. The opposition comes to a head when, in terms of slave morality, a hint of condescension (it may be slight and well intentioned) clings even to those whom this morality designates as 'good', since within a slave mentality a good person must in any event be *harmless*: he is good-natured, easily deceived, perhaps a bit stupid, a *bonhomme*.* Wherever slave morality gains the upper hand, language shows a tendency to make a closer association of the words 'good' and 'stupid'.

A last fundamental difference: the longing for *freedom*, an instinct for the happiness and nuances of feeling free, is as necessarily a part of slave morals and morality as artistic, rapturous reverence and devotion invariably signal an aristocratic mentality and judgement.

From this we can immediately understand why *passionate* love (our European speciality) absolutely must have a noble origin: the Provençal poet-knights are acknowledged to have invented it, those splendid, inventive people of the '*gai saber*'* to whom Europe owes so much—virtually its very self.

261

Among the things that a noble person finds most difficult to understand is vanity:* he will be tempted to deny its existence, even when a different kind of person thinks that he grasps it with both hands. He has trouble imagining beings who would try to elicit a good opinion about themselves that they themselves do not hold (and thus do not 'deserve', either) and who then themselves nevertheless *believe* this good opinion. To him, that seems in part so tasteless and irreverent towards one's self, and in part so grotesquely irrational that he would prefer to consider vanity an anomaly and in most of the cases when it is mentioned, doubt that it exists. He will say, for example: 'I may be wrong about my worth, but on the other hand require that others recognize the worth that I assign—but that is not vanity (rather it is arrogance, or more often what is called "humility", and also "modesty").' Or he will say: 'There are many reasons to be glad about other people's good opinion of me, perhaps because I revere and love them and am happy about every one of their joys, or else perhaps because their good opinion under-scores and strengthens my belief in my own private good opinion, or perhaps because the good opinion of others, even in the cases where I do not share it, is nevertheless useful or promises to be useful to me—but none of that is vanity.' It takes compulsion, particularly with the help of history, for the noble person to realize that in every sort of dependent social class, from time immemorial, a common person *was* only what he was *thought to be*—completely unused to determining values himself, he also attributed to himself no other value than what his masters attributed to him (creating values is truly the *master's privilege*). We may understand it as the result of a tremendous atavism that even now, the ordinary person first *waits* for someone else to have an opinion about him, and then instinctively submits to it—and by no means merely to 'good' opinions, but also to bad or improper ones (just think, for example, how most pious women esteem or under-esteem themselves in accordance with what they have learned from their father con-fessors, or what pious Christians in general learn from their Church). Now, in fact, in conformity with the slow emergence of a democratic order of things (this in turn caused by mixing the blood of masters and slaves), the originally noble and rare impulse to ascribe one's own value to oneself and to 'think well' of oneself, is more and more encouraged and widespread: but always working against it is an older, broader, and more thoroughly entrenched tendency—and when it comes to 'vanity', this older tendency becomes master of the newer. The vain person takes pleasure in *every* good opinion that he hears about himself (quite irrespective of any prospect of its utility, and likewise irrespective of truth or falsehood), just as he suffers at any bad opinion: for he submits

himself to both, he *feels* submissive to both, from that old submissive instinct that breaks out in him.

It is the 'slave' in the blood of the vain person, a remnant of the
slave's craftiness (and how much of the 'slave' is still left, for
example, in women today!) that tries to *seduce* him to good opinions
of himself; and it is likewise the slave who straightway kneels down
before these opinions, as if he himself were not the one who had
called them forth.

So I repeat: vanity is an atavism.

262

A *species* comes into being, a type grows strong and fixed, by
struggling for a long time with essentially similar *unfavourable*
conditions. Conversely, as we know from the experiences of stock-
breeders, a species that is given over-abundant nourishment and
extra protection and care generally shows an immediate and very
pronounced tendency to variations in type, and is rich in marvels
and monstrosities (and in monstrous vices, too). Now let us consider
an aristocratic community, such as the ancient Greek *polis*, say, or
Venice, as an organization whose voluntary or involuntary purpose
is to *breed*: there are people coexisting in it, relying on one another,
who want to further their species, chiefly because they *must* further
it or run some sort of terrible risk of extermination. In such a case,
good will, excess, and protection, those conditions that favour
variation, are missing; the species needs to remain a species, something that by virtue of its very harshness, symmetry, and simplicity
of form, can be furthered and in general endure throughout all its
continual struggles with its neighbours or with oppressed peoples
who threaten rebellion or revolt. From its most diverse experience
the species learns which qualities have particularly contributed to
its survival, to its continuing victory in defiance of all gods and
peoples: these qualities it calls virtues, and these are the only virtues
that it cultivates. It is done harshly, indeed it demands harshness;
every aristocratic moral code is intolerant, be it in educating its
children, in disposing of its women, in its marital customs, in the
relations of its old and young, or in its punitive laws (which apply
only to the deviant); even intolerance itself is counted as a virtue,
going by the name of 'justice'. A type like this, with few but

very strong characteristics, a species of severe, warlike, prudently taciturn, closed and uncommunicative people (and as such most subtly attuned to the charms and nuances* of society) thus becomes established beyond generational change; as mentioned above, its continual struggle with the same *unfavourable* conditions causes the type to become fixed and harsh. Eventually, however, it arrives at a period of good fortune, the tremendous tension relaxes; perhaps there are no longer any enemies among its neighbours and its means for living, even for enjoying life, are plentiful. At one single stroke the coercing bond of the old discipline is torn apart: it is no longer felt to be essential, critical for existence—if such discipline wished to endure, it could do so only as a kind of *luxury*, as an archaic *taste*. Variation, whether as deviance (into something higher, finer, more rare) or as degeneration and monstrosity is suddenly on the scene in all its greatest fullness and splendour; the individual dares to be an individual and stand out. During these historical turning points, we see splendid, manifold, jungle-like upgrowths and upsurges coexisting and often inextricably tangled up with one another; competition for growth assumes a kind of *tropical* tempo and there is a tremendous perishing and causing-to-perish, owing to the wild egoisms that challenge one another with seeming explosiveness, struggling 'for sun and light', and no longer knowing how to derive any set of limits, any restraint, any forbearance from their earlier moral code. It was this very moral code, in fact, that stored up the energy to such a monstrous extent, that tensed the bow so ominously—and now that code is, or is becoming 'obsolete'. The dangerous and sinister point is reached where the greater, more differentiated, richer life *survives beyond* the old morality; the 'individual' is left standing, forced to be his own lawgiver, to create his own arts and wiles of self-preservation, self-advancement, self-redemption. Nothing left but new 'What for?'s and new 'How to?'s; no more common formulae; misunderstanding and mistrust in league with one another; decline, decay, and the greatest aspirations terribly entangled; the genius of the race spilling good and bad out of all the horns of plenty; an ominous simultaneity of spring and autumn, full of new delights and veils that are intrinsic to the new, still unplumbed, still unwearied decay. Danger is present once again, the mother of morality, the great danger, this time displaced into the individual, into the neighbour or friend, into the street, into our own children, into our own hearts, into everything that is most secretly our own of wishing and wanting: what will the moral philosophers who emerge during this period find to preach about? They will discover, these keen observers and idlers, that things are quickly going downhill, that everything around them is turning to decay and causing decay, that nothing lasts past tomorrow, with the exception of one single species of human being, the incurably *mediocre*. The mediocre alone have the prospect of continuing, of having descendants—they are the people of the future, the only survivors. 'Be like them! Become mediocre!' will henceforth be the only moral code that still makes sense, that can still find an ear.

But it is hard to preach, this morality of the mediocre!—it can never admit to itself what it is and what it wants! It has to talk of proportion and dignity and duty and brotherly love it will not find it easy to *hide its irony*!

263

There is an *instinct for rank* that more than anything else is itself the sign of *high* rank; there is a *joy* in the nuances of reverence that hints at a noble origin and habits. The subtlety, kindness, and greatness of a soul are dangerously tested when it encounters something that is of the first rank, but as yet unprotected by awe of authority against crude, intrusive poking; something unmarked, undiscovered, tentative, perhaps capriciously cloaked or disguised, going its way like a living touchstone. A person who has taken upon himself the task and habit of sounding out souls and who wishes to establish the ultimate value of a soul, its irrevocable, inherent hierarchical position, will make manifold use of one particular art above all others: he will test the soul for its *instinct for reverence*. *Différence engendre haine:** when a holy vessel, a jewel from a locked shrine, or a book with the sign of a great destiny is borne past, the commonness of certain natures suddenly splatters forth like dirty water; and on the other hand, there can be an involuntary loss of words, a hesitation in the eye, a quieting of all gestures which conveys the fact that a soul *feels* the proximity of something most worthy of reverence. The way that Europeans have so far more or less continued to revere the *Bible* may be the best part of the discipline and refinement in manners that Europe owes to Christianity: books with this kind of depth and ultimate significance must be protected by a tyrannical external authority in order to win those thousands of years of *duration* that are required for their full exploration and comprehension. Much has been achieved when the great crowd (the shallow and diarrhoeal of every kind) has finally been trained to feel that it may not touch everything; that there are holy experiences in the presence of which it must remove its shoes and keep its dirty hands off—this is virtually its highest ascent to humanity. Conversely, the so-called educated people, believers in 'modern ideas', stir our revulsion most of all perhaps by their lack of shame, their easy impertinent eyes and hands that go touching everything, licking, groping; and it is possible that among the common people, the low people, among today's peasants especially, there is *relatively* more nobility in taste and sense of reverence than in the newspaper-reading intellectual *demi-monde*, the educated.

264

There is no way to efface from a person's soul what his ancestors best and most regularly liked to do: whether they were avid economizers, say, appendages of their desks and money-boxes, modest and bourgeois in their desires, modest too in their virtues; or whether they lived in the habit of commanding from dawn to dusk, enjoying rough pleasures and along with them perhaps even rougher duties and responsibilities; or whether at a certain point they ultimately sacrificed their old privileges of birth and property in order to live for their beliefs (their 'god'), as people of an unshakeable and sensitive conscience that blushes at every compromise. It is simply impossible that a person would *not* have his parents' and forefathers' qualities and preferences in his body—whatever appearances may say to the contrary. This is a problem of race. If we know something about the parents, then we are allowed a stab at the child: a certain repellent intemperance, a certain narrow envy, a clumsy self-righteousness (these three together have ever made up the true rabble type)—these things will be passed on to the child as surely as corrupted blood; and all that the best upbringing or education can achieve is to *deceive* others about such an inheritance.

And what other intention do today's upbringing and education have! In our very popular, which is to say, rabble-like age, 'upbringing' and 'education' *must* be essentially the art of deception—deceiving away the origins, the inherited rabble in body and soul. Nowadays an educator who would preach truthfulness above all else and constantly call out to his charges, 'Be genuine! Be natural! Be yourselves!'—before too long, even such a virtuous and naive idiot would learn to reach for that *furca* of Horace's, in order to *naturam expellere*: with what success? 'Rabble' *usque recurret.**

265

Running the risk of displeasing innocent ears, I would assert that egoism is part of the nature of noble souls—I mean that steadfast belief that other beings must naturally submit to 'our' kind of being and sacrifice themselves to it. The noble soul accepts its egoistic condition without any sort of question mark, also without any feeling of harshness, coercion, or wilfulness, but rather as something that may be based in the primeval law of things: if a noble soul were to seek a name for this, it would say, 'This is Justice itself.' In certain circumstances that at first cause it to hesitate, the soul admits to itself that there are others with entitlements equal to its own; as soon as this question of rank has been clarified, it moves among these equally entitled equals as assured in its modesty or tender reverence as when dealing with itself—according to an inborn, heavenly mechanism that all the stars understand. This is one *more* aspect of the soul's egoism, this subtle self-limitation in the society of its equals (every star is this kind of egoist): in these equals and in the rights that it yields to them, it reveres *itself*; it has no doubt that mutual reverence and rights are the *essence* of all society and also part of the natural state of things. The noble soul gives as it takes, from out of the passionate and excitable instinct of requital that is at its core. The concept of 'mercy' has no meaning *inter pares,** no aroma: there may be a sublime way of letting ourselves be showered, as it were, with gifts from above, drinking them in thirstily like dewdrops—but the noble soul is not adept in arts or gestures of this kind. Its egoism stops it here: it never really likes to look 'up'—preferring to look either *ahead*, horizontal and slow, or downwards: *it knows that it is above.*

266

'The only person we can really respect is one who is not *seeking* himself.'—Goethe to Councillor Schlosser.

267

The Chinese have a saying which mothers even teach their children: *siao-sin*, 'make your heart *small*!' This really is the fundamental tendency in late civilizations: I have no doubt that the first thing an ancient Greek would notice about us contemporary Europeans is that we make ourselves small—for that reason alone he would find us 'offensive'.

268

What does commonness really mean?

Words are acoustic signs for concepts; concepts, however, are more or less precise figurative signs for frequently recurring and simultaneous sensations, for groups of sensations. Using the same words is not enough to ensure mutual understanding: we must also use the same words for the same category of inner experiences; ultimately, we must have the same experiences in *common*. That is why the individuals of one single people understand one another better than the members of different peoples do, even when they are using the same language; or to put it better, when people have lived for a long time under similar conditions (of climate, soil, danger, necessities, work), then something *comes into being* as a result, something that 'goes without saying', a people. In all their souls a similar number of often-recurring experiences has prevailed over others less frequent: because of these experiences, they understand one another quickly, and ever more quickly (the history of language is the history of a process of abbreviation); because of this quick understanding, they are connected, closely and ever more closely. The greater the danger, the greater the need to agree quickly and easily about what is necessary; not to be misunderstood in times of danger—people in society find this absolutely crucial. We carry out this test even in friendships or love affairs: both are doomed as soon as one person discovers that the same words have caused different feelings, thoughts, hunches, wishes, fears in the

other person. (The fear of 'eternal misunderstanding': that is
the benevolent genius that so often keeps people of different sexes
from an over-hasty attachment when their senses and heart are
urging it—and *not* some Schopenhauerian 'genius of the species'—!)
Which of the groups of sensations within a soul come alive most
quickly, to speak or command—that decides the overall hierarchy
of the soul's values and ultimately determines its table of goods. A
person's value judgements reveal something about how his soul is
structured, and what, in its view, constitutes the conditions essential
to its life, its real necessity. If we now assume that necessity has
always brought together only those people who could indicate by
similar signs their similar needs, similar experiences: then this is
as much as to say that the easy *communicability* of necessity (which
ultimately means having experienced only average and *common*
experiences) must, of all the forces that have heretofore controlled
humans, have been the most forceful. The more similar, the more
common people: these have always been and continue to be at an
advantage, while those who are more select, subtle, rare, harder to
understand are readily left alone, come to harm in their isolation,
and rarely procreate. We have to call upon enormous counterforces
in order to thwart this natural, all-too-natural *progressus in simile*,*
the further development of humans who are similar, ordinary,
average, herd-like—*common*!

269

The more a psychologist (an inevitable, a born psychologist and
diviner of souls) turns to the more select cases and people, the
greater is his danger of being suffocated by his pity: he *needs*
harshness and cheerfulness more than other people do. For it seems
to be the rule that higher people come to ruin, that souls that are
constituted differently are destroyed: it is terrible to have this rule
continually before our eyes. The repeated torment of a psychologist
who has discovered this destruction, who has made the initial, and
then *nearly* invariable discovery of all this inner 'wretchedness' in
the higher person, this eternal and all-encompassing 'Too late!'—
his torment may one day make him turn with bitterness against his
own fate and attempt self-destruction—'come to ruin' himself. We
notice that virtually every psychologist prefers the company of

everyday, predictable people: this reveals his constant need of
healing, of a sort of refuge and forgetting, far from the burdens
that his insights and incisions, that his 'handiwork' has laid on his
conscience. He is characteristically afraid of his memory. He easily
grows silent at other people's judgements: he listens with a stony
face as they speak in terms of respect, honour, love, transfiguration
about matters that he has *seen*—or he may hide his silence by
agreeing adamantly with some foreground opinion. The paradox
of his situation may even reach the frightful point where those
cases that have triggered in him great pity as well as great contempt,
have triggered in the crowd, the educated, the enthusiasts a feeling
of great reverence; theirs is a reverence for 'great men' and per-
forming animals, for whose sake we bless and esteem the fatherland,
the earth, the dignity of humanity, and ourselves; men whom we
ask our children to look up to and emulate . . .

And who knows whether the same process has not occurred in
all the great cases: the crowd adored a god—and the 'god' was only
a poor sacrificial animal! Success has always been the biggest liar—
and the 'work' itself is a success; a great statesman, a conqueror,
an explorer is disguised to the point of unrecognizability by his
creations; it is the 'work', whether of an artist or of a philosopher,
that first invents the creator, the one who is said to have created it.
'Great men', as others revere them, are poor little tales written
after the fact; in the world of historical value, counterfeits *predomi-
nate*. Take these great poets, for example—Byron, Musset, Poe,
Leopardi, Kleist, Gogol—just as they are, perhaps as they have to
be: people of the moment, inspired, sensual, childish, frivolous and
precipitous in their trust and distrust; with souls that usually shield
some fracture in need of concealment; often taking vengeance with
their works for an inner defilement; often seeking in flights of fancy
oblivion from their all-too-faithful memory; often lost in and almost
in love with the mire, until they finally become like will-o'-the-
wisps around a swamp and *pretend* to be stars (and then the common
people will likely call them idealists); often struggling with a prolonged revulsion, with the recurrent spectre of disbelief that chills
them, forcing them to yearn for *gloria* and to feed on 'faith itself'
from out of the hands of intoxicated flatterers: what a *torment* these
great artists and all higher people in general are for the person who
once has found them out! It is understandable, then, that *they* are

the ones at whom women especially (being clairvoyant in the world of suffering and, unfortunately, addicted to helping and rescuing far beyond their abilities to do so) like to direct their outbursts of limitless, utterly devoted *pity*, which the crowd, especially the reverent crowd, does not understand and saddles with smug or intrusive meanings. Women are regularly deceived about the power of their pity; they would like to believe that love can do *anything*—that is their true *faith*. A person with true knowledge of the heart guesses, alas, how poor, stupid, helpless, presumptuous, misguided, more easily destructive than redemptive is even the best, the deepest love!

It is possible that beneath the holy tale and camouflage that is the life of Jesus, lies hidden one of the most painful cases of martyrdom out of *knowledge about love*: the martyrdom of the most innocent and desirous heart, one that never had enough of any human love, that *demanded* to love and to be loved and nothing else besides, with harshness, with madness, with frightful outbursts against those who denied him this love. It is the story of a poor man, unsatisfied and insatiable in matters of love, who had to invent hell in order to send there the people who did not *want* to love him—and who, initiated into human love, finally had to invent a God who was all love, all *capacity* for love—who takes pity on human love because it is so very paltry, so ignorant! One who feels like that, who *knows* about love like that—*seeks* death.

But why should we muse about such painful things? Assuming that we are not compelled to do so.

270

The spiritual arrogance and loathing of any person who has suffered deeply (hierarchy is virtually determined by *how* deeply people can suffer), his horrifying certainty, pervading and colouring him completely, that because of his suffering he *knows more* than the wisest or most clever people can, having been recognized and 'at home' in many far-off, frightful worlds about which 'all of *you* know nothing!'—this silent, spiritual arrogance of the sufferer, this pride of the man chosen for understanding, the 'initiate', the near-sacrifice, requires all forms of disguise to protect it from the touch of intrusive or pitying hands and in general from everything that is not its equal in pain. Deep suffering makes us noble; it separates. One of the subtlest forms of camouflage is epicureanism and the display of a certain brave aesthetic taste that treats suffering casually and resists all things sad or deep. There are 'cheerful people' who make use of cheerfulness because it causes others to misunderstand them—they *want* to be misunderstood. There are 'scientific people' who make use of science because it gives them a cheerful aspect, and because scientific work leads us to conclude that humans are superficial—they *want* to seduce us to a false conclusion. There are free, impertinent spirits who would like to conceal and contest their possession of hearts that are proud, shattered, irreparable; and at times folly itself becomes the mask for a wretched, all-too-certain knowledge.

From which we can conclude that it is a sign of a more subtle humanity to revere 'the mask' and not pursue psychology or curiosity in the wrong place.

271

What separates two people most deeply is their differing understanding and degree of cleanliness. No matter how kind and helpful they are to one another, no matter how great their mutual good will: in the end it is always the same—they 'can't stand the smell' of one another! A person burdened with a supreme instinct for cleanliness is put in the strangest and most dangerous isolation, like a saint—for that is exactly what saintliness is: the highest spiritualization of this instinct. A certain complicit knowledge of indescribable fulfilment in the happiness of the bath, a certain avid thirst that continually sends the soul out of the night into the morning and out of the gloom, out of 'gloominess' into light, brilliance, depth, subtlety: just as we are *distinguished* by such a tendency (it is a noble tendency), so does it also *separate* us.

The pity of the saint is a pity for the *filth* of things human, all too human. And there are degrees and heights at which he will even experience pity itself as pollution, filth.

272

Signs of nobility: never to think of reducing our duties into duties for everyone; not to want to transfer or share our own responsibility; to count our privileges and their exercise among our *duties*.

273

A person striving for great things will regard anyone he meets upon his path either as a means or as a postponement and an obstacle—or else as a temporary resting place. His particular, characteristic, highly constituted *kindness* to his fellow humans is possible only when he has reached his highest level and is in command. Impatience and his awareness that he is meanwhile condemned to play-acting (for even war is a play-acting and conceals, as every end is concealed by its means) ruins all company for him: this kind of person knows solitude and knows the most poisonous thing about it.

274

The problem of those who wait.—It takes a lot of luck and much that is unfathomable for a higher person, in whom the solution to a problem is sleeping, to begin to act (or break free, as we might say) at the right time. On the average, it does *not* happen, and in all corners of the earth people are sitting and waiting, hardly knowing the extent of their waiting, and knowing even less that they are waiting in vain. Sometimes, too, the wake-up call—that chance event that gives them 'permission' to act—comes too late, when their best youth and strength for action have already been consumed by sitting still. And how many a one, upon 'springing up', found to his dismay that his limbs were asleep and his mind already too heavy! 'It is too late', he said to himself, no longer believing in himself and forever after useless.

Could it be that a 'Raffael without hands',* taking the phrase in its broadest sense, is not the exception in the realm of genius, but rather the rule?

Perhaps it is not genius that is so rare, but rather the five hundred *hands* it requires in order to tyrannize καιρός, 'the right time', in order to seize the moment!

275

If we do not *want* to see the higher things about a person, we look all the more carefully for the things about him that are low and in the foreground—and by so doing reveal ourselves.

276

Whenever there is injury or loss, the lower and cruder soul is better off than the nobler: the dangers to the latter have to be the greater; in fact, considering how many vital necessities it has, there is a tremendous probability that it will come to harm and perish.

If a lizard has lost a digit, it will grow back again: that's not how it is with people.

277

—More's the pity! The same old story all over again! After we have finished building our house, we notice that we have inadvertently learned something in the process, something that we absolutely *should* have known before we—began to build. The eternal, sorrowful 'Too late!'

The melancholy of everything *completed*! . . .

278

Wanderer, who are you? I see you go your way, without scorn, without love, with inscrutable eyes; misty and sad like a sounding weight that has returned out of every depth into the light again, unsatisfied (what was it seeking down there?), with a heart that does not sigh, with lips that conceal their disgust, with a hand that reaches out only slowly now: who are you? What have you done? Rest here a while: this spot is welcoming to every guest—refresh yourself! And whoever you may be—what is your pleasure now? What will serve to refresh you? Just name it: I'll offer you whatever I have!

'Refresh me? Refresh me? Oh, you curious man, what are you saying! But do give me, I beg of you . . .'

What? What? Just tell me!

'Another mask! A second mask!'

279

People of deep sorrow reveal themselves when they are happy: they have a way of grasping happiness as if they would like to crush and suffocate it, out of jealousy—ah, they know only too well that it will run away from them!

280

'Oh dear! Oh dear! What's this? Isn't he going—backwards?'

Yes! But you misunderstand him if that worries you. He is going backwards as people do when they are about to take a great leap.—

281

'Will you believe what I am going to say now? But I insist that you believe me: I have thought of myself, about myself only poorly, only very rarely, only under pressure, always reluctant to "get to the point", ready to digress away from "me", never believing in an outcome—all this due to my ungovernable distrust of the *possibility* of self-knowledge. This has taken me to the point of feeling that there is a *contradictio in adjecto** even in that concept of "immediate knowledge" accepted by the theoreticians: this whole phenomenon is virtually the surest thing I know about myself. I must have some kind of resistance to *believing* anything definite about myself.

Could a riddle be hiding here? Probably; but not the sort that I myself will chew on, luckily.

Could it explain the species that I belong to?

But not to me: which is how I want it.'

282

'But what happened to you?'

'I don't know,' he said hesitantly, 'perhaps the harpies flew across my table.'

It sometimes happens nowadays that a mild-mannered, moderate, restrained person suddenly starts to rage, smash dishes, upturn tables, scream, fume, insult the whole world—and then finally turns away, ashamed, furious with himself—where to? what for? To starve on the fringes? To choke on his memory?

Anyone who has the appetites of a great, discriminating soul, who only rarely finds his table set and his nourishment provided, will always be in great danger: but today that danger is extra-ordinary. Thrown into a noisy and vulgar age, whose bowl of food he does not wish to share, he can easily perish from hunger and thirst, or—if he finally does 'dig in'—from sudden nausea.

All of us have probably been seated at tables where we do not belong; and the most spiritual of us particularly, those who are hardest to nourish, are familiar with that dangerous dyspepsia that arises from a sudden, disappointing insight about our food or table partners—*after-dinner nausea.*

283

We demonstrate a subtle and also noble self-control—assuming that we want to praise at all—by praising only where we do *not* agree (otherwise, after all, we would only be praising ourselves, which is contrary to good taste). To be sure, such self-control offers a nice impetus and occasion for being constantly *misunderstood*. If we want to grant ourselves this truly luxurious moral and aesthetic taste, we cannot live among intellectual fools, but rather among people who can still be amused by the subtleties of misunderstandings and misconceptions (or else we will have to pay dearly for it!).

'He praises me: *therefore* he thinks I am right'—this sort of idiotic conclusion is always ruining life for us hermits, for it sends the idiots our way, as neighbours or friends.

284

To go through life with tremendous, proud calmness; always beyond . . . To feel or not to feel our emotions, our Pros and Cons, as we see fit, to condescend to them for hours at a time; to *sit upon* them, as we do upon a horse, and often an ass—for we need to know how to capitalize on their stupidity as well as their fire. To hold on to our three hundred foreground reasons; also our dark glasses, for there are times when no one may look into our eyes, and even less into our 'reasons'. And to choose to keep company with that roguish and cheerful vice Courtesy. And to remain master of our four virtues: courage, insight, sympathy, solitude. For we think solitude is a virtue, a sublime, exceeding need for cleanliness, born from knowing what unavoidably unclean things must transpire when people touch one another ('in company'). Somehow, somewhere, sometime, every commonality makes us—'common'.

285

The greatest events and thoughts (but the greatest thoughts are the greatest events) are the last to be understood: the generations that live contemporaneously with these events do not *experience* them: they live past them. Something similar takes place as in the heavens. The light of the farthest stars is the last to reach human beings; and until it has arrived, people *deny* that out there, there are—stars. 'How many centuries does a spirit need in order to be understood?'—that, too, is a measuring stick; with it, too, we can create the sort of hierarchy and etiquette required—for spirit and star.

286

'Up here the view is clear, the spirit exalted.'*

But there is an opposite kind of person who is likewise at the top and likewise has a clear view—but looks *down*.

287

What is noble? What meaning does the word 'noble' still have for us today? As the rule of the rabble begins, under this heavy, cloudy sky that makes everything opaque and leaden, how is a noble person revealed, by what do we recognize him?

It is not his actions that identify him (actions are always ambiguous, always unfathomable). Nor is it his 'works'. There are plenty of artists and scholars these days whose works reveal that they are motivated by a great desire to be noble: but just this very need *for* nobility is fundamentally different from the needs of the noble soul itself, and virtually the eloquent and dangerous sign of its absence. It is not works, it is *faith* that is decisive here and establishes a hierarchy, to take up an old religious formula again in a new and deeper sense: some fundamental certainty of a noble soul about itself, something that cannot be sought or found or, perhaps, lost.

The noble soul reveres itself.

288

There are people who cannot help having spirit, no matter how they turn and twist themselves and hold their hands over their traitorous eyes (as if a hand were not a traitor!)—in the end, it will always come out that they have something to hide, namely spirit. One of the best ways to deceive others as long as possible, at least, and successfully pretend to be more stupid than you are (often as handy as an umbrella in everyday life) is called *enthusiasm*, including what is included in it: virtue, for example. For according to Galiani, who was in a position to know: *vertu est enthousiasme.**

289

We always hear something of the echo of desolation in a hermit's writings, something of the whispering tone and shy, roundabout glance of solitude; out of his mightiest words, even out of his screams, we still hear the sound of a new and dangerous sort of silence, silencing. Anyone who has sat alone, in intimate dissension and dialogue with his soul, year in and year out, by day and by night; anyone whose cave (which might be a labyrinth, but also a gold mine) has turned him into a cave-bear or a treasure-digger or a treasure-keep and dragon; this person's ideas will themselves finally take on a characteristic twilight colour, an odour fully as much of the depths as of decay, something uncommunicative and stubborn that gusts coldly at every passer-by. The hermit does not believe that any philosopher (given that all philosophers have always first been hermits) ever expressed his true and final opinions in books: don't we write books precisely in order to hide what we keep hidden? Indeed, he will doubt whether a philosopher is even *capable* of 'final and true' opinions, whether at the back of his every cave a deeper cave is lying, is bound to lie—a wider, stranger, richer world over every surface, an abyss behind his every ground, beneath his every 'grounding'.* Every philosophy is a foreground philosophy—this is a hermit's judgement: 'There is something arbitrary about the fact that *he* stopped just here, looked back, looked around, that he did not dig deeper *just here*, but set down his spade—and there is also something suspicious about it.' Every philosophy also *conceals* a philosophy; every opinion is also a hiding place, every word also a mask.

290

Every deep thinker is more afraid of being understood than of being misunderstood. In the latter case his vanity may suffer; but in the former it will be his heart, his sympathy, forever saying, 'Oh, why do all of *you* also want to have it as hard as I?'

291

Human beings (complex, mendacious, artificial, impenetrable animals, and disturbing to other animals less because of their strength than because of their cunning and cleverness) invented the good conscience so that they could begin to enjoy their souls by *simplifying* them; and all of morality is one long, bold falsification that enables us to take what pleasure we can in observing the soul. From this vantage point, there may be much *more* to the concept of 'art' than we usually think.

292

A philosopher: that is a person who is constantly experiencing, seeing, hearing, suspecting, hoping, dreaming extraordinary things; who is struck by his own thoughts as if they came from outside, from above or below, as *his* sort of happenings and lightning bolts; who may even be himself a thunderstorm, going about pregnant with new lightning; an ominous person, ringed round by roaring and rumbling, gaping and sinister. A philosopher: alas, a being who often runs away from himself, is often afraid of himself—but too curious not to 'come to himself' eventually . . .

293

A man who says, 'That pleases me, I will make it my own and protect and defend it against everyone'; a man who can spearhead a cause, execute a decision, remain loyal to an idea, hold on to a woman, put down and punish an upstart; a man who has his sword and his anger, and to whom weak, suffering, oppressed people, as well as animals, naturally like to turn and belong; in short, a man who is by nature a *master*: when such a man feels pity—well! *this* pity has value. But why should we bother about the pity of those who suffer! Or of those who may even preach pity! Nearly everywhere in Europe today, there is a sickly, raw sensitivity about pain, and also a disgusting lack of restraint about complaining; a softening that would like to use religion and philosophical gibberish to paint itself as something greater—there is a veritable cult of suffering. The first thing that always leaps to the eye, I believe, is the *effeminacy* of what these fanatical groups christen as 'pity'.

We must be firm and thorough in banishing this newest form of bad taste; and I ultimately wish that people would lay the good charm '*gai saber*'* around their necks and hearts—'gay science', to make it clearer for the Germans.

294

The Olympian vice.—In defiance of that philosopher who as a true Englishman tried to give any thinking person's laughter a bad reputation ('Laughter is a nasty infirmity of human nature that any thinking person will endeavour to overcome.'*—Hobbes), I would actually go so far as to rank philosophers according to the level of their laughter—right up to the ones who are capable of *golden* laughter. And assuming that gods, too, are able to philosophize, as various of my conclusions force me to believe, then I do not doubt that when they do so, they know how to laugh in a new and superhuman fashion and at the expense of everything serious! Gods like to jeer: it seems that even at religious observances they cannot keep from laughing.

295

The genius of the heart, a heart of the kind belonging to that great secretive one, the tempter god and born Pied Piper of the conscience whose voice knows how to descend into the underworld of every soul, who does not utter a word or send a glance without its having a crease and aspect that entices, whose mastery consists in part in knowing how to seem—and seem not what he is, but rather what those who follow him take as one *more* coercion to press ever closer to him, to follow him ever more inwardly and completely: the genius of the heart that silences everything loud and self-satisfied and teaches it how to listen; that smoothes out rough souls and gives them a taste of a new longing (to lie still like a mirror so that the deep sky can mirror itself upon them); the genius of the heart, that teaches the foolish and over-hasty hand to hesitate and to grasp more daintily; that guesses the hidden and forgotten treasure, the drop of kindness and sweet spirituality lying under thick, turbid ice and is a divining rod for every speck of gold that has long lain buried in some dungeon of great mud and sand; the genius of the heart, from whose touch everyone goes forth the richer, neither reprieved nor surprised, not as if delighted or depressed by another's goodness, but rather richer in themselves, newer than before, opened up, breathed upon and sounded out by a warm wind, more unsure, perhaps, more brooding, breakable, broken, but full of hopes that still remain nameless, full of new willing and streaming, full of new not-willing and back-streaming . . . but my friends, what am I doing? Who is it that I am telling you about? Have I forgotten myself so much that I have not even told you his name? Unless, of course, you have already guessed who this questionable spirit and god may be, who demands this kind of *praise*.

Like everyone who since childhood has always been on the road and abroad, I too have had some strange and not necessarily harmless spirits run across my path, but especially the one I was just speaking about; and he has come again and again, the god *Dionysus*, no less, that great ambiguous tempter god, to whom, as you know, I once offered my first-born* in all secrecy and reverence. It seems to me that I was the last to *sacrifice* to him, for I found no one who understood what I was doing then. Meanwhile I learned much, all too much more about this god's philosophy and, as I mentioned, from mouth to mouth—I, the last disciple and initiate of the god Dionysus, may I now be finally allowed to begin to give you, my friends, a little taste, as much as I am permitted, of this philosophy? In an undertone, of course: for we are talking about much that is secret, new, strange, curious, uncanny. Just the very fact that Dionysus is a philosopher and that gods can philosophize too, seems to be something new and not without its dangers, perhaps making philosophers suspicious—you, my friends, have less to object to, unless the news should come too late and at the wrong hour: for they've informed me that you do not like to believe in God or gods these days. And perhaps to tell my tale candidly, I must go further than the severity of your listening habits would always like? Certainly the god I named went further in such dialogues, much further, and always kept many steps ahead of me . . . Indeed, if I were permitted to follow the human custom and call him by beautiful, ceremonious, splendid, virtuous names, I would have to speak in very grand terms about his courage as an explorer and discoverer, his daring eloquence, truthfulness, and love of wisdom. But this kind of a god has no use for all this worthy pomp and rubbish. 'Keep this,' he would say, 'for yourself and your own kind and whoever else may need it! I—have no reason to cover my nakedness!'

Do you think that this kind of godhead and philosopher may be lacking in shame?

Thus, he once said, 'In certain cases I love human beings' (and he was alluding to Ariadne, who was present); 'to me, human beings are pleasant, brave, inventive animals who do not have their equal on earth; they can find their way in any labyrinth. I am well disposed towards them: I often think about how I can help them go forward and make them stronger, deeper, and more evil than they are.'

'Stronger, deeper, and more evil?' I asked, frightened. 'Yes,' he said once again, 'stronger, deeper, and more evil—more beautiful, too.' And at that the tempter god smiled his halcyon smile, as if he had just uttered a charming compliment. This shows us two things at once: shame is not the only thing that this godhead lacks; and there are generally good reasons to assume that in some respects all the gods could do with some human schooling. We humans are—more human . . .

296

Oh, what are you really, all of you, my written and depicted thoughts! Not so long ago, you were still so colourful, young, and malicious, so full of thorns and covert spices that you made me sneeze and laugh—and now? You've already cast off your novelty and some of you, I fear, are at the point of becoming truths: they already look so immortal, so heart-breakingly righteous, so boring! And was it not ever thus? What things do we really write down and depict, we mandarins with our Chinese brush, we immortalizers of things that *can* be written, what things are really left for us to paint, after all? Alas, only that which is about to wither and beginning to smell rank! Alas, only exhausted, retreating storms and late, yellowed feelings! Alas, only birds that have flown themselves weary, flown astray, and have let themselves be caught in someone's hand—*our* hand! We immortalize what cannot live or fly any longer, weary and crumbling things all! And it is only for your *afternoon*, my written and depicted thoughts, that I still have paint, much paint perhaps, many colourful tender words and fifty yellows and browns and greens and reds—but they will not help anyone to guess how you looked in your morning, you sudden sparks and miracles of my solitude, my old, beloved——*wicked* thoughts!

From High Mountains
Concluding Ode*

Oh noon of life! Oh ceremonious hour!
    Oh summer gardens!
A restless joy in standing, watching, waiting—
I look for friends, expectant day and night,
Where are you friends? Oh come! It's time! It's time!

If not for you, why is the glacier's grey
    Now decked with roses?
The brook is searching, longing, wind and cloud
Are straining, streaming higher towards the blue,
To spy you out from up where birds can see.

I set my table for you in the highest:
    Who lives this near
To stars, or to the chasm's greyest depths?
My realm—what realm has ever reached out farther?
And honey like my own—who knows its taste?

—So *there* you are! But friends—am *I* not he
    Whom you are seeking?
You hesitate and stare—would that you'd grumble!
Is it no longer—I? Have hand, step, face been switched?
And *what* I am, to you friends—isn't it I?

Have I become another? Someone strange?
    Sprung off from me?
A wrestler who has pinned himself too often?
His strength too often forced against itself,
And wounded, hampered by his own success?

Did I not seek the place where winds blow sharpest?
    And learn to dwell
Where no one dwells, in lonely ice-bear zones,
Forget all men and gods, and curses, prayers?
Become a ghost that glides by over glaciers?

—You, my old friends! Just see how you turn pale
    With love and fear!
No, go in peace! For *you* could not reside here:
Remote here in the worlds of ice and stone—
A man must be a buck here, and a huntsman.

I've been a *wicked* huntsman!—See how taut
    My bow is spanned!
The strongest man it was who drew it thus——
But now, alas! *This* arrow comes with dangers
Like no *other*—go in haste! Find safety! . . .

You turn away?—O heart, you've borne enough,
    Your hopes were strong;
Hold open now your door to *newfound* friends!
Let old ones go! And with them memory, too!
If you were young once, now—you're better young!

Whatever bound us in one single hope—
    Who reads the signs
That love once wrote into it, all so pale?
To me it's like a parchment that no hand
Will *dare* to touch—being like it browned, and burned.

They are no longer friends, they are—what then?
    Just ghosts of friends!
They knock by night upon my heart and window,

They look at me and say, '*Weren't* we the ones?'
—Oh wilted words, whose scent was once like roses!

Oh youthful longing that was born in error,
    Those *I* longed for,
Imagined as transformed yet true to me,
Their growing *old* has banished them away:
Stay true to me? You must transform yourself.

Oh noon of life! Oh second youthful season!
    Oh summer gardens!
A restless joy in standing, watching, waiting!
I look for friends, expectant day and night,
For my *new* friends. Oh come! It's time, it's time!

*

This song is done—and longing's sweet lament
    Died on my lips:
A good magician helped, a friend in need,
A midday friend—No! Ask not who it was—
It was at midday that One turned to Two . . .

And now we celebrate, in victory bound,
    The feast of feasts:
Friend *Zarathustra* came, the guest of guests!
Now laughs the world, the ancient curtain's torn,
And light and darkness wedded are as one . . .

EXPLANATORY NOTES

PREFACE

3 *subject and ego*: a reference to the distinction between the empirical and the transcendental ego made in the first two sections of the A deduction in the first edition of the *Critique of Pure Reason* (1781) by Immanuel Kant (1724–1804).

I. ON THE PREJUDICES OF PHILOSOPHERS

6 *thing in itself*: *Ding an sich*. In Kant's *Critique of Pure Reason* (1781) this refers to the existent as it exists independently of our knowledge; a noumenon, a thing of the mind rather than of the senses; that which a thing is when there is no human perception of it, that is, when it is in 'essence' rather than in 'appearance'.

de omnibus dubitandum: Latin: everything is to be doubted.

a perspective from below: Nietzsche uses the German art term *Frosch-Perspektive* (literally: 'frog perspective').

7 *niaiserie*: French: foolishness.

the measure of all things: dictum of the Sophist Protagoras (*c*.490–420 BC), quoted by Plato in the *Theaetetus* 152a.

synthetic a priori judgements: judgements not verifiable by experience nor by definition, but known with certainty to be true.

8 *hypocrisy*: *Tartüfferie*, a term derived from the hypocritical priest who is the eponymous hero of Molière's 1664 comedy *Tartuffe*. It recurs in Aphorisms 24, 228, and 249.

categorical imperative: in the *Critique of Practical Reason* (1788), paragraph 7, Kant writes: 'Always act in such a way that the maxims of your will could function as the basis of a universal law of action.'

the love of his wisdom: the literal meaning of the word 'philosophy' is 'love of wisdom'.

9 *kNOwledge*: *Verkenntnis*, a neologism and pun on *Erkenntnis* (knowledge), suggesting mistaken knowledge.

Epicurus: the Greek philosopher (341–270 BC), father of Epicureanism, founded his school in Athens in 306 BC.

10 *adventavit . . . fortissimus*: Latin: the ass entered, | beautiful and most brave.

Stoics: the school of the Stoics (after the *stoa poikile*, the painted porch) was founded in Athens by Zeno of Citium, *c*.300 BC, and held that the world is an ideally good organism all of whose parts interact for the benefit of the whole.

11 *causa prima*: Latin: first cause.

fanatics of conscience: *Fanatiker des Gewissens*, a term that plays with the word *Gewissheit* (certainty), used earlier in the sentence.

12 *facilitated by a faculty*: *vermöge eines Vermögens* (literally: by means of a faculty).

niaiserie allemande: French: German foolishness.

13 *real-political*: a reference to the *Realpolitik* (reality politics) of Otto von Bismarck (1815–98).

Tübingen Stift: academy in Tübingen whose pupils included Hegel, Hölderlin, and Schelling.

'finding' and 'inventing': *'finden' und 'erfinden'*.

intellectual intuition: in the *System of Transcendental Idealism* (1800), part One, section II, by Friedrich Wilhelm Joseph von Schelling (1775–1854).

quia est . . . assoupire: Latin and French: because it has a sleep-inducing faculty – whose nature is to put the senses to sleep. Spoken by the impostor physician in Molière's *Le Malade imaginaire* (1673).

14 *materialistic atomism*: the doctrine of Democritus of Abdera (460–360 BC) that the real world consists of qualitatively similar atoms.

Boscovich: Roger Joseph Boscovich (1711–87), Italian-Serbian Jesuit mathematician and scientist whose *Theory of Natural Philosophy* was published in 1758, advancing a theory of dynamism, that is, that nature is to be understood in terms of force, not mass.

Copernicus: Nicolaus Copernicus (1473–1543) advanced a heliocentric theory of the universe in *De Revolutionibus Orbium Coelestium* in 1543.

metaphysical need: in Arthur Schopenhauer's *The World as Will and Representation* (1818), part 2, book 1, chapter 17.

15 *Spinoza*: the argument concerning self-preservation is in part IV of the posthumously published *Ethics* of Baruch (Benedictus de) Spinoza (1632–77).

16 *least possible energy*: a reference to the extremal principle in Darwin's theory of natural selection, that is, that very slight differences in individual organisms over time will result in very great modifications to the species.

reductio ad absurdum: Latin: reduction to absurdity.

causa sui: Latin: cause of itself; the property possessed only by God, of being His own cause, as in the first definition of Spinoza's *Ethics*.

Schopenhauer's superstition: a reference to Schopenhauer's *The World as Will and Representation*, which holds that the experience of an inner, volitional reality within one's own body is an immediate certainty.

contradictio in adjecto: Latin: a logical inconsistency between a noun and its modifier.

knowing-to-the-end: because the German prefix 'Er-' generally connotes the completion of an action, Nietzsche is playing with the literal meaning of *Erkenntnis* (perception, knowledge) as 'knowing-to-the-end' as opposed to *Kenntnis* (informational knowledge).

17 *There is thinking*: *es denkt* (literally: it thinks). The neutral subject is used much more commonly in German than in English, thus implying a subject-as-cause for general actions. Cf. Freud's concept of the id (*das Es*).

19 *L'effet c'est moi*: French: I am the effect; a play on *L'état, c'est moi* ('I am the state'), the claim of Louis XIV (1638–1715).

21 *Locke's superficiality*: a reference to the *Essay Concerning Human Understanding* (1690) by John Locke (1632–1704). In book III, Locke argues that language hinders access to things themselves, because words stand for nothing but the ideas in the mind of the one who uses them.

causa sui: see above, note to p. 16.

Münchhausen: Hieronymus Karl Friedrich Freiherr von Münchhausen (1720–97), the prevaricating adventurer-hero of Rudolf Erich Raspe's *Baron Munchausen's Narrative of his Marvellous Travels and Campaigns*, published in London in 1785 and translated into German in 1786.

22 *la religion de la souffrance humaine*: French: the religion of human suffering.

Ni dieu, ni maître: French: neither God nor master.

24 *sacrifizio dell'intelletto*: Italian: the sacrifice of the intellect; part of the duty owed by Jesuits who take the vow of obedience.

II THE FREE SPIRIT

25 *O sancta simplicitas!*: Latin: O holy simplicity!

ignorance . . . uncertainty: Nietzsche is playing with various forms of the word *wissen* (to know): *die Unwissenheit* (ignorance), *die Wissenschaft* (science), *das Nicht-wissen* (not knowing), and *das Ungewisse* (uncertainty).

26 *knights of the most sorrowful countenance*: an allusion to the eponymous hero of Miguel de Cervantes' *Don Quixote* (1615).

Giordano Brunos: Bruno was an anti-dogmatic Italian philosopher and astronomer (1548–1600), burned as a heretic in Rome.

28 *Abbé Galiani*: Ferdinando Galiani (1728–87), Italian economist who evolved a theory of value based on utility and scarcity.

gangasrotogati: according to Walter Kaufmann's 1966 edition of *Beyond Good and Evil*, this is a Sanskrit term meaning 'as the current of the

Ganges moves'. The following term, *kurmagati*, means 'as the tortoise moves'.

29 *buffo*: Italian: comic actor.

Petronius: Petronius Arbiter (d. AD 66), Roman writer of the Neronian age, author of the fragmentary comic narrative, the *Satyricon*.

in moribus et artibus: Latin: in morals and arts.

Lessing: Gotthold Ephraim Lessing (1729–81), playwright, literary critic, and theorist of the German Enlightenment.

Bayle: Pierre Bayle (1647–1706), philosopher whose subversive *Historical and Critical Dictionary* (1697) was condemned by the Church. Nietzsche is incorrect in thinking that Lessing was Bayle's translator.

Machiavelli: Niccolò Machiavelli (1469–1527), Florentine writer and statesman, whose *Prince* was published in 1532.

30 *petit fait*: French: little fact.

33 *disinterested contemplation*: a reference to Kant's *Critique of Judgment* (1790), book 1, paragraph 2.

34 *advocatus dei*: God's advocate; a play on the more common phrase *advocatus diaboli* (devil's advocate).

35 *valeurs*: French: values.

il ne cherche . . . le bien: French: he seeks truth only to do good.

36 *intelligible character*: a reference to Plato's world of ideas, capable of being apprehended only by the intellect, not the senses.

38 *Stendhal*: the pen name of the French novelist Henri Beyle (1783–1842), author of works such as *The Red and the Black* (1830) and *The Charterhouse of Parma* (1839).

Pour être . . . ce qui est: French: To be a good philosopher, one must be dry, clear, free of illusions. A banker who has made a fortune has something of the character needed to make philosophical discoveries, that is to say, to see clearly into that which exists.

wicked cunning . . . cunning: a play on the parts of the German word *Arglist* (cunning): *arg* (bad, wicked) and *List* (cunning).

39 *an experiment . . . a temptation*: a play on *Versuch* (experiment) and *Versuchung* (temptation).

41 *'libre-penseurs', 'liberi pensatori', 'freethinkers'*: the French and Italian terms for freethinkers are followed by the German *Freidenker* (freethinker), making clear Nietzsche's distinction between their 'progressive' ideas and those of his own *freier Geist* (free spirit).

III. THE RELIGIOUS DISPOSITION

43 *cognizance and conscience*: Wissen und Gewissen.

homines religiosi: Latin: religious men.

Pascal: French scientist and philosopher Blaise Pascal (1623–62) whose Jansen-influenced *Pensées sur la religion* was posthumously published in 1670.

44 *Phoenicianism*: a reference to self-mutilation, cf. Aphorism 229.

absurdissimum: Latin: the ultimate absurdity.

45 *Kundry*: seductress-turned-penitent in Richard Wagner's late opera *Parsifal* (1882).

type vécu: French: a type that has lived.

46 *sociology*: the French philosopher Auguste Comte (1798–1857) was known as the founder of positivism for works such as *Système de politique positive* (1851–4).

Saint-Beuve: Charles Augustin Saint-Beuve (1804–69), French literary critic and author of *A History of Port-Royal* (1840–60).

Renan: Ernest Renan (1823–92), French historian, published the *History of the Origins of Christianity* in 1890.

47 *Disons . . . le mieux?*: French: Let us say boldly that religion is a product of normal man, that man is most right when he is most religious and most confident of an infinite destiny . . . It is when he is good that he wishes virtue to correspond to an eternal order; it is when he contemplates things in a disinterested manner that he finds death revolting and absurd. How can we doubt that these are the moments when man sees most clearly?

la niaiserie . . . par excellence!: French: the height of religious nonsense!

delicatezza: Italian: delicacy.

unio mystica et physica: Latin: mystical and physical unity.

Madame de Guyon: Jeanne-Marie Bouvier de la Motte-Guyon (1648–1717), French mystic and a religious prisoner from 1695 to 1703.

50 *Mithras Grotto*: Tiberius Julius Caesar Augustus (42 BC AD 37), second Roman emperor, is said to have conducted human sacrifices here after AD 27.

da capo: Italian: from the beginning; a reference to Nietzsche's theory of the eternal return, as introduced in his *Thus Spake Zarathustra* (1885).

51 *circulus vitiosus deus*: Latin: God as vicious circle.

IV. EPIGRAMS AND INTERLUDES

60 *respects himself as a despiser*: a play on *achten* (to respect) and *verachten* (to despise).

62 *bites*: *Gewissensbiße* (literally: bites of conscience) is the German idiom for 'pangs of conscience'.

63 *incarnation as an animal*: *Tierwerdung*, a play on *Menschwerdung*, the incarnation (of God as man in Jesus Christ).

63 *pia fraus*: Latin: pious fraud; a reference to false statements of the Church that encourage piety, such as 'The meek shall inherit the earth', etc., in contrast to the *impia fraus* (impious fraud).

67 *Pharisaism*: hypocrisy; Jesus criticized the Pharisees for following the Torah in a legalistic way instead of valuing justice, mercy, faith (cf. Matthew 23: 23).

68 *Curious counsel*: *Rat als Rätsel*.

Dans le véritable amour . . . le corps: French: In real love it is the soul that envelops the body.

buona femmina . . . bastone: Italian: good women and bad women both need the stick.

Sacchetti: Franco Sacchetti (*c.*1335–*c.*1400), Florentine poet and novelist whose *Novelle* were first published in 1724.

70 *Thy neighbour*: *Nächster* (neighbour in the religious sense) as opposed to *Nachbar* (neighbour in the literal sense), used subsequently.

71 *sheep*: *Hammel* (literally: 'wether', a castrated ram). Nietzsche is playing on *Leithammel* (bell-wether) and *Hammel*.

grimace: *Maul* (literally: 'muzzle').

72 *utile*: French: useful.

V. TOWARDS A NATURAL HISTORY OF MORALS

74 *facta*: Latin: facts.

75 *The Fundamental Problems of Morality*: a reference to the second essay of Arthur Schopenhauer's *Die beiden Grundprobleme der Ethic* (1841). The emphases are Nietzsche's.

neminem laede . . . juva: Latin: harm no one; rather help everyone as much as you can.

76 *laisser-aller*: French: letting things go.

Port-Royal: French Jansenism, as practised at the abbey and school of Port-Royal near Paris, founded in the seventeenth century.

77 *discipline and cultivate*: *Zucht und Züchtung*.

78 *amour-passion*: French: passionate love.

No one wants to do himself harm . . . good: the 'Socratic paradox', in Plato's *Meno* 77b–78b (also in *Protagoras* 345d–e and *Gorgias* 509e).

79 Πρόσθε Πλάτων, ὄπιθεν τε Πλάτων, μέσση τε χίμαιρα: 'Plato in front, Plato behind, and a Chimaera in the middle'; an allusion to Homer's *Iliad* vi. 181, where Chimaera is described as a lion in front, a serpent behind, and a goat in the middle.

80 *Armbrust*: the Latin *arcubalista* means 'crossbow', as does the German *Armbrust* (literally: arm-breast), which imitates the sound of the Latin.

81 *Quidquid . . . agit*: Latin: what has taken place in the light continues in the dark.

82 *Cagliostro*: Count Alessandro di Cagliostro (1743–95), born Giuseppe Balsamo, Sicilian alchemist and adventurer, arrested and imprisoned in Rome in 1789.

Catiline: Lucius Sergius Catilina (108?–62 BC), Roman conspirator, defeated by Cicero in an attempt to be Roman consul.

83 *The Jews . . . them*: this aphorism, like Aphorisms 201 and 202 in this Section, directly anticipates Nietzsche's *On the Genealogy of Morals* (1887).

Borgia: Cesare Borgia (1475?–1507), cardinal, soldier, statesman, and Duke of the Romagna.

85 *Hafis*: Mohammed Shamsuddin (1300–89), called Hafis, the Persian poet who inspired the ageing Goethe's collection of poems, the *West-Östlicher Divan* (West-East Divan), published in 1819.

licentia morum: Latin: moral licentiousness.

86 *Sabbath of Sabbaths*: cf. Augustine's *City of God*, book XXII, section 30.

87 *Alcibiades*: Athenian general (450–404 BC), statesman, and pupil of Socrates, exiled to Sparta for sacrilege, but later elected Athenian commander-in-chief.

Frederick II: brilliant Hohenstaufen ruler (1194–1250), Emperor of the Holy Roman Empire from 1215 to 1250.

res publica: Latin: commonwealth.

90 *ni dieu ni maître*: see above, note to p. 22.

pity . . . suffering: *Mitleiden* (literally: suffering along with) and *Leiden*.

mediocritizes: *Vermittelmässigung*, Nietzsche's neologism.

VI. WE SCHOLARS

93 *montrer ses plaies*: French: to show one's wounds.

science: *die Wissenschaft*; this word, especially in the plural form that occurs frequently in this Section, can also have the broader connotation of 'scholarship' or 'higher learning'.

self-praise smells sweet: a play on the German saying 'Eigenlob stinkt' (self-praise stinks).

most cultured and conceited: *gebildetsten und eingebildetsten*.

otium: Latin: leisure.

94 *Dühring*: Karl Eugen Dühring (1833–1901), German positivist philosopher, who denounced religion and Kantian philosophy in works such as *The Value of Life in an Heroic Sense* (1865).

Hartmann: Karl Robert Eduard von Hartmann (1842–1906), whose

Philosophy of the Unconscious (1869) advances a pessimistic philosophy that incorporates inductive science.

95 SCENT*ipede*: *Tausendfuss und Tausend-Fühlhorn*.

    Cagliostro: see above, note to p. 82.

96 *appreciation . . . recognizable*: a play on *anerkennen* (to appreciate) and its root *erkennen* (to recognize).

97 *ipseity*: Nietzsche's neologism *Ipsissimosität*.

98 *caput mortuum*: Latin: dross.

    Je ne méprise presque rien: French: I despise almost nothing.

99 *substance or content*: Inhalt und Gehalt.

    in parenthesi: Latin: parenthetically.

    nihilism: Nietzsche uses the neologism *Nihilin*, a play on *Anilin* (aniline, a poisonous chemical).

    bonae voluntatis: Latin: of good will.

    What do I know?: 'Que sais-je?'; the motto of the *Essays* (1580) of Michel de Montaigne (1533–92). It was placed on the work's title-page after Montaigne's death.

100 *l'art pour l'art*: French: art for art's sake.

101 *King of Prussia*: Frederick William I (1688–1740), father of Frederick the Great (1712–86).

102 *esprit*: French: wit, intellect.

    cet esprit fataliste, ironique, méphistophélique: French: that fatalistic, ironic, Mephistophelian spirit.

    dogmatic slumber: a reference to Kant's statement that reading Hume had awakened him from his dogmatic slumber.

103 *mannish woman*: an allusion to the French novelist Germaine Necker, Madame de Staël (1766–1817), whose *De l'Allemagne* (On Germany) appeared in 1813.

    Voilà un homme!: French: This is a man!

    the name that I have dared to call them: a reference to Aphorism 42, where Nietzsche calls the new philosophers 'experimenters'.

104 *Chinaman of Königsberg*: a reference to Immanuel Kant.

105 *casual acquiescence*: Sich-gehen-lassen und Sich-fallen-lassen.

VII. OUR VIRTUES

109 *pigtail*: Zopf, a term used by liberals since the end of the eighteenth century to refer to antiquated views.

110 *bêtise bourgeoise*: French: bourgeois foolishness.

111 *homo bonae voluntatis*: Latin: man of good will.

112 *désintéressé*: French: disinterested.

unselfish . . . useful . . . at his own expense: Nietzsche is playing with the component parts of the word *uneigennützig* (unselfish): *eigen* (one's own) and *nützen* (to be of use).

113 *bonhomme*: French: simple man.

pity . . . suffering: see above, note to p. 90.

114 *in moribus et artibus*: see above, note to p. 29.

115 *Saint-Évremond*: Charles Saint-Évremond (1610–1703), French royalist and pupil of the Jesuits, whose writings were published posthumously in London in 1705.

esprit vaste: French: vast spirit.

118 *nitimur in vetitum*: Latin: we strive for what is forbidden (Ovid, *Amores* III. iv. 17).

119 *Bentham's*: Jeremy Bentham (1748–1832), English philosopher, jurist, and reformer, whose *Introduction to the Principles of Morals and Legislation* (1781) espoused the utilitarian idea of the 'greatest happiness of the greatest number'.

a Homeric simile . . . plainly: cf. *Iliad* vi. 424; ix. 466.

Helvétius's: Claude Adrien Helvétius (1715–71), French philosopher, whose thought centred around the idea that public ethics has a utilitarian base and that culture is critical to national development. His *De l'esprit* (1758) incensed the dauphin of France and was condemned by the Sorbonne.

cant: this word is in English in the original.

comfort . . . fashion: these words are in English in the original.

120 *Sans génie et sans esprit!*: French: Without genius and without wit!

158 *milk of pious thinking*: *die Milch der frommen Denkart* in Friedrich Schiller's *Wilhelm Tell*, IV. 3, recalling Shakespeare's phrase 'the milk of human kindness' (*die Milch der Menschenliebe* in the Schlegel-Tieck translation) in *Macbeth* I. v.

121 *sacrifizio dell'intelletto*: see above, note to p. 24.

123 *homo natura*: Latin: natural man.

124 *Fatum*: Latin: fate.

Eternal-Boring: an allusion, the first of several in this Section, to the last line of Goethe's *Faust II*, sung by the Mystical Choir as Faust ascends to heaven: 'das Ewig-Weibliche zieht uns hinan' (the Eternal-Feminine draws us on high).

125 *mulier taceat in ecclesia!*: Latin: Let women keep silence in church (cf. 1 Corinthians 14: 34). The two following variations on this phrase are: 'Let women keep silence in political matters' and 'Let women keep silence about women.'

125 *Madame de Staël*: see above, note to p. 103.

Madame Roland: Manon Jeanne Phlipon (1754–93), self-taught scholar who had a powerful influence in France especially after 1789. Famous for her phrase at the guillotine: 'O liberty! What crimes are committed in thy name!'

George Sand: Amandine Dudevant née Dupin (1804–76), prolific French novelist whose colourful life defied social conventions.

126 *Mon ami . . . plaisir*: French: My dear, never indulge in any follies but the ones that will give you a great deal of pleasure.

ella guardava suso, ed io in lei: Italian: she was looking upward, and I at her.

127 *The speech is short, the meaning long*: *Kurze Rede, langer Sinn*: an inversion of Friedrich Schiller's phrase 'der langen Rede kurzer Sinn' (the short meaning of a lengthy speech) in *Die Piccolomini*, Act I, Scene 2.

130 *the horned animal*: an allusion to the myth of Europa and the bull.

VIII. PEOPLES AND FATHERLANDS

131 *pressure . . . nightmare*: a play on *Druck* (pressure) and *Alpdruck* (nightmare).

132 *metabolism*: here, *Stoffe wechseln* (to exchange matter), playing on the literal meaning of *Stoffwechsel* (metabolism).

That fellow: a reference to Chancellor Otto von Bismarck (1815–98), the architect of German statehood.

135 *two souls . . . my breast*: a reference to a famous passage in Goethe's *Faust I*, line 1112.

Kotzebue: August Friedrich Ferdinand Kotzebue (1761–1819), popular German playwright, theatre director, and political reporter, who was stabbed to death in Mannheim by Karl Ludwig Sand (1795–1820), a fanatical student who believed him to be a Russian spy.

Jean Paul: Johann Paul Friedrich Richter (1763–1825), renowned German Romantic novelist who was sharply critical of the philosopher Johann Gottlieb Fichte (1762–1814) in works such as *Clavis Fichtiana* (1800).

Gemüt: a quality of 'inner warmth' attributed to the German soul.

136 *ad oculos*: Latin: visibly, for the eye.

137 *sand*: the region around Berlin is known for the sandy quality of its soil.

the 'two-timing' people: a pun on an archaic form of the adjective 'German' (*tiusche*) and the verb 'to deceive' (*täuschen*).

138 *Saxon Switzerland*: a scenic mountainous region south of Dresden.

Werther: the suicidal hero of Goethe's *The Sorrows of Young Werther* (1774).

Explanatory Notes 191

noli me tangere: Latin: touch me not.

141 *Sybels and Treitzschkes*: Heinrich von Sybel (1817–95) and Heinrich von Treitzschke (1834–91), the two most significant political historians of their day.

142 *res facta . . . nata . . . res ficta et picta*: Latin: something man-made . . . born . . . something invented and painted.

aere perennius: Latin: more enduring than bronze (Horace, *Odes* III. xxx).

143 *je méprise Locke*: French: I despise Locke.

Carlyle: Thomas Carlyle (1795–1881), Scottish essayist and historian, whose lectures *On Heroes* were published in 1841.

145 *âme française*: French: French soul.

noblesse: French: aristocratic nobility.

146 *Taine*: Hippolyte Adolph Taine (1828–93), French historian and positivist, whose interpretations of history in works such as *L'Histoire de la littérature anglaise* (1864) stressed the influence of environmental factors.

âme moderne: French: modern soul.

l'art pour l'art: see above, note to p. 100.

boulevardiers de Paris: French: Parisian men about town.

voluptate psychologica: Latin: psychological voluptuousness.

Beyle: see above, note to p. 38, on Stendhal.

147 *blood and iron*: another reference to Bismarck and his militaristic ambitions.

Mediterraneans: Mittelländer (literally: people of the middle).

the future of music: an allusion and response to Richard Wagner's theoretical writings about music, as in his essay *The Artwork of the Future* (1849).

149 *in world literature*: *weltliterarisch*, an allusion to Goethe's ideal of a literature that transcends national boundaries.

150 *the French socialists*: an allusion to Mikhail Bakunin (1814–76), charismatic Russian-born revolutionary socialist, and Pierre-Joseph Proudhon (1809–65), French socialist and political philosopher whom Wagner read as a young man.

Rome's Wordless Creed!: *Roms Glaube ohne Worte!*, an allusion to *Lieder ohne Worte* (Songs without Words), composed by Felix Mendelssohn.

IX. WHAT IS NOBLE?

153 *master moralities and slave moralities*: this concept, informing Essay One of the *Genealogy of Morals* (1886), was first introduced in Nietzsche's *Human, All too Human* (1878), 45.

155 *désintéressement*: French: disinterestedness.

156 *bonhomme*: see above, note to p. 113.

gai saber: Provençal: gay science. This concept was first introduced by Nietzsche in the eponymous work of 1882.

vanity: cf. *Human, All Too Human*, Aphorism 89 for Nietzsche's earlier thoughts on vanity.

159 *nuances*: in French (and also English, of course) in the original.

160 *Différence engendre haine*: French: difference engenders hatred.

162 *furca . . . recurret*: a reference to Horace's *Epistles* I. x. 24: Try to drive nature out (*naturam expellere*) with a pitchfork (*furca*), it always returns (*usque recurret*).

inter pares: Latin: among equals.

164 *progressus in simile*: Latin: continuation of the same thing.

168 *Raffael without hands*: a reference to Lessing's *Emilia Galotti*, Act I, Scene 3, in which an artist is identified not by his productions, but by his vision.

170 *contradictio in adjecto*: see above, note to p. 16.

172 *Up here . . . exalted*: Goethe, *Faust II*, v, lines 11990–1.

173 *vertu est enthousiasme*: French, virtue is enthusiasm.

abyss . . . ground . . . 'grounding': *Abgrund . . . Grunde . . . 'Begründung'*.

175 *gai saber*: see above, note to p. 156.

Laughter . . . overcome: in German in the original.

176 *my first-born*: a reference to Nietzsche's first published work, *The Birth of Tragedy out of the Spirit of Music* (1872).

178 *Concluding Ode*: *Nachgesang* (epode). This translation seeks to preserve the rhythmical pattern of the original Greek ode form, but in the interests of fidelity to the content and to the flow of the verse, there has been no attempt to preserve the original rhyme scheme (ABBAA).

INDEX

Numbers refer to aphorisms
P refers to the Preface
F refers to the concluding ode, 'From High Mountains'

A SELECTION OF   **OXFORD WORLD'S CLASSICS**

JANE AUSTEN	**Emma**
	Mansfield Park
	Persuasion
	Pride and Prejudice
	Sense and Sensibility
MRS BEETON	**Book of Household Management**
LADY ELIZABETH BRADDON	**Lady Audley's Secret**
ANNE BRONTË	**The Tenant of Wildfell Hall**
CHARLOTTE BRONTË	**Jane Eyre**
	Shirley
	Villette
EMILY BRONTË	**Wuthering Heights**
SAMUEL TAYLOR COLERIDGE	**The Major Works**
WILKIE COLLINS	**The Moonstone**
	No Name
	The Woman in White
CHARLES DARWIN	**The Origin of Species**
CHARLES DICKENS	**The Adventures of Oliver Twist**
	Bleak House
	David Copperfield
	Great Expectations
	Nicholas Nickleby
	The Old Curiosity Shop
	Our Mutual Friend
	The Pickwick Papers
	A Tale of Two Cities
GEORGE DU MAURIER	**Trilby**
MARIA EDGEWORTH	**Castle Rackrent**

The Oxford World's Classics Website

www.worldsclassics.co.uk

- Information about new titles
- Explore the full range of Oxford World's Classics
- Links to other literary sites and the main OUP webpage
- Imaginative competitions, with bookish prizes
- Peruse the Oxford World's Classics Magazine
- Articles by editors
- Extracts from Introductions
- A forum for discussion and feedback on the series
- Special information for teachers and lecturers

www.worldsclassics.co.uk

MORE ABOUT **OXFORD WORLD'S CLASSICS**

American Literature

British and Irish Literature

Children's Literature

Classics and Ancient Literature

Colonial Literature

Eastern Literature

European Literature

History

Medieval Literature

Oxford English Drama

Poetry

Philosophy

Politics

Religion

The Oxford Shakespeare

A complete list of Oxford Paperbacks, including Oxford World's Classics, Oxford Shakespeare, Oxford Drama, and Oxford Paperback Reference, is available in the UK from the Academic Division Publicity Department, Oxford University Press, Great Clarendon Street, Oxford OX2 6DP.

In the USA, complete lists are available from the Paperbacks Marketing Manager, Oxford University Press, 198 Madison Avenue, New York, NY 10016.

Oxford Paperbacks are available from all good bookshops. In case of difficulty, customers in the UK can order direct from Oxford University Press Bookshop, Freepost, 116 High Street, Oxford OX1 4BR, enclosing full payment. Please add 10 per cent of published price for postage and packing.